Personality, Religion, and Leadership

To Carl Jung and Katharine
Briggs who pioneered the way,
and to Isabel Myers and John Beebe
who made the path

Personality, Religion, and Leadership

The Spiritual Dimensions of Psychological Type Theory

Christopher F. J. Ross and Leslie J. Francis

LEXINGTON BOOKS
Lanham • Boulder • New York • London

Published by Lexington Books
An imprint of The Rowman & Littlefield Publishing Group, Inc.
4501 Forbes Boulevard, Suite 200, Lanham, Maryland 20706
www.rowman.com

6 Tinworth Street, London SE11 5AL, United Kingdom

British Library Cataloguing in Publication Information Available

Library of Congress Cataloging-in-Publication Data Available

ISBN: 978-1-7936-0582-5 (cloth : alk. paper)
ISBN: 978-1-7936-0583-2 (electronic)

Contents

Preface

Reading *Introduction to Jung's psychology* by Frieda Fordham while walking home from Battersea Grammar School drew me to the study and practice of psychology. However, such is the invisible force of collective disciplinary culture that it took me seventeen years, while working at the Southdown Institute, a psychological treatment center just North of Toronto for Catholic priests and religious, and encountering the use of the Myers-Briggs Type Indicator for the first time, to realize that not only had I forgotten this early impetus from Carl Jung's analytical psychology, but I had forgotten that I had forgotten! Soon, in 1988, I had the good fortune to meet San Francisco Jungian analyst, John Beebe and encounter his marriage of Jung's most rarified concept of archetype to Jung's most accessible—psychological type, which John Beebe today identifies as "The eight function-attitude eight archetype model" of type development. My fascination with Beebe's approach remains after many years, and many clients, many courses and many studies later. My transition the same year from fulltime psychotherapy practice in Toronto that had included a variety of "peoples of the cloth"—Jesuits, United Church ministers, and Anglican priests—to research and teaching in the psychology of religion at nearby Wilfrid Laurier University in Waterloo, Ontario, enabled me to test my intuition that particular religious beliefs and practices are associated with the functions foundational to Jungian psychological-type theory. I then went on also to publish studies showing different frequencies for each of the sixteen psychological types within particular Christian denominations.

At the end of my first sabbatical in 1995 I was very pleased to meet fellow psychologist of religion, Leslie Francis whose work was solidly centered on the psychology of individual differences. My enthusiasm for the practical utility of Jungian typology for religious settings met Leslie Francis' openness to empirical evidence, and issued in two decades of rich collaboration in the psychology of individual religious differences. In the middle years during a walk in the foot-hills of Snowdonia I introduced my research colleague to the subtleties of Beebe's model, and following a successful presentation of preliminary findings at the American Psychological Association in Boston in 2008, my future coauthor proffered "I think there is a book here." I agreed if he would write the book with me, and I am deeply grateful for his exactness, industry, and commitment to applying Jungian type to benefit religious individuals and religious communities.

There are many more individuals who contributed to our publication. I am indebted to John Beebe who has been so generous with his time over three decades and enabled me to obtain "an inside feel" for his rich model of type development. Then there are my colleagues in the Department of Religion and Culture who encouraged me to persevere and over the same period have borne with my regular discourses on type, and more recently newer colleagues at Martin Luther University College who have facilitated new applications of type to the exegesis of sacred texts. Gratitude I feel too for: the generous hosting of Mandy Robbins and her colleagues Emyr Williams and Chris Lewis at the Psychology Department of Glyndŵr University, Wrexham, Wales during a six-month sabbatical in 2016 that enabled me to complete the first draft of this book; to Peter Francis for hosting the working conference at the start of our project, "Type dynamics and Christian leadership" at Gladstone Residential Library, Hawarden, Wales, in April 2009, and for providing a residential bursary there at the start of my sabbatical in 2016; to members of the Network for Psychological Type and Christian Faith, who provided a forum for the presentation of findings and ideas for the development of fresh studies through the annual symposium; to the St Mary's Centre and particularly to Emma Eccles who was so patient and conscientious in preparing the final copy for publication; to Judith Muskett for carefully checking the proofs; to Jim Gollnick, formerly of the University of Waterloo, for many talks about all things Jungian, his on dreams and dreaming and mine on personality; to Adam Frey for his direct, helpful, grounding comments; and to John Lougheed for the opportunities for type applications to hospital chaplaincy. I am grateful to the participants in our studies, to the students who asked me questions that took my thinking further and applied type to their lives, and to clients whose openness to life enabled me to go more deeply into this application of psychological type theory.

On a personal level I am indebted to Jeannie Wetheral for her sustained interest and for providing a quietly supportive, introverted feeling environment, and to daughter Julia Ross for her infusion of extraverted feeling enthusiasm.

Christopher Ross

Introduction

Work-related psychological health, vulnerabilities, and well-being among religious leaders are matters of growing concern across religious groups. Increasing secularization and the decline of congregations and of other religious gatherings, together with fewer paid posts for religious leaders, make the demanding vocation of religious leadership even more so. As emotional exhaustion increases, and satisfaction in ministry decreases, so religious leaders may become more vulnerable to their inner psychological weaknesses.

In this book, to help religious leaders understand and deal with their personal spiritual journey in times of stress as well as in times of success, we have—as two psychologists immersed in the psychology of religion—drawn on the insights of Jungian psychological type theory and the dynamic power of Jungian analyst John Beebe's eight function-attitude eight archetype model.

Over the past decades, psychological type theory has played an increasingly important part in the intersections between research in the empirical psychology of religion, research in empirical theology, and applied practice emerging from pastoral theology and practical theology. As colleagues, we have enjoyed moving among these academic disciplines and fields of practical application. Christopher Ross has worked in the psychology of religion at Wilfrid Laurier University for a number of years, as well as in clinical practice, meeting with clergy among his clients and contributing to the work of the neighboring Lutheran seminary. Leslie J. Francis has occupied Chairs in Pastoral Theology, Practical Theology, and Religions and Education, and contributed to programs of initial and continuing professional development for clergy, priests, ministers, and pastors across denominations. Together we have found that psychological type theory illuminates questions of theoretical interest within the academy, raised within the fields both of psychology of religion and empirical theology, and also illuminates individual differences in the experiences of professional joys and stresses and in the experiences of emotional exhaustion and satisfaction in ministry among clergy.

We are aware of the ambivalence with which psychological type theory is held both in the academy and in religious organizations. We are convinced, too, that psychological type theory will remain controversial and contested within the immediate future. More fundamental academic research is required, and psychologists working within the individual differences traditions need to become more open to approaches that challenge their established assumptions. By the same token within seminaries, a fuller rapprochement may be realized between theology and psychology through a two-way dialogue.

Both of us are acutely aware that a superficial grasp of psychological type theory may not only do a disservice to the theory but may also be dangerous for the religious leaders who try to operate with a partial (mis)understanding of the theory. Carl Jung's theoretical understanding of the human psyche is a complex and well-considered system that deserves serious reflection and consideration. Our intention in writing this book is not to provide an easy introduction to psychological type theory for religious leaders, but to offer a sustained and systematic analysis. Such an analysis may make fascinating head-knowledge, but it only begins to illuminate and to transform individual human experience when we apply the model to observe and to interpret how we live our individual lives in encounters with others.

What makes our approach distinctive in this book are two important features of our understanding and presentation of psychological type theory. The first distinctive feature is that we have chosen to focus not on the notion of psychological functions, but on the notion of psychological function-orientation, what Beebe, following Thompson (1996), terms function-attitudes. Some presentations of psychological type theory make the clear distinction between four psychological functions: the two perceiving functions (sensing and intuition) and the two judging functions (feeling and thinking). This concentration just on the functions misses the subtlety of the way in which each function is nuanced differently in the two orientations (introversion and extraversion). It is for this reason that we speak consistently of the eight function-orientations rather than of the four functions. In this book, we argue that psychologically mature individuals are able to draw effectively on the full range of the eight function-orientations described by psychological type theory as

- introverted sensing
- extraverted sensing
- introverted intuition
- extraverted intuition
- introverted feeling

- extraverted feeling
- introverted thinking
- extraverted thinking

Moreover, psychological type theory suggests that the role played by these eight function-orientations varies within each of the 16 psychological types. According to psychological type theory, within different psychological types, each of these functions emerges from the unconscious mind into consciousness at a different stage in life. It is this balance between the function-orientations that gives individuals their distinctive psychological strengths, but also alerts them to their psychological weaknesses. Within each of the 16 psychological types, psychological type theory envisages the eight function-orientations emerging within the conscious personality and the shadow personality within the following structure:

Conscious personality

1. Dominant
2. Auxiliary
3. Tertiary
4. Fourth

Shadow personality

5. Dominant shadow
6. Auxiliary shadow
7. Tertiary shadow
8. Fourth shadow

The second distinctive feature of our approach is that we have chosen to link the hierarchy of the eight functions (from the dominant function to the fourth shadow function) with the powerful imagery of Jungian archetypes drawing on John Beebe's insights from his life-long experience as a Jungian analyst and leading teacher at the C. G. Jung Institute of San Francisco. The imagery of archetypes helps us depict the tone, strength, and quality of each of these eight function-orientations within each individual. The strongest and best developed function-orientation is carried by the archetype of the hero. This archetype characterizes our heroic strength. The weakest and least developed function-orientation is carried by the archetype of the demon. This archetype characterizes our demonic pitfalls.

By examining the unfolding structure of each of the 16 psychological types in turn, this book shows how religious leaders may become more effective in building strong and vibrant religious communities by paying closer attention to developing the full range of the eight function-orientations within their own lives and by recognizing the role of these function-orientations in the lives of others. For readers who would like to discern, clarify, or confirm their Jungian psychological type, the authors recommend consulting some of the following sources: for succinct descriptions that keep closely to Jung's formulations and with liberal quotations from his work, *Personality types: Jung's model of typology* by Jungian analyst Daryl Sharpe; for the refinements provided by Isabel Briggs Myers, her classic *Gifts differing: Understanding personality type*, more briefly her *Introduction to type, 7th edition*, and the *Myers–Briggs Type Indicator: Self-scorable Form M.*

In order to develop our distinctive presentation of psychological type theory that focuses both on the eight function-orientations and on the Jungian archetypes, we have divided this book into two parts. Part one of the book is composed of four chapters that set out the *theory* behind Jungian psychological type and Jungian archetype.

Chapter 1 examines the structure of psychological type theory and introduces the ideas of psychological functions and psychological orientations, distinguishing between the two perceiving functions, the two judging functions, and the two psychological orientations. The two perceiving functions are sensing and intuition. The two judging functions are feeling and thinking. The two orientations are introversion and extraversion.

Chapter 2 examines the four perceiving function-orientations: introverted sensing, extraverted sensing, introverted intuition, and extraverted intuition. The sensing function perceives details and content, and the intuitive function perceives patterns of meaning and content.

Chapter 3 examines the four judging function-orientations: introverted feeling, extraverted feeling, introverted thinking, and extraverted thinking. The feeling function makes judgments or evaluations based on values appraised or felt as relevant to human situations without so much regard for formal consistency, and the thinking function makes judgments or evaluations by reference to consistency and the relationship between causes and effects, based on formal resemblances between phenomena with less regard for the human situation.

Chapter 4 examines the eight archetypes that carry the functions within the dynamic structure of the conscious personality and the shadow (unconscious) personality. The order in which the functions are linked with the archetypes is:

Conscious personality

1. Dominant (Hero)
2. Auxiliary (Nurturing parent)

3. Tertiary (Eternal child)
4. Fourth (Soul friend)

Shadow personality

5. Dominant shadow (Challenger)
6. Auxiliary shadow (Critical parent)
7. Tertiary shadow (Trickster)
8. Fourth shadow (Demon/Angel)

Part two of this book comprises chapters 5 to 20. These 16 chapters take each of the 16 psychological types in turn and work through the development of the eight function-orientations, drawing attention to the location of the specific function-orientation associated with each of the eight archetypes carrying the eight positions within the model: the dominant function, the auxiliary function, the tertiary function, the fourth function, the dominant shadow function, the auxiliary shadow function, the tertiary shadow function, and the fourth shadow function. These chapters illuminate the unique structure of each of the 16 complete psychological types. From a scientific perspective, these chapters exemplify the theory in detail and facilitate predictions to be formulated concerning individual preferences and behaviors. From a practical perspective, these chapters lead to enhanced insights into the self and into other selves. It is through such developing awareness that religious leaders are better equipped to understand and to deal with their personal spiritual journey and to understand and deal with the diverse spiritual journeys of those whom they are called to serve. Each of these 16 chapters begins by summarizing the prevalence of the specific type under consideration among men and among women within the United Kingdom (Kendall, 1998) and within the United States (Hammer & Mitchell, 1996).

In naming the 16 complete types, we have followed the convention established within the psychological type literatures as follows:

- Introverts (I)
- Extraverts (E)
- Sensing types (S)
- Intuitive types (N)
- Feeling types (F)
- Thinking types (T)
- Judging types (J)
- Perceiving types (P)

Chapter 1

Psychological Type Theory

Swiss psychiatrist Carl Jung published *Psychological Types* in 1921 completing a project that started in 1902 when, amidst his word association experiments, he distinguished objective types from subjective-predicate types (Jung, 1973). In Jung's view, individuals differ in regard to the prevailing direction of their attention, something that he termed their conscious orientation. He continued, however, to conflate ways of judging with the direction of orientation of consciousness, pairing feeling with extraversion and thinking with introversion, until in 1916 analyst Maria Moltzer at a presentation to the Psychological Club of Zurich introduced the terms "intuition" and "sensation" as different ways of perceiving (Jung, 1971, p. 454*n*). Jung proceeded to formulate his full theory of four functions of consciousness expressed in extraverted or introverted directions, which he finalized in 1919. After 17 years of observation and deliberation, Jung concluded that individuals primarily orient to—and energetically exchange with—their inner or outer world with one of four functions.

Across the Atlantic, Katharine Briggs had been studying the ways in which the personalities of talented people in Washington DC differed from each other in order to create convincing characters for her novels. A more personal motivation for Katharine Briggs' people project was to "figure out" Clarence Myers with whom her beloved daughter Isabel was in love. In 1923, when she read the English translation of *Psychological Types*, Briggs saw the close identity of the two systems that each observer of human psychological difference had developed independently, but such was the "net woven of sexism, cultural conditioning, and [the isolation imposed by] her own brilliance" that she burned her notes (Saunders, 1991, p. 59). When Briggs met Jung in New York in 1937, he admonished her for destroying such a promising manuscript. It was left to her daughter Isabel Briggs Myers to complete the task her mother started. In 1940, in reaction to the bombing of Pearl Harbor and to contribute to a more effective mobilization of anti-fascist forces through psychologically diverse and balanced teamwork, she retrieved her mother's seminal notes and published the *Myers-Briggs Type Indicator* (MBTI) in 1941 with Education Testing Services (ETS). However, despite Isabel Briggs Myers remarkable industry and ingenuity in validating the instrument, the owners of ETS kept it sequestered for decades as a restricted research instrument, until in 1975 the frustrated pioneer took the MBTI to the then fledgling Consulting Psychologist Press. Within 25 years, it became the world's most frequently used personality instrument with 2.5 million annual administrations, for example, between 2000 and 2005 (Segovia, 2005).

The core of the personality theory of Carl Jung, and of Katharine Briggs and Isabel Briggs Myers, is that there are eight ways of orienting human consciousness, two contrasting ways of perceiving, *sensing* or *intuition*, oriented in an *extraverted* or *introverted* direction, and two contrasting way of judging, *thinking* or *feeling*, each also capable of expression in *extraverted* or *introverted* directions. The sensing function perceives details and content, and the intuitive function perceives patterns of meaning and context; the thinking function determines judgments by reference to consistency, based on formal resemblances between phenomena, while the feeling function makes determinations based on values appraised or *felt* as relevant to human situations without regard for formal consistency. Extraverts habitually turn their consciousness toward the outside world of external objects imbuing them with more reality and spirit, what Jung called "numinal accent" (Jung, 1971, p. 531), whereas introverts turn their energetic attention to the inner world of subjective resonances which are therefore—for them—more real and spirited, being suffused with the numinous.

TYPE DEVELOPMENT

The frequency of use and the degree to which each one of the eight functions is developed in individuals' consciousness at particular points in the human life-cycle depend on the order of each function's emergence from the unconscious. By the age of 20, most individuals have developed (1) one kind of perceiving process that is directed either internally *or* externally and (2) one kind of judging process that is oriented in the opposite direction to that of the developed way of perceiving. Of these two developed functions, Jung considered that the first to develop was clearly dominant or superior and labeled it the *dominant* function, while the second to develop functioned as a modifying *auxiliary* that he designated as the *auxiliary* function (1971, pp. 405–407).

The dominant function is defined in the MBTI type user community as individuals' favorite function oriented to their favorite world and is used to name individuals' type. Thus, an individual with a prevailing extraverted orientation will have a dominant function that is extraverted, for example, extraverted feeling, while someone with an introverted orientation will possess a dominant function that is introverted, for example, introverted feeling. If the dominant function for an individual is an extraverted feeling, then that individual is called an "extraverted feeling type."

According to type theorists Grant, Thompson, and Clarke (1983), our first or dominant function differentiates from the unconscious between the years of six and twelve, roughly corresponding to the latency age of children theorized by Sigmund Freud, and to the school-age Industry *vs* Inferiority stage of the Neo-Freudian pioneer of human life-span psychology, Erik Erikson. The development of a contrasting, but complementary, auxiliary function in adolescence forms part of the changes and possible turmoil of this stage in the human life cycle. True to the alternating principle of type development (Myers, 1980), the second or auxiliary function complements and balances the effect of the individual's dominant function in two regards: for example, a dominant extraverted feeling type will have an auxiliary function that is introverted and, since extraverted feeling is a form of judgment, the auxiliary function will be a form of perceiving, either sensing or intuition.

The third or tertiary function develops in early adulthood, during what life-cycle theorist Gail Sheehy (1995) has termed provisional adulthood. While there has been controversy in the Jungian and MBTI type-user communities, regarding the direction of orientation of the third or tertiary function, the consensus now seems to be that the third function, which Grant, Thompson, and Clarke (1983) considered to be usually developed in the 1920s, is the complete opposite of the auxiliary function and hence oriented in the same energetic direction as the dominant function.

The fourth function to develop was named by Jung the "inferior" function, somewhat problematically because of its disparaging connotations. This fourth function has been long regarded as oriented in the opposite direction to that of the dominant function and hence in the same direction as the auxiliary (von Franz and Hillman, 1971). It is also the dominant's direct opposite in regard to the most favored function. Thus, for an extraverted-thinking type, like one of the authors, who likes to organize everything in the external world in a logical way, his fourth "inferior" function is an introverted feeling that has been described by Jungian analyst von Franz (1971) as having all the intensity and flexibility of molten lava, being slow to start but once started impossible to stop.

Regarding the remaining four functions, a similar pattern of alternation between extraversion and introversion, and between a judging and perceiving function, has been observed by Beebe (2004) among analysands and by Haas and Hunziker (2006) among participants in experiential workshops.

EIGHT FUNCTION APPROACH IN THE CONTEXT OF RELIGION AND SPIRITUALITY

Jung's theory of psychological type has been well explored for its contribution to approaches to developing religious life and community, for the most part Christian, that consider individual personality differences. This book is a response to limitations in such applications of psychological type to religion and spirituality in a mainly Christian context.

The first limitation of these previous applications is structural. As we have seen, Jung articulated eight functions at work in the human *psyche*, Jung's name for our psychological life, by which human consciousness is orientated. However, traditional type theorists—both Jungian analysts and those using the Myers–Briggs Type Indicator (MBTI)—describe, as we have seen, only four levels of type development. The question arises, "What about the other four functions?" Jungian analyst John Beebe was confronted with this discrepancy in 1983 by Laura McGrew, an analyst in training at the Chicago Society of Jungian Analysts. In response to this challenge, he evolved an eight-function, eight-archetype, model of type development which he presented widely and first published in full in the early 2000s (Beebe, 2004) and most recently in *Energies and patterns in psychological type: The reservoir of consciousness* (Beebe, 2016). Leona Haas, Robert McAlpine, and Margaret Hartzler (2001) were the first to publish from within the MBTI community an eight-function approach to type development. Applications of type to religion and spirituality, however, have not included an eight-function approach.

A second limitation of studies applying of Jung's typology to Christian life and ministry is their focus for the most part on the bright side of each psychological type—the positives, the gifts of human difference, to the neglect of the dark side of difference, what Jung called the Shadow. This is out of keeping with the overriding tenor of Jung's inclusive and profound approach to the human condition and at odds with his appreciation of what a religious orientation to life had to offer the modern "soul." For Jung made it clear that anything of substance casts a shadow. By the same token, existentialist philosopher Martin Heidegger's favorite quote of Zhuang Tzu was: "What would shine as brightness only does not illuminate" (Zhuang Tzu, 2002). In fact in most of the global wisdom traditions serious and extensive attention is paid to what may be conventionally regarded as "the negative." Indeed within the history of Western Christian thinking in particular, the problem of evil has a prominent place and a large segment of Christian theology, theodicy, is devoted to this problem. Jung, the son of a pastor of the Swiss Reformed Church, addressed the problem of evil in many of his works but most substantive is his study of Job (Jung, 1977a). Jung considered that the symbolism of mainstream Christianity—the cross and empty tomb—avoided a more thoroughgoing engagement with the dark side of reality, what Jung called the Shadow. For example, to Jung, Jesus crucified between two thieves was a far more complete representation of our human situation than a single cross.

Beebe's eightfold archetypal model responds directly to the shortcomings of a singularly gift-focused application of psychological type to religious and spiritual development. The four levels of the traditional model of type development represented by the dominant, auxiliary, tertiary, and inferior functions merely constitute in Beebe's view the Conscious Personality (Beebe, 2006a, 2016). The four remaining functions constitute the Shadow Personality, being the functions that have the opposite extraverted-introverted orientation to those functions composing the Conscious Personality. It is only this Conscious Personality that has been the subject of previous type studies of Christian ministry and spiritual development.

It is the view of the authors that Beebe's demarcation of two quadrants of functions, one lying in the shadow of the other, is of profound significance and will be of interest both to those within and to those outside Christian religious communities who are concerned with conflict, evil, and negative energy, whether this is encountered on an individual psychological level or within and between groups of people. An encouraging implication of Beebe's approach to the structure of human personality is that the seemingly intractable problem of human evil may be rooted in misunderstanding its actual diverse structure in the human psyche. Beebe's model extends Jung's challenging notion of evil as more than just an absence of good: he encourages us to consider that, while evil may be a singular problem from a philosophical and theological perspective, from a psychological perspective, evil has a fourfold aspect and structure. This aspect of the human problem of evil will be developed in chapter 3 that describes the eight archetypes that mediate the conscious development of the eight functions, including the four shadow archetypes that feature in the Shadow Personality—the challenger, the negative parent, the trickster, and the demon/angel. The 16 portrait chapters describe the specific components of each type's shadow personality which, when not integrated, are frequently projected onto "evil" others or those simply displaying "bad" form. This projective dynamic often presages and legitimizes reprehensible behavior toward the objects and victims of that projected shadow function. Jung's theory of psychological type, with its sets of contrasting and sometimes incompatible psychological functions, is able to inform and illuminate the persistence and paths to resolution of conflict that are encountered in the development of mature Christian spiritualities and communities, and perhaps those of other global wisdom traditions.

A third innovative feature of Beebe's development of Jung's typology is his integration of Jung's concept of archetypes—patterning forces in our psychological life—that add nuance to his theory of personality type. Beebe (2016) states "It is as if they [archetypes] form an interacting cast of characters through which the different functions may express themselves in the ongoing drama of self and shadow that is anyone's lived psychological life" (p. 122). His innovation holds the promise of integrating the structural strength of Jung's psychological type theory focused on how a set of functions become conscious and orient our consciousness, with his discursive concept of archetypes that attempts to articulate, narratize, and organize in order to explain the strong visual and imaginal *motifs* that drive and clash civilizations and which form the collective consciousness.

In Beebe's nuanced model, psychological form and content come together in a theory of personality that is full of promise for insight-yielding application to the complexities and intensities of religious contexts. Religions, Christianity included, are incredibly rich systems of symbols that persist in reaching people in deep lasting ways—often for better, sometimes for worse—because their symbols tap deep currents of psychological life and resonate to individuals' struggles with community and its lack (Jurgensmeyer, 2003). We will see how the eight type-carrying archetypes, along with their complexes, are like a troupe of actors auditioning for different characters that will make up the play of individual lives, including the light-shedding moments, but also those darker ones.

NOTE ON TERMINOLOGY AND CHAPTER OVERVIEWS

In Jung's analytical psychology, the basic building block for psychological development is how we orient our consciousness. Function-type designates the kind of consciousness that turns up most frequently and is used with the most reliability. Archetype designates the place and role that a particular function of consciousness plays in individual lives. While Jung described the four functions (sensation, intuition, thinking, and feeling) in general, nevertheless, in terms of how each shows up in the actual lives and psyches of his analysands or patients, Jung was clear that each function was always oriented in either an extraverted or introverted direction. Accordingly, and in the interests of clarity, John Beebe uses the term function-attitude to describe each of the eight ways of orienting consciousness, following the practice adopted by type consultant Henry Thompson (1996) in *Jung's functions-attitudes explained.* Because, however, "attitude" has a range of meanings in conversational English and in social psychology, the present authors prefer the term "function-orientation" as the more descriptive term of a particular function's direction of energetic focus and engagement—the outer world for extraverted functions and the inner world for introverted functions. Nevertheless, for the sake of flow in reading, we use the single word "function" intending this to refer to one of the eight *directed* ways of orienting consciousness. The terms "process" and "processes," following Jung, are reserved for the context of distinguishing between the perceiving, irrational or non-ordering ways of orienting consciousness, on the one hand, and the judging, rational, or ordering ways of orienting consciousness, on the other hand.

The perceiving and judging processes form the topics of the next two chapters, respectively, followed by chapter 4 that describes each of the eight type-carrying developmental archetypes. The main body of the book is composed of 16 portrait chapters that describe each dominant type as it is modified by one of two auxiliary functions. At the core of each of these portraits is the role and character of each of the eight functions as they are nuanced by the carrying archetype and its implication for Christian ministry and community-building. A concluding chapter draws out the implications of this approach to human difference for understanding ourselves and how people of faith may respond to the challenges and opportunities facing us on this precious fragile planet.

Chapter 2

Perceiving Process

The purpose of this chapter is to provide descriptions of each of the four perceiving functions, how they operate, the characteristics that they tend to generate in people over time, and finally the kind of communication patterns associated with each. By laying out key aspects of each function-orientation in this way, the reader will be empowered to observe and recognize the operation of these functions during their working, loving and living day, both inside and outside their faith community. Furthermore, we hope that this heightened recognition will facilitate acceptance of personality diversity both within ourselves and within others and prevent the destructive projection of the so-called negative qualities we have come to associate with the less developed functions onto others, either onto an individual, small group, or large group basis.

All the functions are most differentiated, refined, and recognizable when they operate in form of the dominant function, and so following the approach of Haas and Hunziker (2006), each function will be described when manifested at that high level of development. Equipped with these descriptions, the reader should be able to approach the functioning of each function at the less developed levels and see how the functioning of each is influenced by the archetypes and by the issues operative at the phase of the human life cycle at which these later functions emerge into consciousness. These archetypes will be described in general terms in chapter 4 and in specific detail in the portrait chapters devoted to each of the 16 Jungian personality types.

There are two kinds of perceiving, sensing and intuition, and each may operate in either the introverted or extraverted direction, According to Jung, perceiving processes are irrational, in that they have no *ratio* (Latin for "order") or ordering properties. Perceiving processes merely register what is there:

> They do not proceed selectively according to principles, but are simply receptive to what happens. But "what happens" is essentially irrational. (Jung, 1971, p. 539)

> But merely because they subordinate judgment to perception it would be wrong to regard them as "unreasonable". It would be truer to say that they are in the highest sense *empirical.* They base themselves exclusively on experience. (Jung, 1971, p. 371)

As Haas and Hunziker (2006, p. 19) explain in *Building Blocks of Personality Type*, the perceiving process is regarded to be irrational because no evaluation is involved.

Sensing is the function that "tells me something exists" (Jung, 1977a, p. 12). Clarity and simplicity at the psychological level are its key contributions to consciousness. Sensing type and type theorist Scott Anchors (1989) claims "Well developed sensation is a comprehensive impression of life as filtered through the five senses. When well developed, this sensing occurs with a purity and clarity that is accurate and clear . . . . It is far more in-depth than a sheer interest in facts" (p. 12). It "is especially useful in relating to immediate reality" (Detloff, 1972, p. 67).

Intuition is a form of perceiving that allows us to "see" the unseen (Ross, 1992, p. 84): "As Jung puts it, 'we must be grateful to heaven that we have such a function which gives a certain light on those things which are round the corners' (Jung, 1977a, p. 16)." There is an involuntary aspect to intuition: "you do not make an intuition. On the contrary it comes to you; you have a hunch, it has to come by itself" (Jung, 1970, p. 41). Intuition connects us to possibilities. Isabel Briggs Myers (1980) describes intuitions as "coming up from the unconscious with enticing visions of possibilities" (p. 57). Intuition fades out detailed impressions in order to draw lines and patterns between the dots. Intuition orients to the context and cognizes "wholes"—an overall configuration that has some kind of meaning. Often language is involved unconsciously in this process of natural clustering that forms in the perceiving awareness of the individual.

EXTRAVERTED SENSING (SE)

According to Jung, "Extraversion is an outward turning of the *libido* . . . , a transfer of interest from subject to object" (Jung, 1971, p. 427). When individuals extravert, they are drawn to and are energized by external objects, persons, or situations, just as when outdoors they may be warmed by the sun (Haas & Hunziker, 2006). According to Jung, sensing in turn tells us "what is there" and so, when extraversion combines with sensing, the effect is to connect consciousness to the surrounding physical world. Most valuably the extraverted sensing function enables us to *delight* in the sights, sounds, smells, tastes, and textures of the five senses. A special relationship is established with external stimuli: "As sensing is chiefly conditioned by the object, those objects that excite the strongest sensations will be decisive . . . . The result is a strong sensuous tie to the object . . . . The sole criterion of value [of objects] is the intensity of the sensation produced by their objective qualities" (Jung, 1971, pp. 362–363). Through extraverted sensing, we are tethered to a shared physical world.

Jungian analyst Mary Loomis (1991), in her study of human psychological difference, *Dancing the wheel of psychological types*, provides examples of extraverted sensing:

> With extraverted sensation, individuals connect to the physical aspects of life, to the aromas and tastes, to the visual, tactile, and audible elements of our environment. It is through extraverted sensation that we enjoy or abhor music, sexuality, food, weather, décor. It allows one to note details and to discriminate, for example, a pelican from a swan or burnt toast from hot apple pie, without judging one to be better than the other. (Loomis, 1991, p. 81)

Furthermore, and in keeping with the purpose of this chapter—which is to enliven awareness of all the perceiving processes whatever our dominant type—Loomis emphasizes the central role of extraverted sensation in the physical life of *all* types: "All interactions in the physical realm are dependent upon the extraverted sensation function [which] keeps our feet on the ground and our mind in the here and now" (Loomis, 1991, p. 82). For her part, Jungian educator and editor Lenore Thomson (1998) in her book *Personality type: An owner's manual* claims the essence of extraverted sensing to be the subtle, but comprehensive, way of dovetailing the interaction of the person with their external environment: "Every time our actions are changing immediately and directly in concert with our surface perceptions" (p. 146), we are drawing on extraverted sensing. No matter what our dominant type, we may all remember a time when we felt effortlessly united with a whole and integrated field of sights and sounds—when driving down a deserted road at dusk, or when preparing bread for the oven adjusting the pressure of hands in accord with the increasing firmness of the dough's texture, or when caressing the yielding surface skin of the beloved.

Extraverted sensing provides a pleasure and satisfaction that cannot be derived from "reading instructions, taking a course or considering the ramification of our actions" (Thomson, 1998, p. 146). Sometimes it is the direct experience of life that matters. This is the gift of extraverted sensing to us all.

Recognizing Extraverted Sensing in Ourselves and Others

Haas and Hunziker (2006, p. 33) define extraverted sensing as (1) "an information gathering process" that (2) "focuses on the current, objective external world" in order to (3) "fully experience the details of the environment through the five senses." Furthermore, extraverted sensing (4) "draws energy and enjoyment directly from people, objects and events."

How do we recognize the activation of extraverted sensing in our own consciousness and those of others? The answer is best approached through observing those for whom it is their dominant function, the extraverted sensing types, in whose *psyche* extravert sensing differentiates early in the life cycle functioning as a "hero" in their psychological life, as described in chapter 4 and elaborated in portrait chapters 19 and 20.

Haas and Hunziker (2006) describe the many ways to recognize extraverted sensing. It is "in play" when there is sheer delight in physical stimulation, what may be called the pleasure orientation. Extraverted sensing seeks immersion in full, pure, and unmediated sensory experience, and its operation is characterized by a here-and-now present disposition, uninfluenced by associations from the past, present, or future (Haas & Hunziker, 2006). Detailed visual perception often plays an important role, which is understandable because the visual cortex forms the largest sensory-specific part of the human brain.

Immediate and ongoing sensation is required to sustain attention within this mode of consciousness. Consequently, second-hand information, other people's stories and use of analogies, will swiftly bore those who habitually employ the function of extraverted sensation as their dominant or auxiliary function (ESFPs and ESTPs, and ISFPs and ISTPs, respectively). The extraverted sensing function only recognizes quickly changing specific stimulation of the external senses, and the livelier the stimulation is the better. For the rest of us when there is a vivid freshness to our external experience, it is likely that our extraverted sensing function is engaging our consciousness. Thompson notes: "When sensing takes on the extraverted attitude the person experiences an expanded range and depth of color, tastes, sounds and smells" (1996, p. 52). Variety and novelty are sought and attention darts easily away to something more sensuously vivid. Among extraverted sensing dominant types, small discrete eye movements and gestures reflect the ever adjusting direction of their attention, both as they respond, and as they re-live the experience in its re-telling that will be replete with specific details and muscle-moving gestures.

For extraverted sensing dominant types, there is an effortless economy of action. They quickly notice all the details of the immediate surroundings, and with this manifold are equipped to respond directly and with relaxed poise to whatever is most relevant in *that* lived moment. There is simple pleasure in action. Predictably in terms of Sheldon's theory of body types, mesomorphs, for whom musculature is most prominent, are overrepresented among dominant extraverted sensing types (Arraj & Arraj, 1988).

With the function of extraverted sensing there is a palpable "thirst" for unfiltered experience: intense is good, but more intense is better for extraverted sensing consciousness. Such excitable poise may be experienced by onlookers as a sense of restlessness, but is felt as "ready energy" by the extraverted sensing hero, who seeks out raw, unsorted, and unaltered experiences in order to feel alive (Haas & Hunziker, 2006), and wants unfettered freedom for embodied spontaneous responses. Extraverted sensing aliveness fills a room with vibrant energy, and there is effortless attuning to the constantly changing immediate environment. For individuals with a different dominant or auxiliary function, however, such energetic pulse may prove tiring after a while, since extraverted sensing is lower in their hierarchy or stack of functions.

In her description of extraverted sensing in *Gifts Differing*, Isabel Briggs Myers (1980, pp. 101–103) concludes that extraverted sensing contributes many valuable qualities to consciousness: it offers us open-mindedness, tolerance, and adaptability, confidence that a solution to problems can be found through a grasp of the facts as they arise. Furthermore, through the acceptance of people and facts as they are, extraverted sensing is adept at bringing conflicting factions together.

INTROVERTED SENSING

To explain introverted sensing, Carl Jung used the example of several painters who paint the same garden but produce a different picture. For Jung, the subjective factor at the core of introverted sensing is decisive because the reactions of the perceiving subject are elevated above the properties of the object that is perceived: "Besides the sensed object, there is a sensing subject who adds his subjective disposition to the objective stimulus" (1971, p. 393). Lenore Thomson (1998) amplifies and illustrates this subjective element in introverted sensing by reminding us how five people watching the same film may hone in on and retain memory of different aspects of the content. Introverted sensing is what happens when the external stimulus is transformed into a mental content.

Isabel Briggs Myers (1980) regarded introverted sensing as providing stability because it anchors the impression of the external object in the familiar field of previous impressions and makes comparisons. "They habitually compare past and present situations" (p. 105). Thus, she concluded that those in whom introverted sensing is dominant "base their ideas on a deep solid accumulation of stored impressions" (p. 104). Jungian analyst and publisher Daryl Sharpe states, "The introverted sensation type is like a highly sensitized photographic plate. The physical sensitivity to objects and other people takes in every smallest shade and detail—what they look like, how they feel to the touch, their state and smell and the sounds they make" (Sharpe, 1987, p. 79). Whereas the extraverted sensing type is the realist painter, the introverted sensing type is the impressionist painter "faithfully rendering . . . the *impression* made by the object on the subject" (p. 80). Introverted sensing dominant types, however, would probably insist that they *were* providing a completely factual, that is, objective version. This may account for heated disputes between people who rely exclusively on introverted sensing to perceive concerning the facts—"What *really* happened?" The *hidden* subjective element in introverted sensing is underscored by Lenore Thomson (1998):

> [T]he facts we acquire by way of Introverted Sensation are more than information. They're part of our self-experience. They define the specific nature of our passions and interests. They become our basis for taking in new data. (Thomson, 1998, p. 170)

Thomson (1998) also reminds us that we all use introverted sensation "to reconcile new impressions with enduring beliefs and commitments" (p. 171). However, to the dominant introverted sensing type—the ISFJ and the ISTJ—it is their primary approach to life and informs their identity.

Recognizing Introverted Sensing in Ourselves and Others

Haas and Hunziker (2006, p. 43) define introverted sensing as (1) an information gathering process, (2) focused "on the subjective, internal world" in which, (3) current sensory experience is compared "to similar past experiences through a vivid detailed . . . database of selectively stored memories", (4) wanting to re-live the past and selectively explore the impact and significance of current events, people, and experiences, and (5) determining "What is different? What is the same? What can be improved?" Confronted with a novel experience, introverted sensing actively seeks something similar to be used for comparison. Introverted sensing is concerned to learn from past mistakes.

Introverted sensing subjectively selects what gets noticed in the present and recalled from the past, using past experience as a guide to current experience. Introverted sensing enables us to recall the exact sequence of events as they occurred. Memories are clear, detailed but subjective, and so may conflict with another's recollection of the same events. What is held as most significant has most impact and may be played over and over again, re-living the actual emotions of the original experience.

Despite the presumption of infallible objectivity, not all experiences are created equal. For instance, it is the sunset with specific associations that is remembered. Accepting another version of an event is usually resisted because that would involve changing the memory, or even the original experience itself. When an individual is operating with introverted sensing, only the individual concerned can change the internal frame, and outside pressure is met with resistance. As Jung stated regarding introverted sensing: "What is perceived is . . . merely *suggested* by the object" (1971, p. 394).

Jungian analyst Wheelwright claimed that introverted sensing types are dominated by the "inner image" and it is impossible to predict from the outside how something will strike them (Wheelwright, 1971, p. 12). Thus, the recollection of past events is automatically and immediately overlaid onto the current experience which may be disregarded altogether. Past events are recalled from a unique perspective with specific details colored by personal experience of the event. Often a specific sound or a specific smell will evoke vivid memories and their related emotions. Whatever the blend of past or present, the internal experience accessed through introverted sensing is very strong and singularly cogent. However, under the sway of introverted sensing, we may be outwardly composed, but in turmoil on the inside. We may sweep into a reverie, lost to what is going on around, and return with a story from our past that may not relate to what others have been discussing.

The familiar is favored over the less familiar, "familiarity has a great impact on making a current event more comfortable" because internal comparison is easier when the present event is somewhat similar to the past event (Haas & Hunziker, 2006, p. 45). Lastly, introverted sensing enables a high level of internal bodily awareness and equips us to be in tune with our physical condition and bodily energy.

EXTRAVERTED INTUITION

For Jung, extraverted intuition seeks out "new possibilities, whereas stable conditions suffocate." This function possesses a "nose for anything new and in the making." For the dominant extraverted intuitive, "it is as though his whole life vanished in the new situation." "The intuitive does have sensations, of course, but he is not guided by them; he uses them as starting points . . . " (Jung, 1971, p. 368). Extraverted intuition grasps "the sensory data as *a pattern of changing* relationships" (Thomson, 1998, p. 197) and envisions possibilities in the external world, experiencing their "irresistible pull" (Myers, 1980, p. 109). This function "strives to apprehend the widest range of possibilities inherent in the objective situation" in contrast to extraverted sensation that "seeks the highest pitch of physical realism" (Sharpe, 1987, p. 60). Projects are for extraverted intuition as responding to facts is for introverted sensing. Extraverted intuition formulates a project, proceeding with confidence that it will provide a way out of a besetting problem or routine. Through the function of extraverted intuition our consciousness is able to create a *context* from the *content* of sensory facts and responds to it with its solution, a project.

Extraverted intuition orients to the future, to what is "not yet." In its orientation to finding patterns, especially patterns of meaning, the extraverted intuitive function seeks connections between events and supports the broad awareness that is available to human consciousness. The broad sweep of extraverted intuitive awareness provides connective energy that inspires individuals to imagine what is possible, to launch projects and realize the potential in a situation. Extraverted intuition is not just comfortable with change, it welcomes change, inspires changes, and derives energy from change; change, however, that comes from a vision of what is possible.

Recognizing Extraverted Intuition in Ourselves and Others

Haas and Hunziker (2006) define extraverted intuition as (1) an information gathering process that (2) focuses on the external world, (3) seeking connections and relationships between the objects, people, and events in the environment, with a view to (4) generating "real-world possibilities" (p. 53).

All of us possess the function of extraverted intuition and use it by choice, necessity, or chance. The role of extraverted intuition in our psychological life, our *psyche*, depends on the *degree* to which it is currently integrated into consciousness, and secondly on the *kind* of archetypal energy that influences its journey of differentiation from the unconscious into a conscious orientation. How do we recognize the activation of extraverted sensing in our own consciousness and those others? An answer is best approached by observing those for whom it is their dominant function, the extraverted intuitive types in whose *psyche* extravert intuition differentiates early in the life cycle, functioning as a "hero" in their psychological life, as we describe in chapter 4 and elaborate in portrait chapters 17 and 18. By identifying its key qualities, we can recognize how extraverted intuition manifests in our daily lives, both within ourselves and as observed in others. In turn differentiating extraverted intuitive function's distinctive ways of operating will allow us to be more conscious of it and the role it plays or could play in our lives and future development.

John Beebe, a rare extravert within the predominantly introverted enclave of Jungian analysts, summed up his dominant function of extraverted intuition in this way: "Extraverted intuition seemed to be involved in picking up what was going on in people's minds, and seeing possibilities that others might not have imagined" (2004, p. 96). At whatever level extraverted intuition rests in our developmental hierarchy of functions, we may all recall a time when we asked the question: "How can I use this information, now I've had this realization, having enjoyed seeing in a single moment how all the pieces being presented fit together?" Or can you recall a time when you were able "to turn on a dime" (Haas & Hunziker, 2006, p. 58), and strike out in a new direction once you "got the message", or have "seen the light" that converted Saul of Tarsus, the tent-maker, into Saint Paul, the strident ecstatic. Such "Aha" experiences show extraverted intuition at work in our psyches—uncharacteristic and uncomfortable for some; predictable, in character, and inspiring for those others who have it as their dominant or auxiliary function. Usually for introverted sensing types, such as Saul of Tarsus, this extraverted intuitive flash of "seeing how it all fits" can only be enjoyed following painstaking absorption of individual facts.

Extraverted intuition ranges freely across all time zones: it is most at home living in the future, in "what is not yet, not quite yet," but enjoys roaming freely back to the past, and then through the present into the exciting speculative future again. Both past and present "patterns and connections are detected and used to shape future alternatives" (Haas & Hunziker, 2006, p. 54). Every fact is explored for the potential embedded within it, through a series of associations triggered by the external world. New possibilities are created. In order to make links extraverted intuition leaps from one datum to another, in no apparent order, effortlessly and automatically clustering information into meaningful patterns and then instantaneously recombining the elements into another form. Because of the way it operates—scanning present events for patterns into the future—extraverted intuition is driven to build future possibilities from the tangible data at hand and to explore what could be. All of us at some time or another take pleasure in imagining specific future events like a loved one's birthday or a vacation destination. This too is only possible as a gift from our extraverted intuition.

For some individuals, the exercise of extraverted intuition will take energy, but for those types for whom extraverted intuition is high in their hierarchy of functions, or when it has been differentiated from unconscious currents and complexes, the mental activity of combining and recombining present factors to yield new possibilities becomes energy enhancing. Moreover, extraverted intuition supplies the fuel and confidence to implement what is envisioned, or at least to *start* implementing the vision, for extraverted intuition energy soon dwindles once the possibility "gets real" and heavy with the details required for implementation and maintenance, for which another function must take over within the person or else be referred to someone else of a different personality type.

INTROVERTED INTUITION

According to Jung, introverted intuition resonates to inner images laid down in what he called the collective unconscious. The images are mediated by archetypes that represent the distillation of intense experiences repeated since time immemorial: "the images of the unconscious are produced in such inexhaustible abundance by the creative energy of life . . . [T]hese images represent possible views of the world which may give life a new potential" (Jung, 1971, p. 400; quoted in Sharpe, 1987, p. 86).

Introverted intuition with its orientation to inner images allows us all to have a sense of the backdrop of accumulated human experience. The images to which introverted intuition resonates are triggered by external objects, but become immediately and decisively detached from them because introverted intuition "searches for grand patterns, themes, and systems in order to understand the meaning and significance of everything" (Haas & Hunziker, 2006, p. 64).

Introverted intuition brings an "*inner* vision of the possibilities" (Myers, 1980, p. 112) and, in contrast to extraverted intuition, "does not concern itself with external possibilities but with what the external object has released within" (Jung, 1971, p. 399; quoted in Sharpe, 1987, p. 84). Introverted intuition affords us the *specie aeternitas* of Spinoza, the perspective of eternity that seems able to perceive the future. Introverted intuition in its extraordinary aspect enables prophecy, and in its everyday form, provides an inner vision that transcends the present moment and sets present trials and triumphs in a wider context.

Recognizing Introverted Intuition in Ourselves and Others

Haas and Hunziker (2006) define introverted intuition as (1) an information-gathering process that (2) "focuses on the subjective, internal world of the unconscious", (3) seeking connections and relationships between the contents of the unconscious, in order to (4) "discover underlying significance, systems and meaning" (p. 63).

Introverted intuition is developed to varying degrees in every individual and is nuanced accordingly by the particular archetype that articulates it. We can all recall asking the questions: "What else is going on here?", or "What does this really mean?", or on occasion when we feel we simply "know" something even though we do not know *how* we know it. Nevertheless, the experience yielded by introverted intuition comes with great conviction of its own truth. Thus, those in whom introverted intuition is dominant may seem arrogant at times. Such kinds of experience indicate the activity of introverted intuition.

Of the four kinds of perceiving functions described in this chapter, introverted intuition is the most self-reflective. Thomson states: "[Introverted intuition] prompts an interest in perception itself – the process of recognizing and interpreting what we take in" (1998, p. 222). Introverted intuition is also the most autonomous of the perceiving functions. "It can be triggered internally or externally or have no identifiable trigger at all," working "in mysterious ways and on its own timetable," "quickly [grasping] the meaning behind the words," and "reading between the lines." The five senses are merely used as "a sources of clues to aid in the pursuit of an inner understanding of the universal truths that the tangible objects represent." Introverted intuition looks for "associations and connection [in order] to identify patterns," seeking to "understand everything as an interconnected whole" (Haas & Hunziker, 2006, p. 65). Using the broadest brush strokes, introverted intuition seeks the most inclusive explanations: "Gathering concrete information is a challenge" and introverted intuitive types tend to move prematurely to overly abstract conclusions (Haas & Hunziker, 2006, p. 65).

Introverted intuition may be recognized as operating in our *psyche* when something comes to us "in a flash" or "out of the blue." As a form of perception, it is—to use Jung's term—irrational. For instance, Haas and Hunziker report from an introverted intuitive they interviewed: "The flash of inspiration comes when it wants to come. I can't consciously summon it" (2006, p. 69). However, while the insight is instantaneous and unpredictable, when introverted intuition is well developed, it is preceded and followed by a sustained seeking-after-meaning which is an aspect of introverted intuition that is more capable of being brought under conscious control. Nevertheless, there is much "searching in the haze" which may account for the fluctuating course of intuition in both its introverted and extraverted forms. Sometimes "it is hard to start a task" when introverted intuition is required by our situation, because we have to wait for the "muse to seize us." For example, Haas and Hunziker quote an introverted intuitive type:

> I need to wait for an understanding of the implications, nuances and broad scope . . . because only then will I know what I need to do and how to do it. People often tell me that I procrastinate. (Haas & Hunziker, 2006, p. 69)

Speed and halting, along with the haze and flashes, make introverted intuition a rough ride for those who are unused to the ups and downs of this perceiving function. By the same token, there is something profoundly human about the passions that are evoked by introverted intuition, and both classical and popular culture is replete with stories of the trials of the suffering creative artist. Contrary to conventional wisdom and everyday parlance, passion is most closely associated with intuition rather than with feeling.

Moreover, the passion of intuition may threaten the grounded operations of sensing perceiving.

Introverted intuition and introverted sensing directly clash in their modes of operating. Thomson writes:

> This is a classic Introverted Sensing approach: material reality is just so much raw experience. It has to be controlled with a stable mental framework. . . . Introverted intuition moves us in the opposite direction. It tells us that changing our frame of mind *can* change the world. . . . This is how Introverted Intuition works. The material facts remain the same, but we organize them in a new conceptual pattern that changes their meaning and gives us new options for behavior. (1998, p. 224)

Thus, the "cognitive reframe," "table turning," and the punch line of a joke are quintessential signs of introverted intuition at work. Thomson adds: "Most types rely on Ni [introverted intuition] to contend with ambiguities of meaning and perception" (1998, p. 225). Introverted intuition naturally orients to and *sees* "the framework of beliefs and expectations that we maintain" and so can challenge or debate them. All the other functions operate *within* these frameworks and so may literally feel unnerved by introverted intuition threatening to change them or even raising the question that they might or should be changed.

Introverted intuition uses surface phenomena to dive deeply: it provides "insight into what is going on beneath the surface through sensing the meaning of what can be seen" (Haas & Hunziker, 2006, p. 68). It is this aspect of introverted intuition that functions to allow us to tune into other people's levels of authenticity and to ascertain if it is safe for us "to be open, honest and vulnerable to them" (2006, p. 68).

Prophets and radical reformers often partake of introverted intuition. Such figures are able to endure and withstand ferocious opposition, for example, Nelson Mandela (INFJ) who led the struggle against *apartheid* in South Africa *or* Pierre Elliot Trudeau (INTJ) the Canadian prime minister who inaugurated bi-lingual federalism in Canada. By the same token, with introverted intuitive types sustained disconnection from their other functions may entail physical death as with John the Baptist.

Chapter 3

Judging Process

There are two ways of coming to a conclusion or *closure* about what is perceived, one based on thinking and one based on feeling. Furthermore, each of these methods is capable of expression in the introverted or extraverted direction. Often we use these conclusions in order to make a decision or form a judgment. Accordingly, Myers (1980) called these judging functions. Jung described these four functions as *rational* functions because following the Latin etymological root—*ratio* (order)—he considered that each of these functions operated in different ways, but with the shared aim of bringing *order* to perceptions. In an interview Jung stated: "Sensation tells you *that* something is. Thinking, roughly speaking, tells you *what* something is. Feeling tells you whether it is agreeable or not, to be accepted or rejected" (McGuire & Hull, 1977, p. 306). Thomson (1998, p. 254) considers that these functions "enable us to make our knowledge systematic, so that we have a basis for concentrating our attention."

The thinking function operates with language and concepts to name, label, or define an experience. The named concept then becomes another object of awareness in its own right. Jung wrote: "[B]y thinking I mean the function of intellectual cognition and the forming of logical conclusions" that "should facilitate cognition and judgment" (Jung, 1971, p. 518). In describing thinking judgment, Myers (1980) highlights the impersonal and purely logical basis on which thinking operates to bring order to perceptions based on consistency (pp. 65–67). Thomson (1998, p. 254) describes thinking as organizing multiple objects of consciousness in order to "establish logical relationships between them." For Beebe (2004, 2016), defining by naming is the key activity of the function of thinking.

Feeling orders perceptions by assigning them value in a particular context (Myers, 1980, p. 6). Feeling for Jung is "a process . . . that imparts to the content [of consciousness] a definite value . . . Valuation by feeling extends to every content of consciousness, of whatever kind it may be" (McGuire & Hull, 1977, p. 435). Thus, feeling is a general ordering function that extends beyond contents that have an obvious affective or emotional component (Ross, 1992). As Pascal claimed, "the heart has its reason that the [thinking] mind knows not" (1670, Section IV: line 277). Whereas thinking needs some distance from what it perceives in order to operate, feeling requires involvement in order to "get a feel" for the objects of its consciousness and decide about them (Ross, 2011a), but both are equally valid bases for organizing our perceptions.

EXTRAVERTED THINKING

Extraverted thinking is concerned with organizing the external world in a logical way. Through extraverted thinking we experience the *objects* to be organized as being supplied by external conditions and relate these directly to the *criteria* by which they are organized (Sharpe, 1987), these determining factors being "objective data, external facts or generally accepted ideas" (Jung, 1971, p. 342).

Extraverted thinking operates when a logical external orientation predominates (Jung, 1971) and is interested in definitions that would hold true for everyone, "according to ideas that everyone might agree with" (Beebe, 2004, p. 96). Myers (1980) describes extraverted thinking as naturally organizing or regulating the external situation through the methodical application of critical analysis. Extraverted thinking simply *loves* making decisions, adopting goals, and "enjoy[s] deciding what ought to be done" and is ready with the appropriate instructions (p. 85).

Extraverted thinking develops relevant standards to guide decisions, and for this reason, when consciousness is under its sway, experiences a drive to structure and organize the external world through a common system of guiding rules. The most universal example might by the law of reciprocity or golden rule that is expressed in most religions: "Do to others what you would like them to do to you" (Luke 6: 36). Extraverted thinking pushes for equality with regard to basic universal moral principles: "Equal treatment before the law" is a *sine qua non* of extraverted thinking. Accordingly, extraverted thinking is more concerned with maintaining systems that effectively take care of people, than with direct one-on-one, person-to-person, care. For extraverted thinking, it is a matter of responsibility and honor to keep faith with certain principles of order.

Extraverted thinking relishes well thought-out conclusions and is at home in the world of formulae and codes that embody basic judgments about the world (Beebe, 2006a, 2016), such as the United Nations Declaration on Humans Rights, and *Roberts Rules of Order*, John Locke's idea of the Social Contract between rulers and the ruled, or the exquisite sonata form of Mozart. Extraverted thinking is concerned with articulating standard operating procedures. It undergirds, even guarantees, the predictability on which civil society rests—calendars, the rules of the road, letters of an alphabet, and rules of grammar.

Extraverted thinking reasons by way of this kind of logic: (1) evaluate the past—when "this" happened, then "that" resulted. Therefore, now (2) if I/we do "this" . . . Then "that" will happen again. If the "that" is a good, that is a chosen goal, then the "if we do this" is transformed by our extraverted thinking into an "ought," a "should" or even a "must." The extraverted thinking function for some of us is so habitual we barely notice it, while for others it is conscious or even alien, depending on where it is located in *psyche*, our psychological life, and under "the genius" or tutelage of which developmental archetype (Beebe, 2016, p. 128).

Recognizing Extraverted Thinking in Ourselves and Others

Haas and Hunziker (2006) define extraverted thinking as (1) a decision-making function (2) directed toward the external world that seeks (3) to institute systems of organization in order to (4) assign information within an appropriate system, through (5) a process of comparison based on objective and preferably quantifiable criteria.

Extraverted thinking surrounds us. It is part of the warp and weave of our lives and reflected in social codes that make living together possible. Depending on the level of conscious, development of extraverted thinking in our personal psychological life, our *psyche*, we will have positive or negative reactions to extraverted thinking's impartial or impersonal way of operating. We may feel that its systematic approach is either very fair or very mechanistic. Recognizing it in ourselves and others will enable us to be more conscious and deliberate in our responses to extraverted thinking and our use of this externally ordering function.

We use extraverted thinking when we rely on conceptual predictability or consistency in order to guide reasoning in a situation, rather than our personal relationship to the situation which is the orientation of feeling. When extraverted thinking is deployed, interpersonal and inner harmony—so dear to extraverted feeling and introverted feeling, respectively—may be temporarily strained, for states of inexpressive neutrality alternate with vigorous verbal critique once the problem is articulated. First the situation is surveyed objectively for consistent elements, and then *critically* and often vociferously assessed for the degree of consistency with the relevant standard (Thomson, 1998).

Extraverted thinking seeks clarity through ordering the environment and is energized by reaching goals and achieving an end result. Extraverted thinking is generally recognized in the observance of laws, rules, regulations, policies, procedures, and standards. If many exceptions become required then our extraverted thinking is dissatisfied and pushes for a better, more comprehensive formulation. This enables the system to be more broadly, even universally, applied, which in turn legitimates the preeminence of "equality" as a pre-eminent value. Equality is honored in the "consistent application of rules" (Haas & Hunziker, 2006, p. 75). Accordingly, extraverted thinking is motivated to find procedures that consider every contingency. However, we may recall an occasion when a concern with equality had been pursued to an extreme by ourselves or others and prompted protest at what was experienced by others as the "imposition of uniformity".

Extraverted thinking enjoys discovering "What causes what?", and then concentrates on designing systems that will apply this knowledge. Extraverted thinking in action has these features: methodical application, proceeding from facts, with intermediate objectives laid out along the path to end result. Extraverted thinking reasons in a stepwise fashion. Defining, labeling, quantifying, and prioritizing are processes integrated toward a chosen end. Satisfaction is experienced when complex problems can be resolved into a sequence of "yes/no" decisions. Completion of the task brings great relief, and movement toward completion is reassuring and needed for well-being, just as set-backs are frustrating and hard to bear for the extraverted thinking part of our psychological functioning. Our extraverted thinking is as interested in "retrodiction" as much as prediction, for sometimes we like to analyze past actions in an attempt "to prepare for similar situations in the future" (Thomson, 1998, p. 265).

Extraverted thinking forms the part of our logical reasoning that needs to think out loud. For example, among extraverted thinking types, vigorous debate is more valued for clarifying their own thinking than persuading others. Haas and Hunziker (2006) recount from one extraverted thinking type, "Discussion gives me new ideas and allows me to work them through with others", while another confessed listening to herself to find out what she thought (p. 78). Extraverted thinking values decisiveness. However, while extraverted thinkers' emphatic tone may sound to others that they have already made up their mind, if extraverted thinkers are still talking, they have not reached a final decision. For with extraverted thinking, talking is thinking and thinking is talking.

Finally, it is extraverted thinking that leads us to be concerned with competence, our own and that of others, for extraverted thinking values knowing what can be done effectively and by whom.

INTROVERTED THINKING

Jung emphasizes the role of the subjective element at the start of his description of introverted thinking: "Introverted thinking is primarily oriented by the subjective factor" (Jung, 1971, p. 380). Beebe amplifies this subjective aspect of introverted thinking: "Introverted thinking has to reflect on whether a particular construction really accords with the conviction of inner truth, regardless of what the received opinion might be" (Beebe, 2004, p. 96). According to Jung:

> Introverted thinking begins with the subject and leads back to the subject, far though it may range into the realm of actual reality . . . . It formulates questions and creates theories, it opens new prospects and insights, but with regard to the facts its attitude is one of reserve. (Jung, 1971, p. 380)

Sharpe (1987) concludes "[W]here extraverted thinking seeks to get the facts straight and then think about them, introverted thinking is concerned with the clarification of ideas" (p. 89). Both extraverted thinking and introverted thinking excel at creating order: one working from the outside in and the other working from the inside out. Isabel Briggs Myers describes introverted thinking as "primarily interested in the underlying principles" (1980, p. 89). These principles organize possibilities when paired with intuition as the auxiliary or organize actions in situations when paired with sensing. The mode of operating of introverted thinking is "analytical and impersonal." "Introverted thinkers use their thinking to analyze the world, not to run it" (Myers, 1980, p. 89).

Introverted thinking is concerned with internal images rather than external facts (Sharpe, 1987, p. 73). Indeed "what seems . . . of paramount importance is the development and presentation of the subjective idea, of the initial symbolic image hovering darkly before the mind's eye" (Jung, 1971, p. 380). When introverted thinking operates, there is an automatic diminution of the object:

> if the object is a person, this person has a distinct feeling that he matters only in a negative way; in milder cases he is merely conscious of being *de trop* [too much], but with a more extreme type he feels warded off as something definitely disturbing. (Jung, 1971, p. 383)

This, however, is in the service of the great gift of introverted thinking to our consciousness, because the de-focus or reduction of the object enables us to "build up the world of ideas, and never shrink from thinking a thought because it might prove to be too dangerous, subversive, heretical, or wounding to other people's feelings" (Jung, 1971, p. 384). By such precision, introverted thinking enables individuals and society to adapt to new situation by having the courage to stand back and coolly reflect on the *new* distinctions most salient to the new situation.

Recognizing Introverted Thinking in Ourselves and Others

Haas and Hunziker (2006) define introverted thinking as (1) a decision-making function, (2) focused on the subjective, internal world of precisely intersecting underlying principles and truths, and to that end (3) creates "original categories and systems, (4) assigning all information to a place within an appropriate framework (5) based upon logical analysis" (p. 83).

Everyone possesses "their own unique framework of internally synthesized concepts, principles and knowledge" (Haas & Hunziker, 2006, p. 84). Individual types differ, however, in the degree of awareness of this internal frame-working apparatus that they possess. Ease and frequency of its deployment varies across individuals, as does the trust and reliance placed on introverted thinking. The structure of its operation is the same: when thinking is introverted, principles are distilled from a network of logical relationships. These principles form the foundation of the analytic framework and are applied to a range of phenomena, in the same way as beliefs form the foundation for values that characterize introverted feeling judgments and are applied to a range of situation.

Principles, generated by introverted thinking, are open to re-negotiation that is based on logical debate or the presentation of new information that cannot be subsumed within the existing operative framework. Thus, when we revise our thinking based on new information introverted thinking is elegantly at work. By the same token, when we are prepared to defend our principles over all else, this is also a sign that our introverted thinking is operative and enabling us to "hold firm".

Moreover, hearing our self say "I think" may trigger us to recognize introverted thinking in our current psychological functioning, since introverted thinking is often aware of its own processing and likes others to know that the words of wisdom that follow are indeed the fruit of careful reflection. However, while holding strongly to their own principles and conclusions, introverted thinking types have no drive actually to persuade others. If asked to present, however, they will want more than a sound-bite moment in order to do justice to their intricate rationale. Furthermore, they will treat the opinions of others with respect, even if they are incorrect, for "everyone has a right to their opinion" (Haas & Hunziker, 2006, p. 87). Introverted thinking types, however, may be surprised that their framework for making a decision is not universally shared (Haas & Hunziker, 2006, p. 87).

Often introverted thinking uses a cyclical zeroing-in thought process and delights in re-fining and re-refining systems of classification. For an object to be identified by introverted thinking, a hierarchical sequence of ever-more precise categorization needs to occur. The assembly of this sequence takes time, but once assembled, the reaction is very quick. Confusion occurs when internal thought processes do not match the external world. Thus, sometimes introverted thinkers need a long time for reflection before a response is forthcoming. At other times, their response is very swift, and generally the impression to others is of someone who is intelligent. However, when they were children, because they were taking their time to put together their carefully customized thought processes, they may have struggled with feeling "slow" compared to the quicker but less reflective responses of their peers (Haas & Hunziker, 2006).

Introverted thinking makes us curious about "how something works." At work, introverted thinking is more interested in understanding work processes than in actual outcomes. Similarly, the process of group interaction is more absorbing than the group goal. Have you ever already made a decision but told no one that you have? That is probably the product of the play of introverted thinking.

EXTRAVERTED FEELING

Extraverted feeling, like extraverted thinking, is a rational, ordering function oriented to the external world that seeks to organize whatever is perceived in the outer environment (Sharpe, 1987). Both extraverted rational functions help construct—and in turn "adapt us to consensual reality"—the standards of reason that characterize a particular society, "which determines its conventions and expectations" (Thomson, 1998, p. 317). However, unlike extraverted thinking that proceeds on the basis of detached cause-effect analysis, the priority for extraverted feeling is to make judgments and determinations in *harmony* with "generally accepted values of some kind" on the basis of human relatedness. According to Jung (1971), extraverted feeling automatically adjusts us to the social situation.

Lenore Thomson agrees with Jung in emphasizing the rational aspect of the feeling functions. She distinguishes feeling from emotion in the following way:

> Extraverted feeling is likely to prompt *disregard* of immediate emotional preference. Consider, for example, the feeling type who dislikes his father's new wife but is obliged by her category of relationship to include her in all family gatherings. What the son "feels" doesn't matter. There is no way to leave out

> his stepmother and also meet conventional, nay obligatory, standards of familial behavior. (Thomson, 1998, pp. 320–321)

Decisions and information are organized in all of us by extraverted feeling according to their relatedness to ourselves and other impacted groups of people—such as family, friend, co-worker, or "other categories of human alliance" (Thomson, 1998, p. 319).

Sharpe warns that without extraverted feeling, "a 'civilized' social life would be virtually impossible" (1987, p. 50), and in support quotes Jung: "This kind of feeling is very largely responsible for the fact that so many people flock to the theatre or concerts, or go to church, and do so with their feelings appropriately adjusted", especially in relation to the feelings of other people (Jung, 1971, p. 355). For extraverted feeling, according to Beebe, actively "seeks to connect with the feelings of others" (Beebe, 2004, p. 96) valuing relating to them "with discrimination, empathy and tact" (Beebe, 2016, p. 223). According to Isabel Briggs Myers, extraverted feeling values "above all, harmonious human contacts" and is invaluable "in situations where needed co-operation can be won by good will" (1980, p. 93).

Recognizing Extraverted Feeling in Ourselves and Others

Extraverted feeling plays an important part in all our lives. It is what connects us warmly to those we love. Extraverted feeling informs us of breakdowns in communication between people and warns us when we feel the chill of indifference from others or within ourselves. For some individuals it is the very life blood of human existence, for others, like both the current authors, extraverted feeling often feels "thrust upon us." It is helpful to recognize the variety of ways extraverted feeling can show up in human life so that we can be more conscious of it, and of its possible contribution to a fully developed human life and community.

Haas and Hunziker (2006) define extraverted feeling as a (1) decision-making function, (2) focused on the objective external world, that (3) creates and draws upon systems of cultural values in which (4) everything is assigned an appropriate place (5) based on a qualitative and relational basis, so that (6) choices can be made and actions initiated that optimize harmony in the outer world (p. 93).

Extraverted feeling maintains that part of ourselves that is concerned about people, situations, events, and objects in terms of their effect on other people and *their* relationship to ourselves and others. Extraverted feeling both provides energy for interaction and derives energy from interaction. Concerned about the needs, desires, and values of others, extraverted feeling attunes us to the human consequences of our actions and decisions and those of others.

Extraverted feeling tries to avoid conflict but "can become unyielding in situations involving a threat to another person" (Haas & Hunziker, 2006, p. 94).

Extraverted feeling informs the part of us that is constantly appraising and evaluating the human implications of actions, plans, and policies. Extraverted feeling fills the room when people are gathered together and creates a social atmosphere and mood. On an individual basis, we are "in" our extraverted feeling when we are "on": we may remember an occasion when we felt our presence brighten a room and were warmed by our awareness of others' response and receptivity to our presence. We may have been surprised that at that instant self-consciousness simply left us.

The drive to "talk something through" is another aspect of extraverted feeling, since conversation from the perspective of extraverted feeling is a form of action. Extraverted feeling enables us "to see value in other people's opinions, even when they are conflicting [with our own]" because extraverted feeling has "faith that somehow harmony can be achieved" through active dialogue (Myers, 1980, p. 94). Consulting and seeking consensus comes easily, courtesy of this function: "What do you think?" or "Are you OK with that?" Extraverted feeling fuels our wish to "get to know each other" whether that is a frequent or a rare experience (Haas & Hunziker, 2006, p. 100).

The function of extraverted feeling is ready with praise and loves receiving it. Through extraverted feeling we experience the wish to nurture and take care of others and to enjoy our positive impact on them. Extraverted feeling enables us to know the right things to say to people and may drive us at times to surprising lengths to maintain external harmony, sometimes at a significant personal cost. By the same token, it is very hard for extraverted feeling even to *hear* criticism, and the extraverted feeling function within us takes conflict and indifference personally, for it feels that the energetic basis of its functioning is shriveled and has died (Haas & Hunziker, 2006). Thomson (1998) argues that extraverted feeling types "will deny negative thoughts or opinions for the sake of social harmony" (p. 336). Accordingly, when exclusive reliance is placed on extraverted feeling, our own less-than-positive feelings are discounted, repudiated, or repressed (Myers, 1980; Haas & Hunziker, 2006).

Extraverted feeling likes things settled (Myers, 1980), and so extraverted feeling types are decisive and "move very quickly to closure" (Haas & Hunziker, 2006, p. 95). Nevertheless, active and developed perceiving functions, either intuition or sensing, are still needed for decisions to be informed, timely, and not just a reflection of standard conventions. Extraverted feeling is inclined also to expect the same consideration from others and may feel hurt when such care and concern is not reciprocated (Myers, 1980).

Extraverted feeling is oriented to maintaining social structure and community standards. Isabel Briggs Myers explains that dominant extraverted feeling types are "idealistic and loyal, capable of great devotion to a loved person, institution or cause" (1980, p. 93). Accordingly, the extraverted feeling function in anyone carries that potential to prize and strengthen individuals and institutions through inspiring idealism, empathy for moral effort, and personal warmth and support. By the same means, extraverted feeling provides energy and inspiration for social causes.

INTROVERTED FEELING

Jung selected the folk-saying "Still waters run deep" to describe an individual's introverted feeling function (1971, p. 388) which captures the hidden warmth lying at the core of this inner function. The aim of introverted feeling according to Jung is "not to adjust itself to the object, but to subordinate it in an unconscious effort to realize the underlying images . . . seen in a kind of vision." Introverted feeling "strives after inner intensity, for which the objects serve at most as a stimulus" (Jung, 1971, p. 387). Jung, an introverted intuitive with thinking, but son of an introverted feeling mother, considered that introverted feeling types are hard to read because "so little appears on the surface" (Sharpe, 1987, p. 75).

The motives deriving from introverted feeling remain hidden since the feelings guiding them are subjective (Jung, 1971). According to Isabel Briggs Myers, "Inner tenderness and passionate conviction are both masked" (1980, p. 97), for introverted feeling shies away from its eliciting object. Haas and Hunziker report that introverted feeling "quietly exudes a peaceful grounded aura" (2006, p. 104). In a similar vein, Jung wrote that, when confronted with "anything that might carry her away or arouse enthusiasm", introverted feeling "observes benevolent though critical neutrality" (Jung, 1977, p. 389). Introverted feeling is the most subjective of the four decision-making functions and the only one of the eight functions that "has a non-negotiable element" (Haas & Hunziker, 2006, p. 103). The beliefs held by our introverted feeling are personal and not influenced by the established value systems of our culture.

Introverted feeling cherishes *inner* harmony above all else. Work and other activities are required to accord with basic values, with what "really matters" as understood by the individual. Introverted feeling is loyal to inner values and the ideals they inspire. Such non-negotiable values provide an inner certainty that is foundational to human life and supply it with great "direction, power and purpose" (Myers, 1980, p. 98). However, introverted feeling requires an extraverted perceiving function of sensing or intuition through which to connect with and adapt to the outer world. Adaptation ceases, however, whenever inner values are threatened.

The experiential aspect of reasoning using introverted feeling offers another contrast to the characteristics of extraverted feeling. Both introverted and extraverted feeling "involve the 'right' ordering of relationship and loyalties." However, whereas "extraverted feeling relies on the outward . . . criteria of custom and law", introverted feeling relies on the inward . . . criteria of experience and empathy (Thomson, 1998, p. 370). Of all the functions, John Beebe (1991) considered the contrasting characteristics following from their contrasting energetic orientations to be the sharpest between the functions of extraverted and introverted feeling. There is subtle but pervading force to introverted feeling.

Recognizing Introverted Feeling in Ourselves and Others

Haas and Hunziker (2006) define introverted feeling as (1) a decision-making function, that is (2) "focused on the subjective internal world of absolute personal value systems, and (3) assesses all things based upon whether they uphold these values, conflict with them, or have no impact", in order to (4) "create and maintain inner harmony" (p. 103), and to be true to self.

For the purpose of individuation and for the sake of authentic relationships, it is helpful to identify where the function of introverted feeling lies within ourselves and others, so that over the course of a life time we may develop this quietly powerful valuing process that is based on personal values. We draw on introverted feeling when we have a gut feeling that something is not right, even though the social custom would indicate the opposite (extraverted feeling), or the pragmatics of the situation (extraverted thinking) dictate otherwise, and even though the proposed action would seem to be based upon internally consistent principles (introverted thinking). Our non-negotiable core values are the provenance of introverted feeling, and we may only become aware of them when strong physical sensations—our pounding heart, for example—shout to us that core beliefs are being violated or compromised. It is our introverted feeling that holds passionately to our internal beliefs and equips us with our sense of right and wrong. Introverted feeling works in the background of our awareness. Thomson (1998) writes:

> It moves us to adjust rationally to a situation while it is happening . . . like using a camera whose lens has been ground by our personal experience of good and bad situations. We are looking through such a lens at the outer world, while also making adjustments for unexpected variables as they exist here and now. (pp. 372–373)

Through the lens of our inner values, adjustments are constantly being made to afford maximum clarity for the discernment and expression of our values in a particular situation.

Through a process of continual adjustment and with the aid of our extraverted perceiving functions, introverted feeling protects our inner emotional life and sees to it that inner harmony is preserved at almost any cost. We feel comfortable and relaxed inside once more when our internal belief systems are re-secured—when we are able to act in accord with our core values. Introverted feeling also provides us with "sensitivity to internal harmony or disharmony in others." While we may be extraverted in other ways, our inner beliefs are guarded by our introverted feeling, while remaining a mystery to others around, even to our life partners (Haas & Hunziker, 2006, pp. 104–105). Introverted feeling comprises our inner integrity that only a few may discern; it is disclosed only when we feel very safe, or under extreme conditions that compel ruthless honesty. Talk, however, is not needed for communication at this introverted feeling level. The salient values are poignantly, tacitly felt, and when they are verbalized it is the usually low-key incontrovertible passion with which they are conveyed that defines them as coming from introverted feeling.

Introverted feeling while internal in its locale of focus may nevertheless be cultivated, enabling a heightened sense of knowing of the authenticity of others. Introverted feeling enables us to tune into the inner life of others; there is a natural awareness of human needs and values. It allows us to be nonjudgmental and tolerant of other people's values, unless they directly conflict with our own. Introverted feeling enables individuals to "take human action transcending conventional extraverted conceptual and social boundaries. But introverted feeling can also precipitate feelings of self-doubt, because . . . ideals generate expectations that are larger than extraverted life can accommodate" (Thomson, 1998, p. 371). Introverted feeling enables us to integrate our inner and outer worlds and suffers when this is not possible (Thomson, 1998, p. 374). We, however, almost reflexively deflect the glare of attention from this very personal inner space, an inner sanctum that few see and of whose existence we may scarcely be aware. Humor and sarcasm may be its protectors when under siege. Our introverted feeling needs "time for private consideration" (Haas & Hunziker, 2006, pp. 106–110).

Chapter 4

Carrying Archetypes

Jung's theory of archetype does not conform to the empiricist assumptions of mainstream psychology and in large measure may account for the neglect of his Analytical Psychology in that discipline. By contrast *Psychological Types* (Jung, 1971) has become the "acceptable face" of Analytical Psychology because it provided the intellectual and descriptive foundation—along with the observations of Katherine Briggs and test development skills and insight of her daughter, Isabel Briggs Myers—for the Myers–Briggs Type Indicator.

Rooted in the allowance of a trans-empirical field afforded by the philosophy of Immanuel Kant, Jung considered archetypes were patterning influences in the human psyche that transcended the usual constraints of time and place, what Kant termed *a priori* categories. In Jung's view, these forces produced common *motifs* that were expressed in great works of art, religious narratives and symbols, folk stories, and individuals' dreams, along with the delusions and hallucinations of those suffering from psychological illnesses. Such *motifs* or themes were part of what he termed the collective unconscious and were established through repeated human experience shared across human cultures, despite variations due to geographical location and historical eras. While the idea of the collective unconscious is dismissed by modernist empiricists as at variance with the Darwinian foundation of the non-inheritance of acquired characteristics, it may be a plausible explanation from the post-modern perspective of post-structuralism. For perhaps, as post-structuralist psychoanalyst Jacque Lacan claimed, "the unconscious is structured like a language" (Lacan, 2001; Berwick & Chomsky, 2016). Simply put, it is possible that as humans we live through language in a world saturated with cultural meaning and embedded images. Humans live and develop in what cognitive developmental psychologist Jerome Bruner (1979) has called a "mythologically instructed community" (p. 36).

The genius of John Beebe's eightfold archetype theory of type development has been to draw on more than 40 years of clinical experience as a Jungian analyst and to reflect, over the course of his life cycle, on the intimate disclosures and dreams of his clients and from his own struggles and dreams toward the Jungian vision of individuation that of becoming undivided. Beebe selected eight archetypes that he considered best conveyed the nuance and nature of each level of development for each function-orientation as each became differentiated into consciousness from the unconscious. Each selected archetype, therefore, is considered to epitomize the role played within an individual's consciousness when that process is differentiated at a particular stage in that individual's life cycle. The process is used to respond and adapt creatively to the demands of an individual's internal and external environments at that stage. As Beebe so eloquently puts it, "functions are carried into consciousness on the backs of the archetypes" (Beebe, 2006b, p. 40). Patterning capacities deep within the human psyche and laid down through the collective unconsciousness' capacity to register repeated human experience in turn organize and shape the unfolding of eight core cognitive processes. The archetype that "carries" a particular function-orientation into consciousness will give inflexion, atmosphere, and flavor to the unfolding of that function at a particular point in the individual's life cycle.

CONSCIOUS PERSONALITY

Dominant Function Carried by Hero Archetype

The dominant function is usually stabilized by late childhood, imbued with the energy of the hero archetype. The hero archetype typifies the challenges that have faced individuals in Western cultures as these have evolved, particularly over the last 1,700 years when the hero motive was incorporated and accentuated with the melding of Roman imperial structure with the Jesus narrative under Emperor Constantine. In Western traditions, there is a strong tendency to identify the hero with the ego. However, from Beebe's perspective of Jungian functions and their development, the hero is merely one character in a cast of eight, but, like any conventional male hero, it does not take kindly to being "overshadowed."

In most Western cultural traditions, humans are required to be singular, unified individuals, and by the time we have ended childhood and commence the move to adolescence, one of the eight psychological functions has been commandeered and drawn into that role. Life for school-age children is frequently experienced as a challenge, and part of their response to this stage of their journey is to come to rely on a particular function-orientation to meet the challenge. This is also the life period when the child may be exposed to the heroic stories. The heroic *motif* is a central element in the narrative of many religions.

Two global religions, Christianity and Buddhism, take their name from the heroic figure at the center of their core narrative. More accessible figures are important too, for example, King Arthur, St George, or the biblical Ruth (see Ragan, 1998). Furthermore, school-age children between five and twelve years develop the narrative memory to recall their hero's stories, which may then be internalized as identities woven into consciousness in adolescence (see Fowler, 1976).

For Beebe, the heroic archetype is that "part of the psyche that welcomes facing challenges, that takes pleasure in recalling its past successful exploits, that revels in its unflagging reliability" (Beebe, 2016, p. 129). Thus, we appreciate the heroic role of our own and others' dominant function because it can be relied upon to cope with many of life's challenges. Nonetheless, according to Beebe, our heroic function on its own can be somewhat of a bore. It insists on being perpetually consulted and is prone to grandiosity. Yet because it is always around, the dominant function becomes invisible and so often goes unnoticed. The dominant function may succumb to megalomania, thinking it to be the "only game in town", the only function available to consciousness. The hero entertains the fantasy that it can function on its own and is a sufficient recipe for complete stability in the face of any event or trial. The perplexity of asking us to experience or "see" our dominant function is akin to asking a fish about water. It is invisible because it surrounds and permeates our psychological life. The stabilization of a dominant function, however, enables the school-age child to feel, and to be seen, as competent and gifted, and, in an acknowledging family, remarkable. Nonetheless, it is reliable and ordinary rather than romantic (Beebe, 2007a).

Auxiliary Function Carried by Nurturing Parent Archetype

The auxiliary function makes two contributions to individuals' personality. First, it is borne into consciousness under the guiding influence of the archetype of the nurturing parent and is the function used most often to give to others and to oneself. In other words, we most easily and most readily nurture with our second function. The auxiliary nurturing parent function enables us to reach out and care for others as well as to care for ourselves. It functions as a leading "right arm" (in right-handed persons; Beebe, 2007b), functioning as a bridge to the world of relationality. Our auxiliary function is both what we have to give and how we enjoy giving to other people. It usually develops in adolescence, and maturing adolescents are aided in their striving autonomy from their actual parents by the development of their own inner nurturing parent as their auxiliary differentiates from the unconscious into a conscious orientation. Through their auxiliary function, adolescents are aided in their struggle to reach out to others and to reach out to the minster to protect their own needs.

The nurturing parental qualities of empathy, understanding, compassion, and caring coalesce in personalized form in the collective unconscious crystallizing into a common archetypal form, the nurturing parent, which finds expression in a variety of overlapping *imagos* across otherwise disparate cultures, for example, as the White Buffalo Woman among the First Nations of the North American Plains or as Mary the Mother of Jesus in Christian Catholic and Orthodox traditions. By the same token, the now slowly changing archetype of the good father incorporates the qualities of both care and protection.

Second, the nurturing parent auxiliary function provides individuals' personality with structural balance by providing a complementary match to features of their dominant function in two respects: in terms of the orientation of its directed energy (introverted or extraverted), and then in regard to the kind of process (perceiving or judging). Thus, if individuals have introverted sensing, for example, as their heroic dominant function, their auxiliary function will be extraverted. Furthermore, as their heroic introverted sensing dominant is a perceiving function, their contrasting but balancing nurturing auxiliary will be a judging function, either extraverted feeling or extraverted thinking.

Because the auxiliary function usually differentiates into consciousness during adolescence, it is a source of change and of potential turmoil both for the emerging adolescents and their parents during this stage of their human life cycle. For example, if an introverted dominant teenager has two introverted dominant parents, both may be shocked at how "loud" their teenage child has become as the extraverted auxiliary differentiates from the unconscious into a consciousness orientation. Conversely the extraverted dominant child, for instance, with extraverted parents may alarm these talkative pairs when their child's introverted auxiliary develops. Without type literacy and awareness it will be hard for the extraverted parents not to react to what they see as withdrawn and sullen behavior. Furthermore, with the shift in adolescence between the relative strength and activity of judging and perceiving processes, parents operating externally with a judging function, for example, may struggle when their hitherto compatible dominant judging and organized child, who now creates messes as an introverted perceiving auxiliary spills into consciousness and into *their* tidy living area.

For the emerging individuals themselves when the dominant function is a judging function then the balancing effect of the perceiving auxiliary function is to moisten and soften the personality, and when a perceiving function is dominant, the judging auxiliary function will serve to "dry" and perhaps toughen and sharpen the edges and angles of the personality overall (Beebe, 1988). Berens and Nardi (2004) note that, when the auxiliary function is overprotective, it may have a stunting rather than a nurturing effect.

Tertiary Function is Carried by Eternal Child Archetype

The third function to integrate into consciousness is called the tertiary function. It constitutes the "other arm" to balance the auxiliary's "right arm"; together with the auxiliary, the tertiary forms the horizontal axis of the conscious personality which enables individuals to establish and extend their relational life. In complementary fashion, the first and dominant function conjoins with the fourth "inferior" function to form the vertical axis or the spine of the personality, providing a sense of identity, a self-sense (Beebe, 2006b, 2016). In terms of emergence from the unconscious and stabilization as a conscious orientation, the tertiary usually follows on from the development of the auxiliary function, and so the earliest opportunity for its differentiation is during provisional adulthood, when individuals are in their twenties.

Jungian analyst John Beebe, drawing on the dreams and reflections of his patients, and his own self-reflection, described the psychological space in which this third function is developed, and the role it has in the individuation process toward wholeness. The tertiary function is mediated into consciousness through the archetype of the eternal child, what Jungian analysts refer to as the *puer aeturnus* among males or the *puella aeterna* among women (von Franz, 1970). The effect of this "endless boy" (Beebe, 2004, p. 102) is to render our third function as a bipolar form of consciousness—brilliant, winning but volatile—where innocence is peppered with vulnerability. Beebe states "the tertiary behaves like a child, either divine or wounded" (2004, p. 102).

The complex of personal characteristics associated with the eternal child archetype is classically illustrated by the ancient Greek legend of Icarus. This juvenile was the son of a beleaguered but ingenious father, Daedalus, who fashioned wax wings for them both to escape confinement on an island in the Mediterranean. However, the youthful Icarus waxed overenthusiastic and got too "pumped" so that his wings took him so close to the sun that the sun's heat rays melted the wax that fastened the wings to the boy's arms. Both Icarus and his wings plummeted. By the same token, our third process is like a little child who oscillates between woundedness, on the one hand, and creativity, on the other (Beebe, 2006b). Often the tertiary function works within the individual as if it needs the protection and approval of another's nurturing parental auxiliary function, since this tertiary function is painfully aware of its need for admiration, guidance, and external strength. According to Beebe, use of the tertiary function can trigger regression to a wounded child that has not fully healed from earlier trauma.

The contradictory qualities of the eternal child of the third function highlighted by Beebe help explain and reconcile the estimation of the role of the tertiary function by Berens and Nardi as providing relief, which contrasts to that articulated by Thomson who considers the effect of the tertiary to be unbalancing. For Berens and Nardi (2004), the tertiary function energizes and recharges the personality and works with the helpful auxiliary. The tertiary adds playful and creative qualities to the personality, contributing diversity beyond the heroic dependability and seriously nurturing of the dominant and auxiliary functions, respectively. In contrast, Thomson (1998) documents how the tertiary function, having the same orientation as the dominant function, often works in a maladaptive way: it may come into play when that dominant cannot cope with a situation and allows individuals to bypass the auxiliary's development of an alternative energetic orientation to that of the dominant, rather than trusting the auxiliary function that works in the other orientation to deal with the situation. This bypass of the auxiliary by the tertiary produces super-introverted or super-extraverted individuals. Familiarity, however, with the tertiary function enables the energy of the eternal child archetype to be integrated into consciousness and moderates the volatility stemming from affective undulations. The highpoints and downfalls of living will attenuate the conscious integration of the tertiary function. These complexities will be explored in the portrait chapters that follow.

Fourth Function Carried by Soul-Friend Archetype

The fourth function to develop, traditionally known as the inferior function in traditional Jungian theories of type development (von Franz, 1971; Quenk, 1993), is the mirror opposite of the dominant function both in regard to process and the direction of expression. A major contribution of Beebe's archetypal theory of type development has been to elevate the role of the fourth function. Beebe (2004) argues that this fourth function is embedded in an archetype of contra-sexual energy, what Jungian analysts had hitherto referred to as the *anima* in men and the *animus* in women. This energy carries the dominant-contrasting fourth function into consciousness. Certain images of the opposite sex that vary from individual to individual possess the power to evoke a certain energy that has been described as "soul", reflected in such terms as soul-mate or soul-friend, terms that hint at the profound and magical connection that transcends mere ego-based contact between the two individuals.

In Beebe's view, the fourth function when eventually made conscious is no longer the inferior of the dominant. Rather the "fourth", through its dynamic connection and conscious connection to the dominant function, provides the foundational structure, or the psychological spine, for the whole conscious personality, composed as it is of the first four functions that have developed into consciousness. Furthermore, the fourth function serves as the bridge and gateway to the unconscious or shadow personality.

Drawing on von Franz' work on the "inferior function" Beebe describes how this fourth function is a doorway through which all figures of the unconscious emerge into consciousness: "Our conscious realm is like a room with four doors, and it is the fourth door by which the Shadow, the Animus or the Anima, and the personification of the Self come in" (von Franz & Hillman, 1971, pp. 55–56, quoted in Beebe, 2004, p. 102). For Beebe, the fourth function, embedded in the "soul" energy of the *anima* and *animus*, serves the ego by connecting it to the needs of the Self wherein all opposites are resolved and reconciled within the human psyche (Beebe, 2004). Beebe claims: "The *animus* and *anima* work, especially through the fourth function, to transmute seemingly opposing forces into a dynamic functioning whole" (Beebe, 2006b, p. 40). Initially, according to Beebe, the inferior function in the young, and those older who have barely started on their road to individuation, may often be the source of shame and finds expression in the accompanying shrill complaining voice of the *anima* in men and the cornered *animus* growl in women. Indeed there is an "uncanny emotionality" to the inferior function "which becomes profoundly upset when its ideals are not met and nearly ecstatic when they are" (Beebe, 2004, p.102).

Familiarity with the function that occupies this soul-friend position in the psyche, along with awareness of the powerful currents of the contra-sexual archetypes, makes possible a transformation within individuals' conscious personality. The rejected "inferior" becomes a firm foundation, as Jesus declared: "The stone that the builders rejected has become the head of the corner" (Mark 12: 10; Psalm 118: 22–23). The hitherto neglected inferior function is enabled to form the basis for a sense of mission that has the capacity to inspire the integration of the four functions of the conscious personality and provide passage to the shadow personality with its own fourfold structure.

SHADOW PERSONALITY

The chapters that follow devoted to portraits of each type show how the structure and content of individuals' shadow personality follow the same sequence of development as the conscious personality, but with each function expressed in the opposite attitude, as outlined in the next section.

> The archetypal complexes of the shadow could sometimes move a stuck situation, but they could also be quite hurtful to others and myself. Specifying these defensive consciousnesses was, however, helpful in getting a handle on them and developing a measure of choice in how I deployed them. (Beebe, 2004, p.109)

The four function-orientations that make up the shadow personality are embedded within and nuanced by four archetypal patterns, and they contrast those four archetypes that orchestrate the function-orientations of the conscious personality. Until we identify these function-orientations within ourselves, bring them into conscious awareness, and use them to orient our consciousness, we know them only indirectly and defensively through projection. During the first half of human life, these archetypes of our later-to-emerge function-orientations operate in their shadow aspect, tending to mislead and "fight dirty" (Beebe, 2004, p. 105).

At the head of our shadow personality, the fifth function attitude is drawn into consciousness by the archetype of the "opposing personality" or challenger; it is the same as our heroic dominant function but oriented in the opposite energetic direction. This function is often experienced as an adversary, opposed to how we routinely operate, and as clashing with our will. The sixth function is managed under the archetypal auspices of the forbidding or negative parent and parallels the auxiliary function managed by the nurturing or good parent, but in its shadow orientation. The psychological location of the seventh function is imbued with the archetype of the trickster, who helps us get out of double binds. This function parallels the tertiary function associated with the eternal child, but expressed in the opposite—and shadow—energetic direction. The last and most challenging function is mediated by the archetype of the demon/angel and is the function opposite to the dominant function but operating in the *same* directional world as the dominant. In its unintegrated aspect, the function in the last position for differentiation for the unconscious serves to *undermine* the individual's dominant way of operating.

In the early days of Analytical Psychology, no-one below 35 was admitted to Jungian analysis. The functions that are expressed in the shadow attitude are seldom developed before mid-life. By mid-life, many of the issues that we face while still intensely personal may have to do more with cultural assumptions of what it means to be a woman or a man and what success and progress mean in the face of illness and death.

The issues arising from the collective unconscious compared to those of the personal unconscious were thought by Jung to be far more challenging and intractable because these issues pervade the whole of Western culture, whereas the complexes of our personal unconscious are more accessible. The latter may be confronted earlier in the human life cycle because they pertain more to the peculiarities of our particular family of origin which become noticeable as the child, adolescent, and young adult encounters the families of friends and other ways of dealing with human psychological issues in other subcultures.

Indeed the issues of the personal unconscious often come quite clearly into focus in our teens and twenties when romance yields to intimacy, and we learn the detailed peculiarities of another's family of origin that rival perhaps our own family in regard to "weirdness." In comparison, the pervading cultural ethos keeps us from such stark confrontations with the challenges of our collective unconscious, particularly if we are part of the dominant culture. In the event of mid-life *malaise* exploration of the shadow function-attitudes may then provide signposts for, access to, and exploration of, the larger shadow which includes the collective unconscious.

Beebe (1988) in his recorded lectures, at the C. G. Jung Institute of Chicago, recounted his sense of progress in his personal analysis that included coming to terms with the issues involved in the integration as an ENTP of tertiary extraverted feeling and inferior introverted sensing. However, he confessed that in other respects he remained "hell on wheels" for the many people who loved him and worked with him. Beebe went on to tell a tale against his "self", that is, his conscious "ego" personality that demonstrated how he projected onto others the unwanted characteristics of those functions directed in the energetic orientation that had been put in shadow by his four more conscious functions. In a real sense, then our shadow personality, even after extensive development, continues to be a story told against our "self." Our shadow personality is *ego-dystonic* "incompatible with . . . what I normally own as part of 'me' and 'my' values" (Beebe, 2006b, p. 42). It is, therefore, helpful to have a chart for navigating these awkward facets of our personality that nevertheless contribute to our total psychological functioning, what Jung termed the big "S" Self. The four shadow archetypes that articulate our four less developed functions provide such a chart.

Beebe, in his eight function-orientations archetypal model of personality type, associates the fourth function with the activity of the contra-gender archetype of the *animus* in women and *anima* in men. However, with the development of humility—if this agony can be endured, and vulnerability experienced—the hitherto inferior function may be brought more into consciousness. Jungian analysts von Franz and Hillman (1971) and Beebe (2004) state that the inferior function is the doorway to the shadow by means of the contra-gender energy of the *animus* and *anima* that has the power to transform what is inferior into something foundationally strong—to become the base of the psychological spine of the conscious personality, which this hitherto "inferior" function forms in combination with the dominant function-orientation. This function then furnishes a sense of mission for the ego and provides the central support for the conscious personality.

Dominant Shadow Carried by Challenger Archetype

The shadow to the dominant function that is expressed in the opposite orientation bears the archetypal character of the challenger. It acts as an adversary toward the heroic dominant function, and seems to enjoy embarrassing it. To show how this fifth function is more difficult to relate to than our fourth function, Beebe quotes von Franz:

> Jung has said that the hardest thing to understand is not your *opposite* type – if you have introverted feeling it *is* very difficult to understand an extraverted thinking type – but it is even worse to understand [extraverted feeling,] the same functional type with the other attitude. There one feels that one doesn't know how the wheels go round in that person's head; one cannot feel one's way into it. Such people remain to a great extent a puzzle and are very difficult to understand spontaneously. Here the theory of types is tremendously important practically, for it is the only thing which can prevent one from completely misunderstanding certain people. (von Franz & Hillman, 1971, p. 52)

This challenger function is often represented in dreams and dramas as a contra-sexual figure as is also the case with the soul-figures that carry the fourth function. However, the archetypal figure in the fifth position is not soul-filled. It is oppositional. Beebe feels phenomena accounted for by Jungians as "negative" *anima* or *animus* projections are more accurately ascribed to the operations of the challenger and the associated process that falls "in the blind-spot", the shadow, of the dominant function. Because of its obscured position, it is hard to see in ourselves and so tends to be projected onto others and *their* "bad" behavior.

The atmosphere surrounding our favorite function in our opposite world is often anything but soulful, bringing avoidant, or passive–aggressive dynamic into play with self and others, evoking resentment and resistance. Thus, a function operating from this position in the psyche often has a competitive, even paranoid flavor to the way it manifests: there is something about how it is deployed that puts other people's backs up. A function under the challenger's influence is "in your face." At other times, the function in the challenger position is just "plain embarrassing."

The function under the archetypal influence of the challenger until such time as it becomes owned in consciousness is "disowned" and plastered onto other people and experienced as *their* problematic and oppositional behavior. Such others are experienced as "spoilers" or "poor sports." The function lying in the challenger position tends to be triggered and lurches forward when our heroic dominant function and "its most cherished values is [perceived to be] under attack" (Beebe, 2007a, p. 5). Our dominant shadow may also be mobilized when confronted with material that requires us to encounter directly the function in the shadow direction of our dominant function. Using our shadow dominant function takes energy. Feeling exhausted may be a sign that our challenger function has been triggered or forced into action under the pressure of circumstance at work or in our home or friendship circle. When the challenger function is integrated, however, there are fewer clashes with certain others; things run more smoothly. We are more comfortable with our selves. More vitally we discover a deeper part to our "selves" that we did not know was there, and we find ourselves able more frequently to take a different perspective from "normal."

Auxiliary Shadow Carried by Critical Parent Archetype

The shadow to the auxiliary function that is expressed in the opposite orientation bears the archetypal character of the critical parent that is concerned with real or imagined threats to the ego's survival and acts to immobilize dangerous threats. Fierce obstructive power flows from the operations of the function placed in this role and is based on the felt sense of a presumed foolhardy fragile child requiring protection either from her or his own mistakes, or else from external malevolent forces. The role of the sixth function in this shadow position is to block whatever threatens by shaming, blaming, and other morally questionable ways of setting limits and boundaries (Beebe, 2004).

The function under the control of the critical parent archetype operates in the shadow of the second, the auxiliary, function that is influenced by the archetype of the *nurturing* parent. Each function is of the same nature but oriented in the opposing direction to the other. Thus, if the nurturing second function is extraverted feeling, the sixth shadow auxiliary function will be introverted feeling.

Because individuals have both mothers and fathers, as either presences or absences in their lives, the critical parent *motif* has a gendered aspect. There is a "witch-like" aspect that is willing to use powers and "cast spells" if need be to meet threats to our survival. The equivalent male archetypal figure is the *senex* or "old man" who dogmatically clings to the "tried and true" and is willing arrogantly to "pull rank" in order to resist change experienced as threatening to the *status quo*. Pompous condescension thwarts youthful exploits and creativity (Beebe, 2004, 2006b, 2007b). The effect on those who are targets of such energy is for them to "doubt the prudence of everything that they are doing" whether expressed in overt criticism in a stentorian voice, physical challenge, or cold silence (Beebe, 2007b, p. 25).

Beebe argues that the energies of both the male and female versions of this archetypal obstructive force are directed against our *animus* or *anima* that takes care of our fourth function. The effect is for individuals to be cut off from their fourth, soul-friend function, and so be deprived of a sense of mission, inducing paralysis by sapping the source of inspiration. Usually for males, "the *senex* archetype, when internally active as a withering self-critic, has the same silencing and deadening effect on the feminine figure inside the man, the anima" (Beebe, 2016, p. 63). Both archetypal images, the *senex* and the witch, may be understood as the critical shadow of the good parent. Their common effect, and perceived intent, is obstruction mainly by means of demoralization.

With differentiation into consciousness, the influence of the critical parent archetype is diminished. This seldom occurs until well into mid-life, and so individuals are usually in that mid-life passage before this liberatory process gets underway. Provisional and even consolidated adulthood (Sheehy, 1995) are sometimes scarred by the unconscious intensity and a history of failed relationships with many moments of empathic failure and emotional disjunction. Some of this misfortune may be attributed to the activities of the critical parent function: an onslaught may be triggered either by other persons who habitually operate with a dominant or auxiliary function that corresponds to the one in the critical-parent location within that individual's *psyche*, or else by the demands of the situation that require the operation of the critical-parent function for individuals' own survival.

Integration of the critical parent shadow function calls for both awareness and considerable moral effort in order to halt the projection of the critical parent onto others. When this defensive dynamic is recognized, conflict and suffering is mitigated, the capacity to face what is negative within oneself is increased, and the effect of internal critical voices diminished. Relationships may become less stormy, or the storms are at least briefer, because apologies within newly "shadow-aware" relationships are more forthcoming. The power that hopefully remains is a protective wisdom—uncanny prescience that warns of problems on the horizon.

Tertiary Shadow Carried by Trickster Archetype

The shadow to the tertiary function that is expressed in the opposite orientation bears the archetypal character of the trickster archetype. Tricksters break cultural rules. Their activities are morally ambiguous: sometimes the intention is to do harm; at other times, the irregular behavior seems accidental. Trickster figures may break (1) norms of "seriousness" by being playful, humorous or simply unpredictable, (2) rules of ownership by stealing—fire for example, by Prometheus in the Greek myth or by Raven among the First Nations of Pacific Northwest America, (3) customs of fidelity—Judas kissing Jesus, or (4) gender patterns—Coyote morphing between male and female among the myths of the First Nations of the North American Plains.

The shadow of our volatile, innocent, and childlike tertiary function works as a trickster to extricate us from double-binds and other "tricky" situations that are often signaled by the thought: "Someone or something is taking advantage of me in this situation." The function in the trickster position of our *psyche* enables us to "reverse expectations" (Beebe, 2006b) and turn the tables on those seemingly intending to manipulate us into compliance. By the same token, our trickster function attitude may *lead us into* "tricky" situations since the function occupying the trickster position is even less consistent and trustworthy than the already volatile innocent child quality of our tertiary function. It is able to deceive us into thinking something is important and worth our attention when it is not (Berens & Nardi, 2004) or conversely mislead us into skipping over something that merits attention.

The function in this position may not be recognized by the rest of our personality—especially our heroic dominant—as deserving trust or any attention at all. This in fact furthers the trickster's aims, who is able to carry on operating in the shadows profiting from neglect by the high-flown and the high-brow functions of the conscious personality. Mistakes, therefore, continue to "just happen" to everyone's astonishment and consternation.

The trickster archetype may have arisen in order to deal with the inevitable conflict—so brilliantly laid out in Sigmund Freud's writings on culture, especially in *Civilization and its discontents* (Freud, 1989) whereby our instinctual desires of sexuality and aggression clash with the need for co-operation in civil society and for human community. The trickster *motif* reflects and derives its energy from the uneasy compromises that societies and individuals were and are required to make in order to mediate contradictory requirements and expectations.

Building community in a distinctly Christian context may be particularly challenged by the function that occupies the trickster position in human psychological development, for historically within the sacred traditions of the global monotheisms of Judaism, Christianity, and Islam the trickster archetype has been collapsed into the demonic archetype. For example, the serpent in the Garden of Eden is often seen as intrinsically evil, while in the New Testament Judas is seen as the irredeemable "betrayer" rather than as a failed trickster character.

In other traditions of the sacred, the trickster archetype has a humorous aspect: Coyote among some First Nations of North America, and Krishna and the *ghoppis* (shepherdesses) in the *Bhagavad Gita* of Hinduism. Through humor we are able to access reserves and provide significant help when neither logic nor morality nor brute force makes any difference. Berens and Nardi describe a function attitude in this archetypal position as providing "comic relief", enabling us, and perhaps others, to "laugh at ourselves" (2004, p. 19), and so the process carried by our trickster may be our surest way to our all-important sense of humor. This is something better appreciated by our friends, loved ones, and those under our authority than to ourselves. So ask around!

Fourth Shadow Carried by Demon/Angel Archetype

The shadow to the fourth function that is expressed in the opposite orientation bears the archetypal character of the demon/angel. This function is the opposite function to the dominant function but oriented in the same direction. These two functions converge in the same world—outer or inner—and directly clash. The function in this position is the least exposed to the sunlight of consciousness because it is the one most frequently overshadowed by the habitual monopolizing tendencies of our heroic dominant function. Integration of the demon/angel function seldom starts before mid-life and is never complete, so that throughout individuals' lives the function's demonic aspect remains liable to be disowned and projected onto other people and experienced as "the problem with *them.*" Its demonic aspect serves to *undermine* what is encountered, as Beebe avers: "The Demonic Personality is usually the locus of our most unyielding and uncompromising flaws of character. When we act beastly, it is often through this archetype and its associated function attitude" (Beebe, 2007a, p. 5).

The fourth shadow function has the same direction as the dominant function. For example, introverted sensing types (ISJs), those with the dominant perceiving process of introverted sensing, will have as their internally competing demonic function, the opposite kind of introverted perceiving known as introverted intuition. Internal focus on details is impossible while introverted intuition ranges across time and space for patterns of significance; this occurs when introverted intuition is triggered in ISJs by individuals with introverted intuition as their dominant or auxiliary function or by the demands of a particular situation. This was the case of an ISFJ who, confronted in an, oncologist's consulting room with a foreshortened life, was completely *internally* disoriented and become prey to powerful archetypal currents and entertained unrealistic fantasies, including an out-of-character extramarital dalliance. Haas and Hunziker (2006) warn that the demonic function generates confusion, created chaos and destroys trust (p. 179), evincing conduct destructive to the self and others (Berens & Nardi, 2004).

Our dominant opposite in our habitual world is the thing furthest from our mind, being crowded out by our insistently capable dominant function and overshadowed by a barely integrated soul-like fourth function in the conscious personality. Opportunity for conscious development of the fourth shadow function is rare, and so when triggered may erupt with no attunement as to intensity or accuracy. We or rather "It" acts out, whether through monstrous action or oaf-like inaction. Regret should follow. Unfortunately, without considerable moral effort, regret is all too readily put aside or seldom entertained—for such is the pain, embarrassment, or discomfort of facing the "beast within."

In rare instances, the fourth shadow functions bring transformation. Acting like an angel it can be "an uncanny source for the infusion of redemptive spirit" into our dealings with self and others (Beebe, 2006b, p. 42; Ross, 2019). Berens and Nardi (2004) aver "when we are open to the process that plays the devilish role [the fourth shadow function] becomes trans-formative" and gives "impetus to create something new" (p. 18). Beebe illustrates the double-nature of this function by reference to the fairytale of Beauty and the Beast. Beauty, the soul-like fourth function that provides depth and mission, requires awakening before the Beast can emerge from the fourth's shadow and transform into a prince. Beebe cautions that such transformation is an infrequent occurrence and not permanent (Beebe, 2016). Nonetheless, ongoing engagement with the contra-sexual *anima/us*, and the function for which it cares, will soften and thin the shadow cast upon the undermining aspect of the last function, allowing merciful liberation from, and some taming, of our monsters. Vigilance is still advised as our last function has at its core a defensive archetypal force, compounded by the three preceding shadow structures that include the deceiving trickster.

Chapter 5

The Thoughtful Idealist

INFP Leaders

INFP Frequency in the General Population of the United States and United KIngdom

	Male (%)	*Female (%)*
UK	3.6	2.7
USA	4.5	4.2

INFP PSYCHOLOGICAL TYPE PROFILE

Leading Functions

Dominant introverted feeling with auxiliary extraverted intuition

Conscious personality
1. Dominant (Hero): Introverted Feeling
2. Auxiliary (Nurturing parent): Extraverted Intuition
3. Tertiary (Eternal child): Introverted Sensing
4. Fourth (Soul-friend): Extraverted Thinking

Shadow personality
5. Dominant shadow (Challenger): Extraverted Feeling
6. Auxiliary shadow (Critical parent): Introverted Intuition
7. Tertiary shadow (Trickster): Extraverted Sensing
8. Fourth shadow (Demon/Angel): Introverted Thinking

CONSCIOUS PERSONALITY

1 Dominant (Hero): Introverted Feeling

The dominant function of INFP leaders is introverted feeling. Introverted feeling is always considering the valuing process and adapting to the situation based on the opportunity to express or realize core beliefs. The daily work of INFPs continually monitor their world for what they believe is of real importance. They readily change daily plans in response to new information and continually sift opportunities in the external environment through their core values, producing unexpected (but to INFPs natural and rational) changes in plans that may be frustrating to those who run their outer life with extraverted judgment, especially to sensing judging types (SJs) who establish plans based on past absorption of accepted facts. INFP leaders do well to remember that there is an abundance of SJs in most religious groups and that often SJs may form the majority at a church council. INFP leaders will need to cope with the exhaustion of explaining everything at a meeting and plan an adequate amount of "down time" afterward.

INFP leaders' talents lie in helping people clarify issues, values, and matters that affect a sense of identity (Berens & Nardi, 2004), and this is done most comfortably on a one-to-one basis. Folk who work with INFP leaders need to remember their preference for private conversation and realize that INFP leaders may not be at their best in a large group meeting. However, in a set role where they have scope to express themselves (e.g., giving a talk or sermon, or writing an account of an event that mattered to them), their ability to connect activities with core religious themes will be a key factor in building a cohesive community over the long term.

INFP leaders stick to their ideals with passionate intensity (Myers, 1987). In view of this, it may be helpful for INFP leaders to engage the pain or awkwardness of possible compromise before a critical meeting that will likely require them to articulate their core values to important stakeholders in the community so that these members will be less surprised when their INFP leaders change from their easygoing flexible style and stick to their principles. INFP leaders tend to do this if one of their core beliefs is in danger of being violated.

There is a natural tendency for individuals in a leadership position to be unaware of the invisible framing of their world and of their responses by the indefatigable activity of their dominant function. The heroic function (in the present case, introverted feeling) is simply so pervasive that it disappears and becomes a bias, or yardstick, by which every other way of seeing things or dealing with life is seen as less than satisfactory. This is the case even with INFP leaders. It may be difficult, however, to persuade them that their introverted feeling function could be dominating in any way.

Leaders with introverted feeling as a dominant function carry within themselves deeply felt values. On the outside they are "flexible, open, complicated, mild, modest and often self-effacing" (Quenk, 1993, p. 91), but their essential personality is hidden from view (Robards, 1986). When in a leadership position, however, that hidden aspect of personality becomes clearly visible. Thus, leaders with dominant introverted feeling present a paradox to themselves and to others. They are surrounded in Western culture by leaders who do not look like how they feel inside, but it is precisely this that matters to INFP leaders. Churches, however, offer a rare cultural opening where introverts may come into leadership roles.

2 Auxiliary (Nurturing Parent): Extraverted Intuition

The auxiliary function of INFP leaders is extraverted intuition. Extraverted intuition provides the means to connect to and nurture what introverted feeling leaders hold dear. Extraverted intuition tunes into the possibilities in the external world by automatically seeing patterns and inter-relationships amidst disparate phenomena. For introverted feeling leaders, this auxiliary radar-like process provides the bridge by which they connect their own inner values to others in their community. Through extraverted intuition INFP leaders are enabled to give to others by sharing with them the possibilities they see in a shared situation. Such possibilities may take the form of programming ventures that reach out to new members or re-engage previous members. Through one-on-one encounters, through talks, and through sermons, INFP leaders are able to point out possibilities even in challenging situations. By reaching out with this extraverted "right arm" of their personality, INFP leaders are effective in re-connecting members to their core beliefs in invigorating ways.

Use of INFP leaders' auxiliary function will tend to excite ENFPs in the congregation, who have extraverted intuition as their dominant function, and who often constitute the largest intuitive type group in churches. Proposals voiced by extraverted intuitive types might seem "a bit sketchy" to the sensing judging types (SJs) in the group, but the proposals may nonetheless be welcome as something explicit to which they can react and attempt to bring down to earth.

For Jungian analyst John Beebe the function in the auxiliary position is influenced by the archetypal energy of the nurturing parent. Whereas our dominant function is our almost reflexive response to dealing with life; our auxiliary function is the one we add when we want to give to others and even to ourselves. In other words, we most easily and most readily nurture with our second function. Moreover, the auxiliary function provides balance and diversity in two ways to the dominant introverted feeling leader.

When the dominant function is a form of judging, Beebe (1988) has observed that the auxiliary function (being a form of perceiving) serves to moisten the personality, by giving it more to feed on as it were. By the same token, introverted feeling is a form of judging, that is used for determining priorities; extraverted intuition is a form of perceiving. Extraverted intuition, therefore, provides balance and diversity in terms of the direction of psychological energy. Extraverted intuition offers material for introverted feeling to feed on and prioritize in terms of its finely honed value system.

Because introverted feeling is so non-negotiable and personalized (Haas & Hunziker, 2006), Thomson (1998) claims that the development of the auxiliary function is particularly crucial for introverted feelings types, and even more so for INFP or ISFP who are leaders. Both types need their extraverted perceiving auxiliary to know what is going on in the outside world, in order to connect and also to nurture both the people around them and, for INFP leaders, the projects they hold dear. Without this moistening and nurturing, INFP leaders may dry up and become isolated, the prisoner of noble but unrealizable ideals.

The kind of perceiving auxiliary, whether sensing or intuition, gives such a decisive stamp to the personality that temperament theorists Keirsey and Bates (1978) regard them as belonging to different temperaments. According to Thomson, whereas ISFPs engage through extraverted sensing and relate to *material reality* as it exists and generate values based on concrete experience, INFPs engage *patterns of meaning* through their extraverted intuition and generate values based on a mixture of direct experience and the mental impressions of alternate patterns (Thomson, 1998).

3 Tertiary (Eternal Child): Introverted Sensing

The tertiary function for INFP leaders is introverted sensing. Introverted sensing is the perceiving function that precisely registers specific details, and selectively records them, favoring those that relate to previously stored details. The integration of introverted sensing into consciousness, therefore, enables INFP leaders to establish an anchor within themselves that rests on registered details and facts and provides relief for them and those around them from the intensity arising from the continuous appraisal of inner values through the dominant function and the scanning of the horizon for the possibility of realizing these values in the external world through the auxiliary function.

As the third function to emerge and differentiate from the unconscious, the course of this integration of introverted sensing is affected by the archetype of the eternal child. Accordingly the development and use of introverted sensing is frequently uneven, having a charming playful innocence at times but proving unreliable at others. Introverted sensing shows up in creative ways, while often at the same time carrying a sense of wounding. The operations of introverted sensing are therefore often volatile, possessing an exuberant idealistic naive flavor one moment, vulnerability the next, and then, lacking stamina, succumb suddenly to the rapid fatigue that we associate with young children.

Nevertheless, the development into consciousness of introverted sensing within INFP leaders has great value for ministry. Introverted sensing contributes real diversity to the functions available for conscious deployment in building Christian community. More specifically, it will enable the quietly inspiring but somewhat mysterious and deep INFP leaders to connect more easily and directly with the large proportion of the congregation who have introverted sensing (the SJs). For instance, one of the principles of a type-informed approach to community building is meeting the minimal bottom line for the dominant function of another particular type. One of the authors recalls in a whole-church feedback session from type-alike groups the murmurings that issued from the SJ group after an imaginative report from some NFPs: "We would have more time for your new ideas if you brought your children to Sunday School on time." Accordingly, when INFP leaders are able to organize in a manner consistent with introverted sensing, the SJ phalanx will feel more respected and become more responsive to innovative proposals from INFP leaders.

With the development of introverted sensing, Berens and Nardi (2004) report that INFPs come to recognize and take comfort in familiar and subtle sensory experiences, preferring "new experiences [that] match old ones that were enjoyable" (Berens & Nardi, 2004, p. 51). Since facility with introverted sensing brings greater interest in reviewing and recalling past experiences, INFP leaders will feel less compromised by couching their proposal for a course on spiritual reflection in terms of past practice and local tradition. By the same token, because of a new interest in the specifics of their own past and that of the community and tradition, INFP leaders' talks and sermons may now include personal reminiscences with a narrative sequence that SJs can more readily follow and enjoy, with details to remember. INFP leaders' advocacy thus gains new legitimacy because it is now grounded in a "real-life experience."

What once may have been seen by INFP leaders as a sentimental and dead tradition may now be regarded as grounded. However, balanced judgment about the right amount of detail may take time to achieve, with enthusiastic INFP leaders going "over the top" on the specifics of a plan. On the other hand, the increased tolerance for details may suddenly hit a limit with the old vagueness and impatience for detail supervening, arousing the SJs' suspicion that their INFP leaders' apparent conversion to their way of doing things was purely cosmetic, mere "window dressing."

4 Fourth (Soul-Friend): Extraverted Thinking

For INFP leaders, extraverted thinking is the fourth function that is integrated into consciousness. Extraverted thinking is the function concerned with organizing the external world in a logically consistent manner. It is an externally directed decision-making function that seeks to establish systems of organization whereby phenomena may be appraised on the basis of objective criteria (Haas & Hunziker, 2006). As the fourth function to develop, it does so according to Beebe (2007a) under the archetypal influence of the soul-friend.

Extraverted thinking for the INFP seldom develops before the onset of mid-life. Indeed being the mirror opposite of the dominant function, its development usually forms an important part of what life-cycle developmentalist Gail Sheehy (1995) has termed the mid-life passage or crossing. When dominant introverted feeling leaders are able to connect with their completely opposite function, extraverted thinking, something magical happens to their personality—a certain completeness and depth is realized. Their conscious personality is rounded out, with their conscious psychological spine being solidified through a firm connection between their dominant function at the head and their fourth function at the base. With INFP leaders being introverted judging types, the advent of conscious extraverted thinking means that a complete range of judging becomes available to them. They become more naturally organized in a way that is expected in organizations in Western culture. INFP leaders find it easier to pay more attention to segmenting and sequencing actions and to optimizing their efficiency (Berens & Nardi, 2004).

With the development of this extraverted thinking, INFP leaders discover that they enjoy implementing their values through tangible programs with which other personality types are able to identify and in which they can involve themselves. It is very satisfying to INFP leaders to see programs express their deeply held values and observe them making a clear difference in people's lives in ways that matter. As a result, they feel happier within themselves. Since introverted feeling types are keenly aware—sometimes painfully aware—of the discrepancy between their inner ideals and the state of the outside world (Myers, 1980a), the development of extraverted thinking with its ability to segment, systematize, and organize (Berens & Nardi, 2004) provides a soul-bridge that connects internally with their values and externally to goals and programs to which many others may relate.

Other types may feel relieved because now they have a practical basis on which to interact with a person whom they may have long respected but for whom topics for conversation seemed hard to come by on a daily social basis. Consolidation of extraverted thinking will enable INFP leaders to develop more "street cred" and a stronger connection with what is likely to be the largest male type group in the congregation, the practical and logical ESTJs and

ISTJs. Furthermore, this type grouping will appreciate the greater patience of their INFP leaders to bother enough to back up their proposals with facts and provide explanations that they are able to understand. However, it may take time for INFP leaders themselves and others in their church and life to get used to and find poise with the more structured, logical assertive style, in place of one solely based on maintaining an unassuming inner harmony.

SHADOW PERSONALITY

5 Dominant Shadow (Challenger): Extraverted Feeling

For INFP leaders, the dominant shadow function is extraverted feeling—an externally focused function that makes judgments and determinations based on systems of shared values, which promotes harmony so that human relatedness is sustained (Haas & Hunziker, 2006). Integration of extraverted feeling into conscious awareness only starts for INFP leaders some years into the mid-life passage and does so under the archetypal influence of the challenger.

Since this function is subject to the "twist" of challenger archetypal energy, extraverted feeling takes on an adversarial and somtimes paranoid aspect. Indeed for introverted feeling leaders, extraverted feeling has a competitive flavor because it is constantly put in shadow by their frequent exercise of dominant introverted feeling. Each of the two kinds of feeling functions, while sharing a common concern for valuing and appreciation, is adapted toward two quite different worlds and tasks: introverted feeling is directed within, toward intensely held core values with a view to internal congruence, while extraverted feeling targets relationships between people with a view to external harmony.

Because extraverted feeling exists as a part of the shadow personality, until it becomes "owned" in consciousness, it is "disowned" by INFP leaders, projected onto other people and experienced as *their* problematic and oppositional behavior. This is more likely to occur with those who have extraverted feeling as a dominant function (ENFJs and ESFJs). For example, INFP leaders may feel awkward or even anxious faced with having to articulate their feelings to others, and in turn feel overwhelmed when confronted by others' extraverted feeling. Encountering extraverted feeling will be a frequent occurrence since among religious joiners extraverted feeling is second to only introverted sensing as the most frequent dominant or auxiliary function (Ross, 2011a) accounting for 60 percent of the congregation in three Ontario Catholic churches (Ross, 1995).

INFP leaders may appear "in their own world" or simply unrealistic and run the risk of being sidelined because of their delayed response when crises come. There is much incentive, therefore, for INFP leaders to be aware of their instinctive oppositional response to overt feeling, whether experiencing fear at the display of negative feelings or manipulation in face of positive ones. The dawning mindful awareness of this tendency will reduce their feeling of constant emotional invasion in their chosen work setting.

Introverted feeling leaders may feel frequently exhausted when they deal with so many extraverted feeling types who want to find agreeable ways of operating that reflect prevailing cultural patterns. In contrast *their* priority is to search out projects that may be in tension with prevailing culture inside and outside the church, which nonetheless espouse values they feel are a more profound expression of core Christian or universal values.

INFP leaders will probably have to fight a tendency to withdraw, and instead make efforts to find support for their personalized way of going about ministry. There are, however, a number of antidotes. Acknowledging resentment is an important element in preventing burnout after years in the demanding situation of a traditional church setting. Furthermore, INFP leaders should be prepared, on the one hand, to seek other INFPs outside the local congregation for mutual support, particularly in regard to their creative ways and innovative projects. On the other hand, inside their religious group, INFP leaders will profit from embracing the challenge of reaching out to and cultivating a closer relationship with a few individuals who have extraverted feeling as an auxiliary (ISFJs or INFJs) or dominant function (ESFJs or ENFJs).

6 Auxiliary Shadow (Critical Parent): Introverted Intuition

For INFP leaders, the auxiliary shadow function is introverted intuition. Introverted intuition provides "insights into the unknowable" and discerns "patterns and connections that are not related to external events" (Hartzler & Hartzler, 2005, p. 27). Ranging across time and space, the inward-turned mind's eye discerns deep themes spanning human culture and civilizations, including phenomena from experience formed in the past to possibilities shaping the future. The insights so generated transform and re-frame situations.

As the auxiliary shadow for the INFP, introverted intuition is carried into consciousness by the archetype of the critical parent. It is concerned with threats to the ego's survival and acts to immobilize such threats. The function seldom differentiates into consciousness until mid-life, and so early in INFPs' careers remains in the shadow of the nurturing-parental function of their auxiliary extraverted intuition which looks for possibilities in the external world and offers them to others. The operations of *introverted* intuition, however, forming part of their shadow personality, and filtered through the archetype of the negative parent, are often critical and forbidding, using clumsy, misguided, and morally questionable means such as shaming and blaming to protect a presumed fragile inner child.

Before conscious integration, therefore, a distinctly negative aura surrounds the exercise of introverted intuition, sometimes taking the form of self-criticism "for not knowing enough, [or] for not understanding something sooner." Furthermore, when others use their introverted intuition, or when a certain vision is expressed for the community, INFP leaders may struggle hard to restrain themselves from ridicule on the grounds of it being based upon beliefs that lack empirical data. They may use introverted intuition defensively in crass power-oriented ways to resist change—thwarting new energy, demoralizing agents of innovation, and invoking a protective wisdom that "knows best." Members with strong introverted intuition as a resource (INFJs, INTJs, ENFJs, and ENTJs) may trigger these reactions in INFP leaders. The frequent abstract language of these type groups is often stressful to INFP leaders, who become frustrated, feeling such formulation stand in the way of the natural unfolding and articulation of their own ideas and values.

When these patterns are recognized, conflict and suffering decrease. The integration of any part of the shadow personality, however, requires significant moral effort and a capacity to face what is negative within oneself. INFP leaders do well to befriend some of the few with well-developed, introverted intuition. INTJs and ENTJs often gravitate into policy development positions at a national or regional level, while INFJs gather into spiritual direction. In one-on-one conversations, the rapport may enable the INFPs to validate, accept, and harness this introverted intuitive aspect of themselves.

In later life when introverted intuition may operate within a fuller consciousness, INFP leaders may find introverted intuition helpful in transforming difficult situations, both those posed on an intellectual level by theological trends or on a practical level by the conflicting demands of different groups in the immediate or wider community.

7 Tertiary Shadow (Trickster): Extraverted Sensing

For INFP leaders, the tertiary shadow function is extraverted sensing. It is the function that carries our capacity for here-and-now grounded awareness. Delighting in the senses, extraverted sensing takes in the surrounding sights, sounds, smells, textures, and tastes and is the only function rooted solely in the present moment. When developed it enables INFP leaders to orient to and gather specific information from their immediate external environment. However, in the tertiary shadow position for INFP leaders extraverted sensing is infused with trickster qualities, such as playing with reality, deception, and mistaken truths. It is often associated with unintended error and unforeseen results.

Extraverted sensing seldom stabilizes within INFP leaders before the mid-life passage (Sheehy, 1995), and so for much of their personal and professional life remains in the shadow of their tertiary "up and down" childlike detail-focused function of *introverted* sensing. Extraverted sensing, however, as part of the shadow personality and filtered through the trickster archetype, is not only unreliable like the tertiary, but also mischievous and deceptive being oblivious to its own shortcomings. Before mid-life when compelled by pressing physical circumstance, INFP leaders resort to extraverted sensing and make a variety of errors.

Trickster-like extraverted sensing can both literally and figuratively trip up INFP leaders in their ministries. Attendance at important events, for example, may be impaired because of difficulties with following travel instructions. Furthermore, INFP leaders tend to ignore the physical realities of a situation that might pose potential threats to projects close to their heart: for example, in relation to scheduled outdoor church event, bad weather warnings are ignored, so that a mere inconvenience—like shifting the venue—becomes a disappointment or disaster—a cancelled event.

INFP leaders are prone to be cavalier about their unreliability in regard to this essential function, and more tellingly, uncharacteristically indifferent to the effects on others as well as themselves. Their "devil may care" attitude may shock the numerous sensing judging (SJ) types in the congregation who lay such store by reliable appraisal of the facts of the situation. Hitherto this large subgroup in most congregations, while skeptical of their INFP leaders' pet projects, had been impressed by the serious way they pursued them. Thus, in terms of building trust and community, there is an incentive for INFP leaders to become more aware of their trickster-like use of extraverted sensing and reduce physical mishaps, program failures, forfeited trust, discontent, and gossip.

Fortunately, the likelihood of being triggered by the extraverted sensing of others is slight for INFP religious leaders, since there are so few dominant extraverted sensing types in most religious groups, especially compared to their frequency in the general population. However, there may be a few ISFPs with auxiliary extraverted sensing, and this warm reserved practical type group may be quietly supportive, softly chuckling at their INFP leaders' misfortune or temporary disorientation, even while helping them to recover their composure.

For most of their life and work, INFP leaders will tend to discount the pleasurable sensuous side of life, interrupted sporadically by impulsive acting out. However, with more awareness, they may come to be bemused at their lack of comfort in this generally accident-prone domain and gradually relish the joys that come their way with an external focus in the present (Berens & Nardi, 2004) even as the physical dangers and stress recede. As a result, the parents of adolescents in the youth program may breathe a sigh of relief and become more confident about the safe return of their INFP leader who so kindly volunteered for a weekend camping trip with the church youth group that included their children.

8 Fourth Shadow (Demon/Angel): Introverted Thinking

For INFP leaders, the fourth shadow function is introverted thinking. Its differentiation into consciousness seldom occurs until after the mid-life passage is well underway. Introverted thinking is the inwardly focused decision-making function concerned with discerning truth by attending to an inner world of underlying abstract principles whereby individuals may precisely define and name situations (Haas & Hunziker, 2006). Through introverted thinking, phenomena are sorted into logical categories and organized according to the consistent application of principles and criteria relevant to the situation. Introverted thinking may be the last function to emerge into consciousness for INFP leaders and falls under the influence of the archetype of the demon/angel, whose fundamental effect is to undermine.

Introverted thinking, being the opposite judging function to that of introverted feeling (the dominant function of INFP leaders), *directly* clashes with the operations of introverted feeling since both operate in the same (introverted) world. Introverted thinking, therefore, has a disruptive impact on INFP leaders. Occasionally, however, introverted thinking functions like an angel to redeem or transform a situation. According to Beebe (2007a), our fourth shadow function, operating in our dominant world but in a demonically opposing way, is "usually the locus of our most unyielding and unconscious flaws of character" (p. 5).

Whereas INFP leaders are accustomed to reflecting based on quietly but passionately held values, introverted thinking proceeds coolly to reflect on situations on the basis of the most salient set of underlying abstract principles. INFP leaders may encounter few situations that call for introverted thinking. However, formulations of policy and implementations of procedures require logical consistency and the development of precise definitions which are the speciality of introverted thinking, and consequently very taxing for INFP leaders. For this reason, they may procrastinate regarding the revision of bylaws for a church or committee. INFP leaders "may become caught up pointing out others' inconsistencies" (Berens & Nardi, 2004, p. 51). Furthermore, missing sensitivity to "fine distinctions between principles", they may "dogmatically adhere" to a system of thought that they appear to have swallowed whole (Berens & Nardi, 2004, p. 51). Other types may be shocked at this marked departure from their habitual quiet and measured manner.

Fortunately, INFP leaders' demonic introverted thinking is rarely triggered by others. INTPs and ISTPs who depend on this cool critical function to manage their lives are not drawn to organized religion, nor are ENTPs or ESTPs, whose auxiliary offers relevant distinctions as a way to nurture others. The social draw of organized religion lacks traction for all these four types, while its system of belief fails to hang together when submitted to the scrutiny of introverted thinking. Consequently, INFP leaders are unlikely to encounter the cool critique of this function.

Nevertheless, for the sake of their individuating journey toward wholeness and for religions' wider intellectual appeal, it is important for "demonic" introverted thinking to lose its sting for INFP leaders. Occasionally, introverted thinking is allowed its place and succeeds where no other process could: INFP leaders tap "into universal principles that can transform their daily lives" (Berens & Nardi, 2004, p. 51). Nevertheless, most of the time stepping back into cool reflection takes remarkable maturity for the introverted feeling leader—the courage to confront the most challenging aspect of the shadow personality, the demonic/angelic archetype.

Chapter 6

The Versatile Supporter

ISFP Leaders

ISFP Frequency in the Population

	Male (%)	*Female (%)*
UK	3.7	7.9
USA	2.3	6.4

ISFP PSYCHOLOGICAL TYPE PROFILE

Leading Functions

Dominant introverted feeling with auxiliary extraverted sensing

Conscious personality

1. Dominant (Hero): Introverted Feeling
2. Auxiliary (Nurturing parent): Extraverted Sensing
3. Tertiary (Eternal child): Introverted Intuition
4. Fourth (Soul friend): Extraverted Thinking

Shadow personality

5. Dominant shadow (Challenger): Extraverted Feeling
6. Auxiliary shadow (Critical parent): Introverted Sensing
7. Tertiary shadow (Trickster): Extraverted Intuition
8. Fourth shadow (Demon/Angel): Introverted Thinking

CONSCIOUS PERSONALITY

1 Dominant (Hero): Introverted Feeling

The dominant function of ISFP leaders is introverted feeling. Introverted feeling is always considering the valuing process and adapting to the situation based on the opportunity to express or realize core beliefs. Leaders with dominant introverted feeling, contrary to conventional leadership theories, embody an effective dynamic of leading from behind or rather of leading from *within*. For these introverted feeling types, a core of inner values constitute their source of energy as well as their inspiration. ISFP leaders will not meet the expectations of effusive friendliness savored by the many with extraverted feeling preferences that are found in a Christian community. Nor will ISFP leaders meet the expectation of straight-talking decisiveness that STJs revere.

ISFP leaders naturally monitor the priorities of daily work so that these accord with what they believe is of real importance. Accordingly, daily plans are readily and joyfully changed in response to imperceptible shifts in the external environment which are sifted through their core values. Unexpected (but to ISFP leaders natural and obvious) changes in plans may frustrate community members who run their outer life with extraverted judgment, especially the SJs. It does not come naturally to ISFPs to explain why they are doing it, but members who are judging types will be grateful for these explanations especially when change is involved. ISFP leaders have to work hard to remember and respect the security that Js find in having "set plans." By the same token, ISFP leaders also need to cope with their exhaustion at having to explain everything, by planning "down time" for themselves following these meetings and encounters. Others can help ISFPs by encouraging them to feel entitled to "times away" from their responsibilities.

For some ISFP leaders, the contrast between their inner ideals and their actual accomplishments may burden them with a sense of inadequacy, giving rise to painful feelings of self-doubt, when they ask, "Am I worthy?" In the face of self-doubt they may withdraw, since ISFP leaders need to feel good about themselves in order to feel comfortable with others (Brownsword, 1988; Myers, 1980). Members of the community, who observe this, may feel in a quandary as to how to respond to such drawing inwards. ISFP leaders, therefore, need to sustain relationships outside the specific faith community with friends and family to whom they may turn with less fear of feeling emotionally exposed.

Community members need to know that ISFP leaders enjoy the present moment and do not like to spoil it by rushing. ISFP leaders may have to verbalize this characteristic to all but the small number of ISFPs in their community. Other aspects of their personality may be helpfully communicated as well, if not by ISFP leaders themselves, then by a kind intermediary who knows their preference for quietness and privacy. ISFP leaders "stick to their values with passionate conviction, but can be influenced by someone they care deeply about" (Myers, 1987). Though it may be difficult for ISFP leaders to do so, it may be helpful to articulate some of their core values to important stakeholders in the community so that they will be less surprised when these leaders change from their easygoing flexible style and stick to their principles. ISFP leaders tend to do this if their core beliefs are in danger of being violated. They are accustomed to seeing many events and interactions in the outside world that are discrepant with their inner values, but will act decisively to prevent direct harm to another.

2 Auxiliary (Nurturing Parent): Extraverted Sensing

Extraverted sensing as the auxiliary function for ISFP leaders is the next function to differentiate into consciousness. This occurs for the most part during adolescence. Extraverted sensing enjoys "scouting" the external environment for experiences (Hartzler & Hartzler, 2005), taking pleasure in sights, smells, tastes, sounds, and textures. Extraverted sensing solidly connects ISFP leaders to the outer world and gives balance to their personality by providing a form of perceiving that yields an abundance of information on which to base their dominant function of inner valuing: it moistens, grounds, and informs introverted feeling judgment. Through extraverted sensing, ISFP leaders come to trust their firsthand experiences and so "they require hands-on contact in order to know something well" (Thomson, 1998, p. 392).

As the second function to develop fully into consciousness, extraverted sensing proceeds under the guiding influence of the archetype of the nurturing parent. It becomes the way in which ISFP leaders give to others. They love activities and give to others through directly involving them in working together. Their joy of movement is infectious. Their ministry may include the arts, music, or dance. An activity will capture them and their energy will pour out. This joyful energy of action is a real gift to a community—like a breath of fresh air, one rare and neglected, and therefore much needed for balance in most Christian communities. ISFP leaders, however, need "space that allows them to do what they feel called to do" (Thomson, 1998, p. 393). With too much structure and rigid external expectation, they may dry up.

ISFP leaders need to develop their auxiliary extraverted sensing, for it provides an essential bridge to the external world and can save them from being trapped in an inner world of deeply human ideals that have no outlet in an apparently inhospitable outer world. Extraverted sensing enables ISFP leaders to see that it is possible to compromise and find expression for their values without selling out. Thomson (1998), using the analogy of a house, says that ISFP leaders would really like a house on the shore by the sea, but are warned off by townspeople's dire warnings of flooding waves. However, ISFP leaders' extraverted sensing, with its attention to details, allows them to build a house by the sea of their inner world but is now a dwelling appropriately adapted to the world and culture in which they find themselves. Their extraverted sensing nurtures thoughtful poise between reflection and action.

When others use extraverted sensing, ISFP leaders can feel a close bond with these individuals as they dwell together in the joy of the present moment. However, this is likely to be a rare event. For while there is a moderate number of ISFPs in most religious groups who would quietly affirm the tactical realism that comes naturally to ISFP leaders, there are very few of the other types with auxiliary (ISTPs) or dominant (ESTPs and ESFPs) extraverted sensing with whom to share "the simple joy in doing."

For affirmation of this important aspect of their personality, it is important for ISFP leaders and all sensing perceiving types (SPs) to take the time to seek company in the wider community in order to avoid resentment, burnout, and fatigue and to continue to feel nurtured and be nurturing as leaders in their faith group.

3 Tertiary (Eternal Child): Introverted Intuition

The tertiary function of ISFP leaders is introverted intuition. In their twenties and thirties, ISFP leaders may experience an attentional shift back again to the inner world, not in order to prioritize values (the inner judging of dominant introverted feeling) but to see the inner splendor of hidden possibilities. This new function balances the practical present-centered orientation provided by auxiliary extraverted sensing. Outward engagement yields on occasion to "an accent on inner exploration through . . . imagination" (Grant, Thompson, & Clark, 1983, p. 237). Introverted intuition yields insights into the unknowable. This can make ISFP leaders "doubly introverted", and even more inscrutable to extraverts in their community. Thus, it becomes especially important that their extraverted auxiliary function is developed. Otherwise, tertiary introverted intuition can be deployed defensively to avoid outside engagement. However, following the differentiation into conscious personality of auxiliary nurturing extraverted sensing, the development of the inner seeing and inner wisdom of introverted intuition can bring real diversity to the conscious personality of ISFP leaders.

As the third function to develop, introverted intuition is mediated into consciousness through the archetype of the eternal child. As such, introverted intuition takes on a playful and creative aspect and enables ISFP leaders to play inside, and not just wrestle introvertedly with their inner values. Relief is provided by the development of a third function. The development of introverted intuition can validate ISFP leaders' inner values, even when they cannot find a way to express them, especially amidst the "busyness" of running a church or program and amidst the external deadlines imposed by the majority Js in a Christian community. Furthermore, through introverted intuition ISFP leaders are freed from a purely present focus to envision a future in which their ideals can have time now to be realized: "It does not have to be this instant."

With the development of introverted intuition comes an appreciation for complexity, accepting just how many factors and considerations come into play in order to find expression for real values in the external world. Introverted intuition enables ISFP leaders to develop the patience to plan long-term strategies and may enable ISFP leaders to engage the few intuitive thinking types in the Christian community who are looking for a role to play and for an outlet for their skill and interest in abstraction, in strategy, and in planning. At this point in their lives and careers, ISFP leaders may find themselves paying more attention to their dreams and to their own inner potential and capacity to develop.

The eternal child-like play of this "inner knowing" may have a seductive aspect. While the discovery of inner vision may be very attractive, newly developed introverted intuition may latch on to and be mesmerized by a particular symbol or image that gains an obsessive hold on the ISFP leaders' attention. This may distract them from practicalities that require attention. Berens and Nardi (2004, p. 27) warn that ISFP leaders may "lock into a vision ignoring their usual need for some tangible data." This may particularly alarm the loyal and kindly but structured ISFJs. The hard-headed thinking types in the community can make a contribution in this situation by offering a critical perspective that is not seen as a personal attack, but as an argument for balance and perspective.

4 Fourth (Soul-Friend): Extraverted Thinking

Extraverted thinking is the fourth function of ISFP leaders that is integrated into consciousness. Extraverted thinking is the function concerned with organizing the external world in a logically consistent manner. It is an externally directed decision-making function that seeks to establish systems of organization so that phenomena may be compared on the basis of objective criteria

(Haas & Hunziker, 2006; Ross, 2015). As the fourth function to develop, it does so according to Beebe (2007a) under the archetypal influence of the soul-friend.

Extraverted thinking seldom develops for ISFP leaders before the onset of mid-life. Indeed, being the mirror opposite of their dominant function, it usually forms an important part of what life-cycle developmentalist Gail Sheehy (1995) has termed the mid-life passage or crossing. When dominant introverted feeling leaders are able to connect with their completely opposite function, extraverted thinking (organizing the external world in a logical way), something magical happens to their personality, a certain completeness and depth is realized. Their conscious personality is rounded out: their conscious psychological spine is formed, consisting of their dominant function at the head with their fourth function forming the supporting seat at the base. With this development of extraverted thinking, a complete range of judging becomes available for ISFP leaders (as an introverted judging type). They become more naturally organized in a way that is expected in any organization. ISFP leaders find it easier to pay more attention to segmenting and sequencing actions and optimizing their efficiency (Berens & Nardi, 2004).

When ISFP leaders develop extraverted thinking, they discover that they enjoy implementing their values through tangible programs in which other personality types are able to involve themselves. It is very satisfying for ISFP leaders to see a program unfold that expresses their deeply held values and to observe it making a clear difference in people's lives in ways that matter. As a result, they may feel happier within themselves. Introverted feeling types generally, and those with auxiliary sensing in particular, are keenly aware—sometimes painfully aware—of the discrepancy between their inner ideals and the state of the outside world (Myers, 1980). The development of extraverted thinking, with its ability to segment, systematize, and organize (Berens & Nardi, 2004), provides a soul-bridge that connects internally with their values and externally to goals and programs to which many others may relate.

The variety of externally judging types that prevail in most congregations feel relieved, because now they have a practical basis on which to interact with their shy warm leader whom they may have long respected, but with whom topics for conversation seemed hard to come by on a daily social basis, unless engaged in some shared activity. The increased capacity to organize and programatize will enable ISFP leaders to develop more "street cred" and a stronger connection with what is likely the largest male type group in the congregation, the practical and logical ESTJs and ISTJs. This group also appreciates the greater patience of ISFP leaders to back up their proposals with reasoning and explanations that they are now able to understand and support. However, it may take time for ISFP leaders, and for others in their church, to get used to a more structured, logical assertive style, in place of one solely based on maintaining an unassuming inner harmony.

SHADOW PERSONALITY

5 Dominant Shadow (Challenger): Extraverted Feeling

For ISFP leaders, the dominant shadow function is extraverted feeling—an externally focused function that makes judgments and determinations based on agreed-upon systems of shared values, and so promotes harmony so that human relatedness is sustained (Haas & Hunziker, 2006). Extraverted feeling is concerned to connect with others, wanting to affirm and support them for the sake of harmonious relationships both between individuals, and within a group. Integration of extraverted feeling into conscious awareness only starts for ISFP leaders some years into the mid-life passage and does so under the archetypal influence of the challenger.

When a function is subject to the archetypal "twist" of the challenger, it takes on an adversarial and sometimes paranoid aspect. Indeed, for introverted feeling leaders, extraverted feeling has a competitive flavor because it is constantly put in shadow by the frequent exercise of dominant introverted feeling. Each of the two kinds of feeling functions, while sharing a common concern for valuing and appreciation, is adapted toward two quite different worlds: introverted feeling is directed within, toward intensely held core values with a view to internal congruence, while extraverted feeling targets relationships between people with a view to external harmony. In early adulthood, ISFP leaders invariably find encounter with extraverted feeling tinged with embarrassment and challenge.

Since extraverted feeling exists as a part of the shadow personality, until it becomes "owned" in consciousness, it is "disowned" by ISFP leaders, projected onto other people and experienced as *their* problematic and oppositional behavior. Projection is more likely to be triggered when encountering those with extraverted feeling as a dominant function (ENFJs and ESFJs). For example, ISFP leaders may feel awkward or even anxious when faced with having to articulate their feelings to others, and in turn feel overwhelmed when confronted by others' extraverted feeling.

ISFP leaders may appear to others as "out of it," "in their own world," or simply unrealistic, and they risk being sidelined because of their delayed response when a crisis comes. There is much incentive, therefore, for ISFP leaders to become aware of their instinctive oppositional response to overt feeling, be it experiencing fear at the display of negative feelings or manipulation in the face of positive ones. Dawning mindful awareness of this tendency will reduce their feeling of constant emotional invasion in their chosen work setting, for indeed many active in Christian churches do possess extraverted feeling as a dominant or auxiliary function: ISFJs and ESFJs are especially numerous in most religious groups.

Introverted feeling leaders may feel frequently exhausted when they deal with so many extraverted feeling types who want to find agreeable ways of operating that reflect prevailing cultural patterns. In contrast, ISFP leaders draw on what they feel are profound core Christian or universal values, and so the priority for them is to respond spontaneously in a direct manner to human needs whether in keeping or in tension with prevailing culture.

ISFP leaders will probably have to fight a tendency to withdraw. There are, however, a number of antidotes. Acknowledging resentment is an important element in preventing burnout after years in the demanding a situation of a traditional church setting. Furthermore, ISFP leaders should be prepared, on the one hand, to seek ISFPs outside the local congregation for mutual support. On the other hand, inside their religious group ISFP leaders will profit from embracing the challenge of reaching out to and cultivating a closer relationship with a few individuals within their religious group who have extraverted feeling as at least an auxiliary (ISFJs or INFJs) or even dominant function (ESFJs or ENFJs).

6 Auxiliary Shadow (Critical Parent): Introverted Sensing

For ISFP leaders, the auxiliary shadow function is introverted sensing, the function that registers, reviews, and recalls minute detailed impressions, including the subjective affective response to those details (Hartzler & Hartzler, 2005; Berens & Nardi, 2004). Introverted sensing naturally recalls the specifics of a situation and considers these to be objective facts. For ISFP leaders, introverted sensing is carried into consciousness by the archetype of the critical parent that is concerned with threats to the ego's survival and acts to immobilize such threats.

As the auxiliary shadow function, introverted sensing does not usually become more conscious until well into the mid-life passage (Sheehy, 1995), and consequently earlier in ISFP leaders' careers this detail oriented, ostensibly purely factual function, remains in the shadow of the nurturing parental function of their auxiliary extraverted sensing. Introverted sensing, a part of their shadow personality, is filtered through the archetype of the negative parent that is critical and forbidding, using clumsy and misguided means to secure a perceived fragile child's survival, such as shaming and blaming. It is used to thwart new energy and works to demoralize threatening agents of change.

For ISFP leaders, the realm of past recorded facts, accessed by introverted sensing, has a negative aura, and they prefer to avoid focusing on the past (Berens & Nardi, 2004). Such *old* details are felt to be stale and dead, overshadowed by comparison with the manifest usefulness and excitement of extraverted sensing delights and ISFP leaders' swift elegant responses to them. When ISFP leaders do refer to the past, this is often when they feel stressed or threatened in some way. They use it defensively, for example, to demonstrate factual mastery in the face of criticism. Because past performances lack the live energy of the moment, they tend to be viewed in a negative, critical manner. Previous negative experiences are then used to fuel present objections to experimenting with something different. Paradoxically, use of this murky lens upon the past with such exaggeration of negative aspects serves to drain energy in the present and thwarts innovation. Contrary to their usual openness to the present, under stress ISFP leaders may simply refuse to try something again if it has failed in the past.

Until introverted sensing becomes more conscious, the operation of this function is unlikely to build a bridge to the large number of community members who have introverted sensing as their dominant or auxiliary. The generally more conservative SJs will regard ISFP leaders' disparaging use of past experience as inaccurate or as too biased in the negative direction, and this will furnish grounds for distrust. This negative attitude to past experience, that serves to block change, may also surprise and concern more progressive groups in the community.

Conscious familiarity with introverted sensing and how it operates takes time for ISFP leaders. It is better, therefore, if the numerous congregants with introverted sensing function as their dominant or auxiliary (the SJs) give a wide berth to their normally easygoing leader and discover a way around the obstacle rather than arguing about past facts and their interpretation. By the same token, other introverted feeling members in the church can help ISFP leaders by quietly coming forward and exploring with them possible sources of the threat that they experienced, especially as these may relate to their ISFP leaders' core values. The community will welcome the likely swift change of heart in ISFP leaders with a return to their customary quiet warmth and openness.

7 Tertiary Shadow (Trickster): Extraverted Intuition

For ISFP leaders, the tertiary shadow function is extraverted intuition. This is a perceiving function that enables ISFP leaders to be aware of patterns, connections, and inter-relationships in the external world, including those within their religious community. Through extraverted intuition, they interpret situations, assign meanings, and make connections to other supposedly related contexts (Berens & Nardi, 2004). As the tertiary shadow function, extraverted intuition is influenced by the archetype of the trickster, who plays with truth and is often associated with deceptive implications and unintended error. This function seldom stabilizes within ISFP leaders before the mid-life passage (Sheehy, 1995), and so for much of their personal and professional life, this externally oriented meaning-making function remains in the shadow of the tertiary "up and down" childlike function of *introverted* intuition. Extraverted intuition, however, as part of the shadow personality and filtered through the trickster archetype, is not only unreliable like the tertiary, but also mischievous.

ISFP leaders are often deceived in terms of extraverted intuition's reliability for them. Before mid-life, in those rare instances when, compelled by circumstance, ISFP leaders draw on extraverted intuition, they are prone to mistakes. Berens and Nardi (2004) delineate different kinds of errors. Subtle connections not tied to concrete experience go unnoticed or else are ignored or given erroneous or idiosyncratic interpretations. They may fail to consider the future implications and wider impact of their actions. Trickster activity is also revealed in unintended and awkward results. Other mistakes involving extraverted intuition include misinterpreting social and personal relationships and seeing connections between different situations that do not apply.

ISFP leaders use humor to mask the impact of errors, distract others, and lighten the situation. Extraneous allusions come into use to escape double binds, such as situations in which competing congregational factions hold conflicting expectations of pastoral and priestly ministries. Moreover, ISFP leaders' own unconscious mischievous use of this function may actively land them in tricky situations. Because of the tricky aspect of their use of this function, ISFP leaders may inadvertently mislead members and forfeit trust.

When ISFP leaders do draw upon their extraverted intuition, often an attribution of negative intent is made (Berens & Nardi, 2004) that is discrepant with their usually warm trusting demeanor. This may shock and confuse community members with a feeling preference and establish causes for skepticism among those with sensing and judging or thinking preferences. Ripples of tension may arise within a religious community, especially among the ENFPs and INFPs. Thus, there is significant incentive for ISFP leaders to be aware of the unreliable "tricksterish" quality to their capacity to interpret situations, for the NFP groups comprise potential allies who are likely to enjoy and be attracted to the more free-wheeling style of ISFP leaders. Moreover, the NFP group may well be happy to act as a sounding board, especially since they share the inner moral compass of well-developed introverted feeling as an auxiliary or dominant function. When extraverted intuition finally becomes more consciously developed, ISFP leaders are enabled to laugh at their "strange" interpretations (Berens & Nardi, 2004) and their tendency to make wild predictions under stress.

8 Fourth Shadow (Demon/Angel): Introverted Thinking

For ISFP leaders, the fourth shadow function is introverted thinking, and this seldom occurs until after the mid-life passage is well underway. Introverted thinking is the inwardly focused decision-making function concerned with discerning truth by attending to an inner world of underlying abstract principles whereby situations may be precisely defined and named (Haas & Hunziker, 2006). Through introverted thinking, phenomena are sorted into logical categories and organized according to the consistent application of principles and criteria relevant to the situation. Introverted thinking may be the last function orientation to emerge into consciousness for ISFP leaders and falls under the influence of the archetype of the demon/angel, whose fundamental effect is to undermine.

Introverted thinking, being the opposite judging function to that of introverted feeling (the dominant function of ISFP leaders), *directly* clashes with the operations of introverted feeling since both operate in the same (introverted) world. Introverted thinking, therefore, has a disruptive impact on ISFP leaders. Occasionally, however, introverted thinking functions like an angel to redeem or transform a situation. According to Beebe, our fourth shadow function, operating in our dominant world, but in a demonically opposing way, is "usually the locus of our most unyielding and unconscious flaws of character" (2007a, p. 5).

Whereas ISFP leaders are accustomed to reflecting based on quietly but passionately held values, introverted thinking proceeds coolly to reflect on situations on the basis of the most salient set of underlying abstract principles. ISFP leaders may encounter few situations that call for introverted thinking. However, formulations of policy and implementations of procedures require logical consistency and the development of precise definitions which are the speciality of introverted thinking, but very taxing for ISFP leaders. Accordingly, they may procrastinate on revising the bylaws of a church or committee. While "usually unconcerned with definitions and consistency", ISFP leaders "may become caught up pointing out others' inconsistencies" (Berens & Nardi 2004, p. 27). Other types may be shocked at this marked departure from their habitually easygoing style and mild and measured manner.

Fortunately, ISFP leaders' demonic introverted thinking is rarely triggered by others. INTPs and ISTPs who depend on this cool critical function to manage their lives are not drawn to organized religion nor are ENTPs or ESTPs, whose auxiliary offers relevant distinctions as a way to nurture others. The social draw of organized religion effects little traction with these types, while its system of belief under scrutiny fails to hang together. Consequently, ISFP leaders are unlikely to encounter the cool critique of this function from within their religious community.

Nevertheless, for the sake of their individuating journey toward wholeness and for religions' wider intellectual appeal, it is important for "demonic" introverted thinking to lose its sting for ISFP leaders. Occasionally, introverted thinking is allowed its place and succeeds where no other function could, enabling them to "tap into universal principles that . . . transform their daily lives" (Berens & Nardi 2004, p. 27). Stepping back into cool reflection, however, takes remarkable maturity—the courage to confront the most challenging aspect of the shadow personality, the demonic/angelic archetype.

Chapter 7

The Conceptual Planner

INTJ Leaders

INTJ Frequency in the Population

	Male (%)	*Female (%)*
UK	2.5	0.5
USA	4.8	2.2

INTJ PSYCHOLOGICAL TYPE PROFILE

Leading Functions

Dominant introverted intuition with auxiliary extraverted thinking

Conscious personality

1. Dominant (Hero): Introverted Intuition
2. Auxiliary (Nurturing parent): Extraverted Thinking
3. Tertiary (Eternal child): Introverted Feeling
4. Fourth (Soul-friend): Extraverted Sensing

Shadow personality

5. Dominant shadow (Challenger): Extraverted Intuition
6. Auxiliary shadow (Critical parent): Introverted Thinking
7. Tertiary shadow (Trickster): Extraverted Feeling
8. Fourth shadow (Demon/Angel): Introverted Sensing

CONSCIOUS PERSONALITY

1 Dominant (Hero): Introverted Intuition

The dominant function of INTJ leaders is introverted intuition. Introverted intuition has the capacity to draw lines automatically between the dots, to see patterns, to follow hunches, and to generate insights. INTJ leaders deal with everyday reality by accessing their capacity for insights into the unknowable and by discerning patterns and connections in daily life which they apply then in a creative and imaginative way to external events (Hartzler & Hartzler, 2005). Often this is to the surprise, puzzlement, and even consternation of other types who struggle to catch up. Meanwhile fellow INTJs, in the unlikely event that they are around, look on, bemused, and instantly imagine an alternative (and to them superior) "take" on the situation.

INTJ leaders are not content with insightful imaginings alone. They enjoy putting their ideas to work. It is an imperative, which if not followed breeds dissatisfaction producing frustration and exasperation, often experienced by others as irritability, since others are rarely informed as to what is going on in the INTJ leaders' eternally active imagination. In fact, it is hard for INTJ leaders to imagine that there could be any other satisfactory approach to life. Freedom to implement their vision is essential, and so a wide swathe of personal autonomy is a pre-requisite for their happiness. Autonomy is vigilantly and vigorously protected. INTJ leaders are the most independent of types.

INTJ leaders are the prophets of the everyday. On a daily basis, they endure the patience (sometimes the impatience) of seeing how things will unfold before others around them do and they need freedom to act in order to develop a response that is in keeping with *their* vision of what is possible.

INTJ leaders have difficulty putting their vision into words; in part because their vision is holistic and nonverbal, originating from primordial images that resonate to the archetypes of the collective unconscious (Jung, 1971). Their hesitancy and even reluctance may also be traced to memories of past experiences of people either not understanding them or else not being convinced, often because INTJ leaders' explanations are too abstract: bereft of examples for the sensing types, failing to spell out the human implications for the feeling types, and seemingly too vague, passionate, arbitrary, and complex for the thinking types.

For INTJ leaders, their primary relationship is to their inner world. Nurturing their relationship to that world may be at the expense of the numerous and frequent social relationships demanded by contemporary religious ministry and neglect the art of harmonious compromise that is expected by the numerous congregants with extraverted feeling preferences. Developing a conscious awareness of their own specific preference for the inner world at the expense, the demands and expectations of extraverted ministry, may help INTJ leaders meet some of these expectations, while still reserving revitalizing private time.

INTJ leaders have difficulty dealing with the visions of others, as well as with others' objections to their own vision. It is tempting for INTJ leaders to see others' objections as negatively motivated, rather than taking them at face value. Thomson, an *extraverted* intuitive and therefore "the opposing personality," probably overstates the challenge facing INTJ leaders when she writes: "It takes a fair amount of experience to recognize that merely pointing out the limits of whatever happens to be in place is ultimately destructive." However, because of the great potential power of INTJs' vision, Thomson's supportive conclusion seems merited: "INJs have a distinct responsibility to develop their secondary [i.e. auxiliary] function, because their Intuitions transcend well beyond their interests" (Thomson, 1998, p. 234).

Rather than sharing their vision directly, INTJ leaders prefer to share their program for implementing their vision, which requires the development of their auxiliary extraverted thinking function.

2 Auxiliary (Nurturing Parent): Extraverted Thinking

The auxiliary function of INTJ leaders is extraverted thinking. Extraverted thinking is concerned with practical logic that makes it possible for introverted intuitive types to implement their visions. Through a cause and effect analysis of the external world, INTJ leaders use their auxiliary extraverted thinking to derive guiding principles. They then apply these principles and segment the processes required for implementing the vision into a sequence of elements. These elements are first systematized and then organized into a program that is most efficient for a particular situation.

Extraverted thinking is managed in the auxiliary position by the archetype of the nurturing parent and becomes the right hand of INTJ leaders' personality. Extraverted thinking contributes to INTJ leaders' relational life by offering them a process through which they can give to others, and at the same time nurture the relational part of themselves. Their ability to make an accurate estimate of both the time and the steps required and the best sequence of the steps will be valued for different reasons by different types in their community.

The significant NFP subgroup (ENFPs and INFPs) in many Christian communities values this practical aspect of INTJ leaders. However, INTJ leaders need to make a point to spare the time and labor to share their vision with this inspirational, inspiring, but unstructured group. Becoming more transparent regarding their vision will pay dividends. The NFPs will enjoy the INTJ leaders' programmatic structure to convey their vision as long as it also incorporates their concerns, namely the personal dimensions of the program, both in its conception and implementation. The large sensing judging constituency (SJs) will be happy to have something tangible that gives shape to the INTJ leaders' mysterious and complex ideas, as long as the cost and labor of fundraising has been considered. Again, learning to and bothering to consult on these issues will pay off and earn allies with this significant subgroup and enable more of their visions realized together with a richer sense of community.

INTJ leaders can sometimes "go over the top" with extraverted thinking, when, especially under stress, they become too tightly wedded to a particular system for implementing their vision. At such times, they alienate the perceiving types by their rigidity, the feeling types by their exclusive reliance on logic rather than sensitivity to human factors, and the extraverts by their aloofness. Development of the tertiary function, introverted feeling, will make such isolation and conflict less likely. Introverted feeling may start to differentiate into consciousness in their twenties and brings a welcomed and needed background warmth and diversity to the strength and power of INTJ leaders and their formidable will and independence.

In conclusion, the nurturing parent of extraverted thinking will contribute to the ministry of INTJ leaders in a variety of ways. While congregants may not understand the subtleties of their theology, they appreciate the unique, efficient organization, and the INTJ leaders' sheer capability, versatility, and resilience. Their power to organize is a gift that continues giving no matter what.

3 Tertiary (Eternal Child): Introverted Feeling

The tertiary function of INTJ leaders is introverted feeling. The development into consciousness of introverted feeling presages the possibility of broadening INTJ leaders' intensity of purpose to include such personal qualities as inner warmth, greater inner harmony, and the subtle sense of connection and attunement to the experience of others. The emergence of a third function into full consciousness has the archetypal quality of the eternal child. Accordingly, introverted feeling, as it secures its position in consciousness of INTJ leaders, often has the qualities of being charming, playful, and even seductive. Introverted feeling is the most bi-polar of the INTJ leaders' functions: brilliant but distracting and unreliable, exhilarating but fatiguing easily, disarmingly self-confident at times but wounded and unsettling at other times, endearingly innocent one moment but petulant the next.

The process of stabilizing introverted feeling within INTJ leaders is a winding road but with clear rewards for both the leader and those in the community who come or stay close. According to life-cycle type theorist Harold Grant:

> You found yourself, somewhat surprisingly, basing your decisions on the personal values and the feelings of yourself and others. You began to express your emotions with greater freedom, at least to a few trusted friends. . . . Many [however] would be unaware of your developing compassion and sensitivity. (Grant, Thompson, & Clarke, 1983, p. 245)

These developments will bring relief to feeling types, who form a majority in most Christian communities, and connect these feeling types more satisfyingly with INTJ leaders, enabling them to trust INTJ leaders' intuitive insights and feel less railroaded by their schemes. However, employing introverted feeling can be disruptive and unsettling, as INTJ leaders get used to the feeling of being "caught up in believing something that they had [hitherto] been purely objective about" (Berens & Nardi, 2004, p. 39).

For tertiary introverted feeling to lead to greater balance, Thomson (1998) emphasizes the importance of the prior development of the extraverted auxiliary. Otherwise, without this extraverted out-turned right arm, the more retiring left arm of introverted feeling can be used defensively to strengthen the already strongly established introverted orientation of INTJ leaders' dominant function, introverted intuition. In this case, introverted judgment simply convinces INTJ leaders that they have no need to establish an investment in their outer situation. Then, in the case of INTJ leaders, introverted feeling merely confirms their prejudice that the complicated inner stuff of introverted intuition can never be put into words.

In summary, the tertiary function, in this case introverted feeling, is managed by the eternal child archetype and has fetching innocence, but tires easily. Its emergence, often in the twenties, may be imperceptible to all but those closest to INTJ leaders, and such quiet warmth readily disappears at the hint of stress or conflict, but if cultivated may make a real difference, especially so in pastoral situations.

4 Fourth (Soul-Friend): Extraverted Sensing

The fourth function of INTJ leaders is extraverted sensing. Extraverted sensing connects directly with the immediate physical surrounding through the five senses of sight, sound, touch, taste, and smell. This extraverted perceiving function (sensing), as the mirror of the heroic dominant function (intuition), is mediated by the contra-sexual archetype of the soul-friend and becomes suffused with the magic and turmoil of what is "different."

When not integrated into consciousness, extraverted sensing in this "inferior" position, to use the term of early Jungian type theory (von Franz & Hillman, 1971), becomes a parody of what extraverted sensing is in the dominant position. For example, whereas the extraverted dominant sensing type delights in the play and flow of the senses, the extraverted sensing of INTJ leaders may be troubled by a periodic obsessive focus on the sensual experience, accompanied by an ambivalent attitude, that is indulgent one minute and adversarial the next, with the outer world being regarded as a danger, as a threat, and as solely the source of frustration and obstacles.

Fortunately, from a short-term perspective, INTJ leaders are likely to encounter few extraverted sensing types (ESFPs and ESTPs) in their faith community, since extraverted sensing types shy away from organized religion. The few extraverted sensing types that are willing to struggle with the challenge of sitting still in a pew for an hour will probably just accept the intensity of INTJ leaders as long as they show some appreciation for their relaxed and casual approach to almost everything. Unfortunately, from a longer term and more inclusive perspective, the rarity of extraverted sensing types in Christian community means that INTJ leaders may not be challenged to integrate extraverted sensing until much later in life, so that the struggle becomes a very solitary one. However, although there may be a few ISFPs who have extraverted sensing in a congregation, these ISFPs may be so quiet and retiring that INTJ leaders have to work really hard not to overlook them and their quiet joy in living.

As patience for the senses develops, so does greater joy in the present. When the mirror opposite of the dominant is integrated into consciousness, the vertical connecting axis between the dominant and inferior functions forms a psychological spine that brings a solidity and firmness to the conscious personality. The fourth function provides a capacity for profound connection and a deep sense of mission. In the case of INTJ leaders, the integration of extraverted sensing into consciousness gives grounding and a sense of settled-ness that brings satisfaction and happiness to INTJ leaders themselves and greater comfort and ease to those in their community.

In summary, for INTJ leaders, the fourth function of extraverted sensing has the support and magnetism that the contra-gender energy of the soul-friend archetype provides, and its conscious development may reduce the risk of unconscious acting out. Orientation to this joy and pleasure-seeking function may have to be provided for INTJ leaders by pre- and post-ordination training because there are few dominant extraverted sensing types in the seminary, the church hierarchy, or congregation to share its wisdom and perspective. Such grounded wisdom is in short supply in most Christian groups.

SHADOW PERSONALITY

5 Dominant Shadow (Challenger): Extraverted Intuition

For INTJ leaders, the dominant shadow function is extraverted intuition. Of the four perceiving functions extraverted intuition is the one that connects us to the possibilities in the external world. Extraverted intuition enables INTJ leaders readily to identify patterns and inter-relationships and to make connections (Hartzler & Hartzler, 2005) in the immediate social environment formed by their faith community, as well as in the wider context and culture of which that community is a part.

Extraverted intuition is not only alert to what can be done but, because it is an extraverted perceiving function, also provides the energy in the interpersonal shared environment for it to be realized. As such, extraverted intuition is an excellent companion and complement to introverted intuition. They both can see and are energized by future possibilities that are experienced as real to them, much to the dismay and disbelief of sensing types. However, the companionable relationship between the two forms of intuition (with their contrasting directions) is a major achievement. The relationship does not start out that way.

Extraverted intuition and introverted intuition first encounter each other as antagonists. Dominant introverted intuition queries, "How could someone do all that intuiting and speculating about the future out there in the public domain like that?" Extraverted intuition vocalizes back "Well at least I consult others and just don't cook up a scheme out of 'nowhere' (that is in the introverted realm), and then use a judging function to impose it on everyone." As extraverted intuition is mediated by the archetype of the challenger, it frequently has a challenging tone to the ego of INTJ leaders, provoking avoidant or stubborn behavior. For example, while extraverted intuition is still becoming stabilized in consciousness (which rarely happens before midlife), INTJ leaders may simply fixate upon one interpretation of a situation (Berens & Nardi, 2004). When this occurs in a church context, INTJ leaders will hear protest from the extraverted intuitive types in the congregations, for they constitute a small but significant group in most liberal Protestant (Ross, 1993) and Catholic churches (Ross, 1995).

While the passage to reconciliation may not be quiet, the rewards are great if both forms of intuition can be married. Jungian analyst John Beebe defines genius as the functional integration of the two directional orientations of the same process. He thought Jung was a genius not least because as an INTJ with dominant introverted intuition he had, nevertheless, integrated extraverted intuition.

In summary, extraverted intuition, the dominant shadow carried by the archetype of the challenger is likely to be disruptive to the usually more internalized inspiration of dominant introverted intuition. Conscious awareness of the radar antennae of extraverted intuition may mitigate its mobilization in aggressive and paranoid ways. It is likely to be triggered sporadically by ENFP colleagues or congregants who form a significant subgroup in all but conservative evangelical Christian contexts. There is a difference between inspiring change (extraverted intuition) and driving change (introverted intuition). The two forms of intuition take time and struggle to correlate.

6 Auxiliary Shadow (Critical Parent): Introverted Thinking

For INTJ leaders, the auxiliary shadow function is introverted thinking. Introverted thinking is the judging function that classifies perceptions based on an internally generated set of logical categories that are judged to be most salient and precise. While those with dominant or auxiliary introverted thinking are a small group in any Christian community, they are also a small group in Western societies as well. Introverted thinking is not called forth routinely in the development and maintenance of religious communities. Nevertheless, there are particular situations that come up in the life of a community when a keen discernment of how a number of factors relate together in a situation (quite apart from how people feel about the matter) may make a real contribution to a community that is going through a new and perhaps critical stage in its life. The development of introverted thinking, therefore, may equip a community leader to lead at a time of crisis.

Introverted thinking orients naturally to internal structure. When there are basic changes of scale, rapid growth or marked decline in membership for example, the underlying structure of relationships between important factors change, for example, rate of participation and financial generosity. Only introverted thinking discerns this. The prevailing feeling ethos of Christian communities, based on both theology and type composition, very understandably focuses on the human impact of the changes. Thinking functions, in both their introverted and extraverted modes, may be marginalized but yet required for the development of an effective response. Introverted thinking is essential for developing an appropriate set of categories for analyzing the situation or crisis, while extraverted thinking is essential for determining the specific cause-and-effect relationships.

The development and deployment of introverted thinking by INTJ leaders, because of their status, can contribute greater clarity and rigor to the transactions of their religious communities and may help overcome resistance to their own visionary programs with new capacity for a more detached way of dealing with things. Moreover, INTJ leaders may carry weight because of their reputation as an "ideas person." However, INTJ leaders are using a much "cooler" process when introverted thinking is deployed, compared to the quiet but intense passion that stems from dominant introverted intuition. This coolness and clarity may be welcomed by the STJs because the leader appears more logical and by the SFJs because the leader seems less of a "bulldozer."

The development of introverted thinking by INTJ leaders requires facing and coming to terms with some challenging archetypes that Beebe associates with introverted thinking within the introverted intuitive type. However, the gains may be significant both for the individual and for the community as indicated above. The mediating archetype for this process (critical parent) may take more dramatic archetypal form in depiction as "female" witch or "male" *senex.* These figures function to stop threats or perceived threats to the ego's survival. Thus, INTJ leaders tend to deploy introverted thinking in order to block or immobilize what is experienced sometimes accurately, sometimes mistakenly, as dangerous. In the early stage of conscious differentiation, introverted thinking may be used for purely defensive purposes. Logic may be used at the annual meeting of the church to thwart enthusiasm for a new program.

As introverted thinking is made more conscious, so the effect of introverted thinking will be more adaptive. For example, congregants, colleagues, and superiors, long familiar with the involved complex speech of their INTJ leader, may be astounded at the elegant articulation of a key discrimination from their resident INTJ that cuts through to the core of the crisis, stopping the threat and much else in its tracks.

7 Tertiary Shadow (Trickster): Extraverted Feeling

For INTJ leaders, the tertiary shadow function is extraverted feeling. Extraverted feeling works to harmonize the values of individuals with one another, and with the conventions of the culture, so that optimally harmonious relationships prevail. For INTJ leaders, however, extraverted feeling is seldom integrated into conscious awareness before mid-life, and so most of the INTJ leaders' life falls very much under the influence of the trickster archetype. The function in the "trickster position" for any dominant type tends to be inflected, or rather subverted, by the archetype of the trickster, who plays with truth, often involving some kind of deception. Mistakes are made or unintended results produced. The trickster tries to get away with this through the use of humor.

As the tertiary shadow, extraverted feeling is used by INTJ leaders to fix or unfix otherwise impossible situations in which they feel pressed by competing commitments or conflicting expectations. Extraverted feeling is used to get out of double binds, but can also get INTJ leaders *into* tricky situations. At least it may feel that way to INTJ leaders from their introverted intuitive perspective. Berens and Nardi (2004) report that INTJ leaders "usually disregard others' opinions" (p. 39), over-valuing their own independence.

Often INTJ leaders make mistakes in the extraverted feeling domain of social and personal relationships. Their intent to charm does not charm. Miscalculation leads to offence. Balance and stability in this process may be gradual. Once they get into the extraverted feeling mode, INTJ leaders may become stuck in it and may fail to make subtle distinctions regarding authentic and manipulative feeling. They may indeed be deceived or "taken in" by the "sincere" feelings of others and over-react with a sense of betrayal, rather than merely feeling disappointed, by what turned out to be a misunderstood level of closeness.

Gradually INTJ leaders may realize their limitations regarding extraverted feeling (Berens & Nardi, 2004). Feedback from a trusted friend with extraverted feeling preferences (FJ) may avert disaster and prevent dismissal or avoidance of this important interpersonal aspect of human life. INTJ leaders (like most NTs) value competence and so would prefer to avoid an area in which they feel stretched rather than confront feeling vulnerable. Avoidance of this function, however, is nigh impossible because of the strong extraverted feeling element that is inevitably involved in building community, the more so in the case of community building in a Christian context where extraverted feeling may be a preference (as either dominant or auxiliary) for as many as 44 percent of women (Ross, 1995). However, if INTJ leaders apply their characteristic persistence, they come to experience the pleasure in relating well together.

Humor is a quality of the function in the trickster position, and when the function is integrated, their use of extraverted feeling can be more naturally expressive of a genuine warmth, less coy and less strategic. INTJ leaders' humor becomes more appropriate in this domain, stemming from the joy of connection rather than a distraction from the discomfort of learning how to connect.

In summary, development of extraverted feeling in the *Trickster* archetypal position may be a pleasant surprise for the many in Christian circles who favor this function. For example, few expected their serious minister to develop so swiftly such *bonhomie* with someone who had put the church in an awkward situation. Many, including the minister, may be ambivalent about such deft duplicity, but are happy with the results.

8 Fourth Shadow (Demon/Angel): Introverted Sensing

For INTJ leaders, the fourth shadow function is introverted sensing, and this development seldom occurs until after the mid-life passage. Introverted sensing is the perceiving function that precisely registers specific details, and selectively records them, favoring those that relate to previously stored details. Introverted sensing registers the subjective impression of sensory experiences and readily "re-views" and "re-calls" detailed sensory aspects of what has been registered of these past experiences. As the last function to be integrated into a conscious orientation by INTJ leaders, it is carried into consciousness by the archetype of the demon/angel.

Introverted sensing is the opposite of the dominant function (introverted intuition) but operates in its same (introverted) world. It is impossible to perceive with introverted sensing and introverted intuition simultaneously. Therefore, introverted sensing takes on the undermining character of a demon that, nevertheless, occasionally turns angelic and becomes redemptive. In this psychological situation, it is often the last function to start the journey of differentiation into conscious awareness. Introverted sensing disrupts the smooth functioning of introverted intuition on which the ego (conscious personality) of INTJ leaders has become accustomed to rely over the course of a lifetime.

There will always be a dissonance between the two opposing functions operating in the same world. However, increasing awareness of this conflict can mitigate the effects, by instituting strategies to avoid or minimize clashes and intransigence. INTJ leaders lack a storehouse of past data so beloved and crucial to SJs (Berens & Nardi, 2004). They therefore appear to SJs to disregard the past completely.

Details may drive introverted intuitive types crazy, or they may be the threshold for transformation. INTJ leaders will encounter many in Christian communities who have this preference for introverted sensing. The demonic/angelic personality of introverted sensing for INTJ leaders (the opposite function of the dominant but which operates in the same world) is probably triggered and deployed very frequently in religious groups because there are many with introverted sensing as a dominant or auxiliary function among the clergy and in Christian congregations. The quintessential experience of demonic archetypal energy is that of being undermined. The frequency of such a dynamic between introverted intuitive ministers and many of their colleagues, superiors, and congregations who have introverted sensing may be a major factor in burnout for clergy with dominant introverted intuition. The yearning is for resolution. However, acceptance of some continuing level of conflict and undermining is probably more realistic. The angelic, or salvific, aspect should be remembered, for introverted sensing often saves the day in terms of avoiding bankruptcy and collapsing buildings.

Recognizing the role of the fourth shadow function of introverted sensing in themselves helps to protect INTJ leaders from projecting their own demonic/angelic tendencies onto the numerous introverted sensing types in the community. With creative and conscious oscillation between dominant introverted intuition and demonic/angelic introverted sensing, INTJ leaders are able to tap into a universal knowing of how things have always been. The insights generated from this perspective, *sub species aeternitatis*, have transformative power "when woven into the context of their work or lives" (Berens & Nardi, 2004, p. 39).

Chapter 8

The Insightful Visionary

INFJ Leaders

INFJ Frequency in the Population

	Male (%)	*Female (%)*
UK	1.6	1.7
USA	2.0	3.1

INFJ PSYCHOLOGICAL TYPE PROFILE

Leading Functions

Dominant introverted intuition with auxiliary extraverted feeling

Conscious personality

1. Dominant (Hero): Introverted Intuition
2. Auxiliary (Nurturing parent): Extraverted Feeling
3. Tertiary (Eternal child): Introverted Thinking
4. Fourth (Soul-friend): Extraverted Sensing

Shadow personality

5. Dominant shadow (Challenger): Extraverted Intuition
6. Auxiliary shadow (Critical parent): Introverted Feeling
7. Tertiary shadow (Trickster): Extraverted Thinking
8. Fourth shadow (Demon/Angel): Introverted Sensing

CONSCIOUS PERSONALITY

1 Dominant (Hero): Introverted Intuition

The dominant function of INFJ leaders is introverted intuition. Introverted intuition provides insights into the unknowable and discerns patterns and connections that are not related to external events (Hartzler & Hartzler, 2005). For INFJ leaders, introverted intuition is carried into consciousness through the archetypal energy of the hero. The effects of the heroic archetype on how introverted intuition operates in INFJ leaders are recognized by the qualities of reliability, hard work, and stability. When introverted intuition occupies the heroic position in an individual, the capacity to see patterns, follow hunches, and reflect on everything from a timeless perspective is depended upon as *the routine way* of dealing with life.

The INFJ leaders' heroic dominant function of introverted intuition is concerned with the background process of consciousness where unconscious images acquire the dignity of things (Jung, 1971; Beebe, 2006a). Fascination with their own complex imagination may draw some introverted intuitive types to the systems of symbols found in the myths and rituals of religions. These aspects of religious life mirror their own complexity and inspire INFJ leaders to inspire others with a transcendent aspect to life.

INFJ leaders carry a strong sense of the future. In many respects, the future is where they live, and "they struggle with how often people don't listen to the implications that they see" (Berens & Nardi, 2004, p. 46). They enjoy putting their ideas to work. In fact, it is hard for them to imagine that there could be any other satisfactory approach to life.

Adequate autonomy is a pre-requisite for happiness for INFJ leaders. They naturally "see" how a situation will play out; especially in terms of the effects on people (Berens & Nardi, 2004). Often INFJ leaders seem to know what actions need to be taken before other types grasp the situation. This may create problems in the community, especially with the major enclave of the "more grounded" and slower moving sensing judging types (SJs) whose introverted sensing compares everything with the past.

INFJ leaders struggle with impatience when they lack the freedom of action to develop a response that is in keeping with the vision that they have of what is possible. Conflict in their community may be compounded, however, because INFJ leaders have difficulty putting their vision into words. Their vision is holistic and nonverbal. They may be reluctant even to try to communicate their vision because of previous experiences of people not understanding them.

Of all the four discovery functions of perceiving, introverted intuition is the least accessible to others (Thomson, 1998). Because introverted intuition is their most trusted function, they may overuse it. Furthermore, rather than sharing their vision directly, INFJ leaders prefer to share their program for implementing their vision, which requires the development of their auxiliary extraverted feeling function. The numerous sensing-feeling types in many Christian communities will be happy to follow their program as long as they can see the human benefit of it.

2 Auxiliary (Nurturing Parent): Extraverted Feeling

The auxiliary function of INFJ leaders is extraverted feeling. Extraverted feeling is concerned to affirm and support others, and this quality is enhanced when it develops in the auxiliary position under the influence of the archetype of the nurturing parent. When developed into consciousness (which usually occurs in adolescence), extraverted feeling becomes an important part of the personality of INFJ leaders, particularly as they reach out to give to those around them.

In religious communities, there are many with extraverted feeling as a dominant heroic or auxiliary nurturing function, and so the development of this function in religious leaders is an important cohering factor for the community and for the wider religious tradition. This fact may account in part for the significant overrepresentation of INFJs in religious leadership (Francis, Craig, Whinney, Tilley, & Slater, 2007). In short, introverted intuitive types with auxiliary extraverted feeling seem drawn to religious ministry. They are keenly aware of the invisible energies that link all human beings, but rarely talk about these directly. Religious ministry provides a cultural space for expressing this strongly felt reality.

The nurturing parent quality of their auxiliary extraverted feeling makes INFJ leaders natural harmonizers in their congregations, well able to calm problems. They are vulnerable, however, to being overwhelmed and exhausted when confronted with conflict. They are easily wounded by criticism and prone to feeling "hard done by." They wrestle with the tension between expressing emotional truth and maintaining harmonious relationships. Through the combined effect of their strongest functions, INFJ leaders derive satisfaction from the opportunity for public reflection in religious talks and sermons on issues of identity and authenticity. Through their use of metaphor and symbol, they inspire others to grapple with the complexities of acting in a world that may not support their values.

It is important for introverted intuitive types to develop extraverted judgment, not least because it forces them to make compromises that their heroic dominant introverted intuition does not want to make, but which are essential for building community with other types, especially when a significant majority of Christian communities will be down-to-earth introverted sensing types. INFJ leaders will need to face down their inner hero that insists that they are selling out, being hypocritical, or (worst of all) inauthentic (Thomson, 1998). With adequate extraverted judgment, however, INFJ leaders can play a reconciling role in community by showing, for example, "how widely divergent political positions are derived from the same moral principle" (Thomson, 1998, p. 238).

There are some problems that may arise from over-reliance on extraverted feeling. INFJ leaders can become overextended and forget their own needs in the face of those of others whose needs always seem more pressing and deserving. Others may feel confused by a resentment that arises in the relationship when the high level of self-sacrifice offered by INFJ leaders is not reciprocated. By the same token, INFJ leaders may become overprotective of others and not leave enough connective slack for the development of healthy autonomy in the other person, producing what has been described as co-dependency.

3 Tertiary (Eternal Child): Introverted Thinking

The tertiary function of INFJ leaders is introverted thinking. Introverted thinking is the process *par excellence* that organizes information according to an internal framework, distilling the formal essence of a phenomenon and giving it a name. For INFJ leaders introverted thinking is the third function to develop. In this position, introverted thinking falls under the archetypal influence of the eternal child, the *puer aeternus* for males and the *puella aeterna* for females. While this function is still being differentiated into consciousness, something that rarely commences before early adulthood, it has an idealistic, naive quality, inspiring but lacking stamina, and unreliable like a tired child.

The child-like innocent but unreliable tertiary function of introverted thinking enables INFJ leaders occasionally to free themselves from the anxiety and continual tussle between inner vision of their dominant introverted intuition and the desire for harmonious relationships emanating from their auxiliary of extraverted feeling. From introverted thinking, INFJ leaders can draw on an archetypal critic that is unafraid to think the "dangerous, subversive or heretical" (Jung, 1971, p. 384; quoted in Beebe, 2006a, p. 135) and so they become able to operate with more autonomy. Introverted thinking enables INFJ leaders to speak with an independent voice. Others often take note because INFJ leaders are anything but habitual naysayers, and their voice comes from a place of integrity. However, when met with opposition, the developing neophyte introverted thinker may lack the stamina to persist amidst the ensuing politics.

There are ups and downs in the INFJ leaders' journey of integrating introverted thinking into consciousness. For instance, courageously innocent free-thinking may quickly plummet when confronted with prolonged disapproval of the traditionalist SFJs, and so may betray the few introverted thinking types around who *had* thought their minister had at last gained some intellectual fortitude and rigor. At other times, INFJ leaders may seem to be fervently clinging to their beliefs and espousing causes past the point of possible success. Another eddy of incomplete integration is that they may feel drained by those thought systems of colleagues and superiors that they cannot internalize (McAlpine, Shumate, Evers, & Hughey, 2009). Furthermore, when confronting introverted thinking in others, INFJ leaders fluctuate in their response, sometimes prematurely submitting to others' reasoning instead of first taking time for their own processing. At other times, however, they may peremptorily write off another's rationale as too impersonal.

With the integration of introverted thinking, INFJ leaders may come to experience the exhilaration of a variety of learning theories, applying models from many disciplines and using their own analytical function to select the most appropriate framework for solving the problems that confront them in their personal life and ministries (Berens & Nardi, 2004). With a child-like honesty, they may penetrate to the truth of a situation. As introverted thinking develops, INFJ leaders fervently persist in their framework, even when it is not accepted by others, which contrasts with their more customary deference to what matters to others. They come to "enjoy analyzing the rich mental images they experience, such as from dreams and symbols" (Berens & Nardi, 2004, p. 47), and demonstrate prophetic leadership by their brilliance in "naming" what they sense is happening inside the community or society at large.

4 Fourth (Soul-Friend): Extraverted Sensing

The fourth function of INFJ leaders is extraverted sensing. Extraverted sensing connects directly to the immediate physical surroundings through the five senses of sight, sound, touch, taste, and smell. Since this extraverted perceiving function is the mirror of the heroic dominant function, it is mediated by the contra-sexual archetype of the soul-friend and becomes suffused with the magic and turmoil of what is "different."

When not integrated into consciousness, extraverted sensing in this "inferior" position—to use the term of early Jungian type theory (von Franz & Hillman, 1971)—becomes a parody of what extraverted sensing is in the dominant position. For example, whereas dominant extraverted sensing delights in the play and flow of the senses, extraverted sensing as the fourth function of INFJ leaders may be troubled by a periodic obsessive focus on sensual experience, accompanied by an ambivalent attitude that is indulgent one minute and severe the next. Accordingly, the outer world may be regarded as a danger and threat, and a source of frustration and obstacles.

Fortunately, from a short-term perspective, INFJ leaders are likely to encounter few extraverted sensing types (ESFPs and ESTPs) in their faith community, since extraverted sensing types shy away from organized religion. The few extraverted sensing types who are willing to struggle with the challenge of sitting still in a pew for an hour will probably just accept the intensity of their INFJ leaders and be satisfied if their leader accepts their more easygoing casual approach to life. Unfortunately, from a longer-term and more inclusive perspective, the rarity of extraverted sensing types in Christian community means that INFJ leaders may not be challenged to integrate extraverted sensing until much later in life, if ever, and consequently the struggle remains a solitary one. Although there may be a few ISFPs (who have auxiliary extraverted sensing) in a congregation, they tend to be so quiet and retiring that INFJ leaders have to work really hard not to overlook them.

As patience for the senses develops, so does greater joy in the present. When the mirror opposite of the dominant is integrated into the conscious personality, the vertical connecting axis between the dominant function and the fourth function forms a psychological spine that brings a solidity and firmness to the conscious personality. The fourth function provides a capacity for profound connection and for a deep sense of mission. This gives grounding and a sense of settled-ness that brings surprising satisfaction and happiness to INFJ leaders and greater comfort and ease for those in their community.

In the fourth position, extraverted sensing has the support and magnetism provided by the contra-gender energy of the soul-friend, the *anima* and *animus*, and its conscious development may reduce the risk of unconscious acting out. Orientation to this joy and pleasure seeking function may have to be provided through pre- and post-ordination training because there are few dominant extraverted sensing types in the seminary, the church hierarchy, or congregation to share their wisdom and perspective. Such grounded wisdom is in short supply in most Christian groups.

SHADOW PERSONALITY

5 Dominant Shadow (Challenger): Extraverted Intuition

For INFJ leaders, the dominant shadow function is extraverted intuition. Of the four perceiving functions, extraverted intuition is the one that connects us to the possibilities in the external world. Extraverted intuition enables INFJ leaders readily to identify patterns and inter-relationships and makes connections (Hartzler & Hartzler, 2005) in the immediate social environment formed by their faith community and in the wider society. Integration of extraverted intuition into conscious personality seldom starts for INFJ leaders before mid-life.

Extraverted intuition is not only alert to what can be done but also (because it is an extraverted form of perceiving) provides the energy in the interpersonal shared environment. As such, extraverted intuition is an excellent companion and complement to introverted intuition. They both can see and are energized by future possibilities that are experienced as real to them, often to the dismay and disbelief of many sensing types. However, the companionable relationship between the two forms of intuition, with their contrasting directions, is a major achievement. The relationship does not start out that way. Extraverted and introverted intuitions first encounter each other as antagonists. Dominant introverted intuition queries, "How could someone do all that intuiting and speculating about the future out there in the public domain like that?" Extraverted intuition vocalizes back, "Well at least I consult others and just don't cook up a scheme out of 'nowhere' (i.e. the introverted realm), and then use a judging function to impose it on everyone."

As extraverted intuition is mediated by the archetype of the challenger, it frequently has a challenging tone to the ego of INFJ leaders, provoking avoidant or stubborn behavior. For example, while extraverted intuition is still becoming stabilized in consciousness, which rarely happens before mid-life, INFJ leaders may simply fixate on one interpretation of a situation (Berens & Nardi, 2004), and regard brainstorming, searching for alternative ideas, an activity beloved by extraverted intuitive types, as a waste of time. When this insistence on a singular interpretation occurs in a church context, INFJ leaders will hear the protests from the extraverted intuitive types in the congregations, for ENFPs constitute a small but significant and articulate group in most liberal Protestant and Catholic churches. INFJ leaders tend to feel overwhelmed by the possibility of too many different future directions and tend to be dissatisfied with the ideas they suggest themselves. However, when they can schedule and therefore prepare for brainstorming, INFJ leaders may use it to pose valuable questions that bring direction. In response to others' use of extraverted intuition, INFJ leaders may feel immediate annoyance: feeling overwhelmed by too many possibilities.

In summary, carried by the challenger archetype, extraverted intuition is likely initially to be disruptive to the usually more internalized inspiration of the dominant introverted intuition. Conscious awareness, however, of the radar-like antennae of extraverted intuition may mitigate its mobilization in oppositional ways. Nevertheless, early in ministry, it will likely be triggered sporadically by ENFP colleagues or congregants who form a significant subgroup in all but conservative evangelical Christian contexts. The two forms of intuition take time to correlate.

6 Auxiliary Shadow (Critical Parent): Introverted Feeling

For INFJ leaders, the auxiliary shadow function is introverted feeling. Introverted feeling is an inwardly directed decision-making function concerned with inner valuing. Introverted feeling assesses everything on the basis of non-negotiable personal values with a view to optimizing inner harmony. Introverted feeling finds expression in INFJ leaders through the archetype of the critical parent. Accordingly, introverted feeling performs the role of the critical parent (*senex* or witch) and is often mobilized in order to block what is experienced as threats to survival. The *senex* or witch quality of introverted feeling may show itself in an inexplicable but deeply felt forceful hostility to innovation. The *senex* or witch quality of introverted feeling contrasts with INFJ leaders' usual openness to at least entertaining new ideas, with their usual non-hierarchal style.

Introverted feeling as critical parent is likely to occur when INFJ leaders sense that their personal values may be violated. They become moralistic and self-righteous, and individuals under their suspicion are decried and made to feel *persona non grata.* This may undermine the sense of community and shock members who have accepted their leaders' sometimes hard-to-fathom vision because of their usual warmth and caring attitude. By the same token, when this strong reaction is to a *commonly agreed* community threat, members may be amazed and grateful for INFJ leaders' vehemence in the face of threat.

Another way that introverted feeling shows up under the influence of critical parent energy is in the guise of a brutal perfectionism that neither they nor others can ever attain. This is a special problem for INFJ leaders in religious roles, since, because of their elevated status, members of their community are unlikely to challenge them or their expectations. While the instances may be few that trigger such severe reactions, their intensity argue for pre-emptive education and the value of introverted feeling being integrated into conscious awareness. The rewards are there and are not solely preventive or remedial. When INFJ leaders are more in contact with their personally held inner values, they have access to the power that accompanies a resultant *owned sense of self*: whereas before they cared naturally and passionately about their vision for the community and the wider world, now they are empowered to be even more active and initiating.

With the critical parent energy of their introverted feeling integrated into a conscious orientation, INFJ leaders become more dynamic, and widen their base of support in the community. For example, they begin to acknowledge more *openly* those types who speak with that same integrity that they themselves have begun to share. This will secure their relationship with a quiet but powerful element in any religious community—the introverted feeling types.

Introverted feeling types were described by Isabel Briggs Myers, herself an INFP, as constituting the moral backbone of a society, the "moral minority", whose spirituality has been described, for the INFP, as "meeting the heart's yearning to love the quiet mystery of love through insightful service" and, for the ISFP, as "delighting in being the quiet hands and feet of the divine, or whatever has supreme value." This latter approach to spirituality is surprisingly close to that of the ISFJ that has been described as "Living the joy of bringing harmony through loyal service to others" (Ross, 2011b, p. 140).

7 Tertiary Shadow (Trickster): Extraverted Thinking

For INFJ leaders, the tertiary shadow function is extraverted thinking. Extraverted thinking is an externally directed decision-making function that seeks to establish systems of organization so that phenomena may be compared on the basis of objective criteria (Haas & Hunziker, 2006; Ross, 2015). For INFJ leaders, extraverted thinking lies in the shadow of the tertiary function which for INFJ leaders is *introverted* thinking. Accordingly, extraverted thinking finds expression in INFJ leaders through the archetype of the trickster whose activity and effect is recognized by deception, mistakes, unintended results, abrupt reversal of fortunes, and humor. Trickster energy can be effective in escaping double binds and other seemingly "impossible" situations.

Extraverted thinking is a prevailing function in Western societies with their deeply embedded technocratic culture. In contrast, religious groups with their prevalence of extraverted feeling rather than extraverted thinking represent an alternative or counter-cultural way of organizing institutions. Nevertheless, most religious leaders will feel pressure at times to be "efficient and effective," the trademarks of extraverted thinking. When INFJ leaders yield to this pressure, there may be unintended trickster-like results. At other times, INFJ leaders are likely to treat logic as irrelevant, making fun of logical thinking. Such "tricky behavior" may provide comic relief to the minority of perceiving types in the congregation who are hungry for humor and spontaneity, but is likely to annoy many others and lower the credibility of INFJ leaders. In particular, their attitude may erode the trust of the STJs who tend to be on important financial subcommittees of organizations. Moreover, ISTJs are usually the most frequent type groups in church congregations after INFJs and SFJs.

When under stress, INFJ leaders may feel pressured to use extraverted thinking and then spend inordinate time establishing order. When others use extraverted thinking, INFJ leaders may feel obliged to make a decision too quickly. Furthermore, when others use extraverted thinking to impose a program, INFJ leaders may begin to undermine the program's value. Such undermining may create a crisis within the community by eroding trust in the leader. The risk of this dynamic points to the wisdom and the necessity of developing conscious awareness around the play of the trickster archetype, in general, in religious communities, and then, in particular, corrosion of trust that may be perpetrated by INFJ leaders' unconscious trickster-like relationship to extraverted thinking when it comes to programming.

When extraverted thinking is more integrated into a conscious orientation, INFJ leaders report enjoying systematizing and planning (Berens & Nardi, 2004). Moreover, their trickster may fruitfully appear in extraverted thinking form in finding rationale and developing arguments for breaking the rules in an otherwise seemingly impossible situation. This may have the side benefit of feeling like a breath of fresh air to members who respect their INFJ leaders but hitherto had found them too serious and intense.

Generally without conscious commitment to personal growth, the *trickster* aspect of extraverted thinking is seldom consistently developed. It may come in handy in extricating INFJ leaders from the frequent occasions in which they feel themselves in double-binds on account of the numerous factional forces within a congregation, the wider church, and the local community.

8 Fourth Shadow (Demon/Angel): Introverted Sensing

For INFJ leaders, the fourth shadow function is introverted sensing and that seldom occurs until after the mid-life passage. Introverted sensing is the perceiving function that precisely registers specific details, and selectively records them, favoring those that relate to previously stored details. Introverted sensing registers the subjective impression of sensory experiences and readily "re-views" and "re-calls" detailed sensory aspects of what has been registered of these past experiences. As the last function to be integrated into a conscious orientation by INFJ leaders, it is carried into consciousness by the archetype of the demon/angel.

Introverted sensing is the opposite of the dominant function for INFJ leaders (introverted intuition) but operates in its same world of introverted awareness. It is impossible to perceive with introverted sensing and introverted intuition simultaneously, just as photographs cannot be "close-ups" and "pan-shots" at the same time. Thus, introverted sensing takes on the undermining character of a demon that, nevertheless, occasionally turns angelic and becomes redemptive. In this psychological situation, introverted sensing is usually the last process to start the journey of differentiation into conscious awareness. Introverted sensing disrupts the smooth functioning of introverted intuition on which the ego (conscious personality) of INFJ leaders has become accustomed to rely over the course of a lifetime. The stakes are heightened at this point in the human life cycle, especially if the other aspects of the shadow personality have not been encountered or even touched. The temptation is to disown this "beastly" demonic aspect of our cognitive processing and project it onto others.

When other introverted intuitive types using introverted sensing are encountered, INFJ leaders, forgetting their own ineptitude, are prone to show contempt for others for their loose grasp on the facts. In terms of their own past experiences, they may exaggerate insults that they have received, mistakes that they have made, and other embarrassing moments. Under stress, INFJ leaders may over-compensate by engaging in compulsive list-making, creating archives of factual information, or ruminating on past events.

Details may drive introverted intuitive types crazy, or they may be the threshold for transformation. The demonic/angelic personality of introverted sensing (the opposite function of the dominant but which operates in the dominant's same world) is probably triggered and deployed very frequently in religious groups because there are many with introverted sensing as a dominant or auxiliary function among the clergy and in Christian congregations. The quintessential experience of demonic archetypal energy is that of being undermined. The frequency of such a dynamic between introverted intuitive leaders and many of their colleagues, superiors, and congregations who have introverted sensing may be a major factor in burnout for clergy with an introverted intuitive dominant. The yearning is for resolution of this conflict. However, acceptance of some continuing level of conflict and undermining is probably more realistic. And the demonic/angelic, salvific aspect should be remembered, for introverted sensing often saves the day in terms of avoiding bankruptcy and collapsing buildings.

In order to avoid projection onto the numerous introverted sensing types in their community, considerable vigilance, patience, and moral effort is called forth in INFJ leaders as they struggle to own their own beastliness that is so readily provoked and dramatized by those with introverted sensing and the requirement of a grasp of details in many aspects of religious leadership. The personal and professional rewards, however, are significant. With creative and conscious oscillation between dominant introverted intuition and demonic/angelic introverted sensing, INFJ leaders on occasion tap into a universal knowing of how things have always been.

Chapter 9

The Responsible Realist

ISTJ Leaders

ISTJ Frequency in the Population

	Male (%)	*Female (%)*
UK	19.7	8.6
USA	19.4	12.3

ISTJ PSYCHOLOGICAL TYPE PROFILE

Leading Functions

Dominant introverted sensing with auxiliary extraverted thinking

Conscious personality

1. Dominant (Hero): Introverted Sensing
2. Auxiliary (Nurturing parent): Extraverted Thinking
3. Tertiary (Eternal child): Introverted Feeling
4. Fourth (Soul-friend): Extraverted Intuition

Shadow personality

5. Dominant shadow (Challenger): Extraverted Sensing
6. Auxiliary shadow (Critical parent): Introverted Thinking
7. Tertiary shadow (Trickster): Extraverted Feeling
8. Fourth shadow (Demon/Angel): Introverted Intuition

CONSCIOUS PERSONALITY

1 Dominant (Hero): Introverted Sensing

The dominant function of ISTJ leaders is introverted sensing. Introverted sensing is an information gathering function that focuses on particular elements that compose the subjective internal world of present experience, which are then compared to previous related experiences (Haas & Hunziker, 2006). For ISTJ leaders, introverted sensing is carried into consciousness through the archetypal energy of the hero. The effects of the heroic archetype on how introverted sensing operates in ISTJ leaders are recognized in the qualities of reliability, hard work, and stability. The heroic archetype that manages the dominant function emerges by late childhood and equips the growing individual to cope with the challenges of life by providing a function that is reliable, stable, and competent. Consolidated so early in their life-cycle, introverted sensing becomes the function upon which ISTJ leaders instinctively rely.

ISTJ leaders cope with life by relying on introverted sensing to register details—both the physical and emotional aspects of experience—that are stored in arrays, ready for accurate recall when prompted by present but familiar experiences. When perceiving phenomena in the present, the past is used as a basis for comparison. ISTJ leaders use introverted sensing reflexively and often. The assumption is that with enough accurate facts, all important problems can be solved.

By the same token, what seems "objective data" to them is often affected by the emotional tone of past experiences that have been evoked again in the present. However, it is the sense of this past experience as securely rooted and grounded that leads to feeling assured about the facts. This deep-seated sense of assurance is then something that others find it very hard to challenge or to disturb.

Introverted sensing is the most frequent function in the dominant heroic position for churchgoers across Christian denominations (Francis, Robbins, & Craig, 2011). For some clergy, too, introverted sensing was also found to be the most frequent heroic dominant function (Ross, 2011a). These are the "salt of the earth" ministers who are comfortable with the familiar, since introverted sensing reliably registers the minutiae of life and finds spiritual worth in dealing with the facts that make others feel grounded. And what better way to sacralize what is known and familiar than through the beliefs and practices of religious traditions. The tried and true is commended and trusted and institutions that protect traditions evoke loyalty and deserve it in their view.

Community leaders with dominant introverted sensing rely on and lead through their seemingly unerring grasp of detail. Life is treasured by ISTJ leaders for its vividly experienced and precisely remembered concrete experiences, and so their sense of community too must be built on a solid basis of commonly agreed facts.

Implications for ISTJ leaders flow from the high frequency of ISTJs among lay and clergy groups. First, how they approach life (including religious life) will find resonance with a significant group of resilient, even tough, traditionalists in the congregation (Bramer & Ross, 2012). Second, ISTJ clergy will constitute a significant subgroup within their own denomination at diocesan, presbytery or conference level, or within the local groups of clergy and leaders of diverse religious traditions. Thus, they will tend to have significant peer and very often institutional hierarchical support for their straightforward traditional perspectives and priorities. Moreover, they will be respected by many in the community for their reliability, patience with routine, and willing application of and attention to detail.

2 Auxiliary (Nurturing Parent): Extraverted Thinking

The auxiliary function of ISTJ leaders is extraverted thinking. Extraverted thinking is an externally directed decision-making function that seeks to establish systems of organization so that phenomena may be compared on the basis of objective criteria (Haas & Hunziker, 2006; Ross, 2011b). When extraverted thinking develops in the auxiliary position, usually in adolescence, it is influenced by the archetype of the good parent. The good parent archetype is recognized by the ways in which the function it carries is used to protect, guide, direct, and nurture others. Accordingly, extraverted thinking becomes an important part of the personality, especially as a bridge to reach out and connect with others in a helpful way.

Extraverted thinking provides practical outgoing balance to ISTJ leaders whose introverted sensing on its own might otherwise leave them immersed in their own world of vivid impressions. Extraverted thinking, with its ability to segment, sequence, and systematize, makes ISTJ leaders into formidably practical individuals, especially when combined with their heroic introverted sensing that can focus on the salient details of the immediate solution.

For many members, ISTJ leaders inspire confidence, especially regarding practical matters. Their ability to make an accurate estimate of the time and the steps it will take and the best sequence of the steps will be valued for different reasons by different types in the community. Members with the same type (up to 18 percent of the congregation) expect such problem solving from their leader. The numerous SFJs will respect ISTJ leaders even though they often find them lacking in tact. Up to 59 percent of congregations comprise those with extraverted feeling preferences who may feel offended by ISTJ leaders' insensitivity on a number of occasions (Ross, 2011b). The significant NFP subgroup (ENFPs and INFPs) in many Christian communities value the practical wisdom of ISTJ leaders, but tend to be worried too by a lack of sensitivity at times. Of greater concern, however, may be ISTJ leaders' lack of openness to their more holistic approach to spirituality (Ross & Francis, 1998). Again learning to consult on these issues will pay off and earn allies with this significant subgroup.

All type groups in the congregation come to depend on the practical grasp of situations displayed by ISTJ leaders and take their practical presence for granted. This may register resentment within conscientious ISTJ leaders, but such resentment will surface only with like-minded members of the community on an individual basis, but constitutes a significant source of gossip that is a prevailing undermining dynamic to religious community.

ISTJ leaders can sometimes "go over the top" with extraverted thinking, when, especially under stress, they become too tightly wedded to a particular way of doing things. At such times, they alienate the perceiving types by their rigidity, the feeling types by the exclusive reliance on logic rather than sensitivity to human factors, and the extraverts by their diffidence regarding socializing and consulting. Reliance on extraverted thinking alone can lead to control issues emerging in community meetings. Those who value their own autonomy may be alienated, especially NTs who combine intuition with thinking.

The archetypal good parent of extraverted thinking empowers community building for ISTJ leaders, albeit in a traditional mode. If the congregation has become used to this traditional style of leadership, it may continue to be effective.

3 Tertiary (Eternal Child): Introverted Feeling

The tertiary function for ISTJ leaders is introverted feeling. Introverted feeling is an inwardly directed decision-making function of inner valuing. Introverted feeling assesses everything on the basis of non-negotiable personal values with a view to optimizing inner harmony. The development into consciousness of introverted feeling broadens the focus of ISTJ leaders on details and practical problem solving to include such personal qualities as inner warmth, greater inner harmony, and the subtle sense of connection and attunement to the experience of others.

In the tertiary position, introverted feeling falls under the archetypal influence of the eternal child, the *puer aeternus* for males and the *puella aeterna* for females. The eternal-child archetype is recognized by the ways in which extraverted sensing shows up for ISTJ leaders in innocent, playful, creative ways, while at other times it carries a sense of wounding along with sensitivity.

Because of its association with the eternal child archetype, in ISTJ leaders, introverted feeling is volatile, having an innocent, exuberant flavor one moment, vulnerable the next, then succumbing suddenly to the rapid fatigue that we associate with young children. It has an idealistic, naïve quality, inspiring but lacking stamina and showing unreliability like a tired child. The sometimes child-like innocence of their emerging introverted feeling may soften seriously reliable ISTJ leaders, much to the relief of feeling types who form a majority within most Christian communities. More conscious contact with introverted feeling will enable ISTJ leaders to connect more satisfyingly with feeling types. Feeling types may then feel less railroaded by ISTJ leaders' insistence on orderly progression for any change, enabling feeling types to relax, admire the steady realism of their ISTJ leaders, and accept their respect for factual information.

Some members, however, may have to adjust to a growing intensity to their ISTJ leaders, as they start to *feel* what is right and select from their tradition those elements that seem most worthwhile. This helps ISTJ leaders to narrow their wide ranging sense of responsibility into more manageable and specific roles (Berens & Nardi, 2004). Contact with inner feeling produces energy that ISTJs may embrace with child-like enthusiasm. However, they may also show more overt signs of reactivity to hurt and rejection. Furthermore, while ISTJ leaders are getting used to being aware of this fresh emotionality, they may use sarcasm to create a protective distance. Indeed "engaging in introverted feeling can be unsettling and disruptive at times" (Berens & Nardi, 2004, p. 31) with the ISTJ leaders reacting with hasty indignation to felt violations of their values. A period of painful reexamination may ensue as ISTJ leaders work toward a new balance in the way in which they deal with their deep feelings of loyalty to tradition and to others. The feeling majority in most religious communities will feel relieved that their practical leader is sporadically aware of the emotional layer that exists in all communication between members, but which when unacknowledged sustains tension.

For tertiary introverted feeling to lead to greater balance, Thomson emphasizes the importance of the prior development of the extraverted auxiliary. Otherwise, without this extraverted out-turned right arm, the more retiring left arm of introverted feeling can be used defensively to strengthen the already strongly established introverted orientation of ISTJ leaders' dominant function, introverted sensing making for a readier intransigence (Thomson, 1998).

4 Fourth (Soul-Friend): Extraverted Intuition

The fourth function of ISTJ leaders is extraverted intuition. Extraverted intuition is an information-gathering function that seeks connections and relationships between objects, peoples, and events in the external world with a view to generating "real-world possibilities" (Haas & Hunziker, 2006, p. 53; Ross, 2015). The integration of extraverted intuition into conscious awareness seldom starts before the mid-thirties, and according to Beebe (2007a, 2016), does so under the archetypal influence of the *anima/ animus* or soul-friend.

The archetype of the soul-friend, usually imaged as an opposite gendered figure, is recognized by its capacity to forge profound and deep connection, providing a sense of mission on the one hand, and a bridge to the unconscious, on the other. The influence of the soul-friend archetype is expressed, when fully integrated into consciousness, by suffusing extraverted intuition with qualities of mission, intensity, and depth. Accordingly, when extraverted intuition is integrated into consciousness, it forms, along with the dominant function of introverted sensing, the spine of the personality.

Before the integration of extraverted intuition into consciousness, when ISTJ leaders are under stress, the threatening aspects of this function may erupt in the manner that Quenk (1993, 2000) has characterized as "being in the grip." One expression of this phenomenon by stressed ISTJ leaders is catastrophizing. Intuition is concerned with the future, but for ISTJ leaders the future is full of foreboding at the best of times, because it has yet to be directly experienced. Under stress, ISTJ leaders become even "more wildly imaginative about disastrous outcomes" (Quenk, 2000, p. 38). Paralysis and procrastination may result or at the other extreme impulsive activity.

Much is to be gained by ISTJ leaders becoming more familiar and practiced with intuition. An impetus may come from within the religious community when ISTJ leaders see at first hand the utility of, for example, the creative improvisation and *brio* of committed ENFP church members in dealing with an unforeseen circumstance. If ISTJ leaders can accept their anxiety of not requiring everything to be immediately practical and worked out in detail, then the magic of their expansive and creative fourth function can act as a gateway to the power, depth, and breadth of their largely unconscious resources. With such courage, ISTJ leaders become patient with brainstorming and become more spontaneous. They become open to seeing possibilities and exploring multiple meanings, rather than riveting upon a single interpretation of reality. ISTJ leaders are aided in this risky process if they are not subjected to nor themselves succumb to premature problem solving by the sizeable sensing-judging enclave, but rather have their own reservations taken seriously and are allowed to ventilate fears and worries, without being patronized (Quenk, 2000).

Harnessing the rich connectivity of extraverted intuition is not a smooth process for ISTJ leaders. When intuitions occur, some ISTJ leaders report over-excitement with intuitions coming too fast for accurate processing. In the early stages of integrating extraverted intuition, ISTJ leaders experience great difficulty attending to the big picture until all the details are accounted for and understood. When others use extraverted intuition, ISTJs often feel overwhelmed, fearing that the outflow of possibilities will never cease.

Nevertheless, despite the challenges to allowing time and space for the sometimes unmanageable and chaos-producing exercise of extraverted intuition, ISTJ leaders become more rounded people. Moreover, from a developmental perspective, in the journey toward individuation, the struggle to integrate what is opposite brings to such contained and containing ISTJ leaders, the promise of a sense of self that is open to "archaic and mystical qualities" (Spoto, 1989, p. 73; Jung, 1970, p. 121). Thus, for ISTJ leaders coming to a living conscious relationship with extraverted intuition is the most accessible doorway to the shadow personality, promising greater wholeness on the inside and a religious approach to life outside that is more inclusive of other types and their offerings and perspectives.

SHADOW PERSONALITY

5 Dominant Shadow (Challenger): Extraverted Sensing

The dominant shadow function for ISTJ leaders is extraverted sensing. Extraverted sensing enjoys "scouting" the external environment, taking pleasure in the experience of sights, smells, tastes, sounds, and touch through the five senses. Integration of extraverted sensing into conscious awareness seldom starts for ISTJ leaders before mid-life and does so under the archetypal influence of the challenger, often captured by a contra-gender image. Because extraverted sensing comprises a part of the shadow personality, before such time as extraverted sensing is integrated and "owned" in consciousness, it is "disowned" and projected onto others who are experienced as "bad" characters and decried as prone to displaying oppositional and generally problematic behavior. The impact of this oppositional projective process, however, is limited in the case of ISTJ leaders within religious communities because of the low frequency of extraverted sensing as a dominant or auxiliary process among members of religious communities.

There exists a competitive tension between sensing in its introverted and extraverted aspect. For example, ISTJ leaders may be put off by the casual manner and "irreverent" remarks of extraverted sensing types (ESFPs and ESTPs). They may view them as behaving inappropriately if not downright irresponsibly. When they themselves indulge in the delight of the senses, they may feel that they are being wasteful and experience feelings of guilt. Immediately responding to sensory experience without taking time for reflection may feel to introverted sensing types (ISFJs and ISTJs) to be an invitation to physical or ethical disaster. They feel that such intense focus on the present without reference to the past will be perceived by others—as well as by themselves—as operating without integrity.

Before extraverted sensing is integrated into consciousness, ISTJ leaders tend to demand that the present be made relevant by referring back to the past. Shorn of the opportunity for such checking, ISTJ leaders may simply reject, or even deny, current reality in the moment, looking down at the ground with a frown rather than seeing what is happening. This will be quite disturbing to other types who hitherto have come to respect and expect the reasonable realism of ISTJ leaders. However, awareness and appreciation of the different character of sensing in its introverted and extraverted aspects (clarity as opposed to delight) can reduce conflict and misunderstanding, enabling ISTJ leaders to value the contribution of extraverted sensing to a sense of joy, while not ignoring their usual need to reflect and absorb the facts before responding.

The integration of extraverted sensing into a conscious orientation will be a personal journey for most ISTJ leaders. It is likely there will be little positive encouragement from members of their community to develop this important function since very few have it as a well-developed function. They may be less threatened by the quiet fun-loving groups of ISFPs that are present in small but consistent numbers in most congregations. However, if ISTJ leaders rise to the personal growth challenge through their commitment to wholeness and balance in themselves, they will make an immense contribution to the viability and the attractiveness of religious community to the wider society, since extraverted sensing types are a middle frequency type group in the general population of both the United States and the United Kingdom (Hammer & Mitchell, 1996; Kendal, 1998).

Integration of extraverted sensing that otherwise may show up in an oppositional way both inside and outside religious communities is a significant accomplishment for ISTJ leaders: it magnifies their effectiveness, as leaders whose realism and gathered presence cannot be ignored. The grounded reflectiveness of their dominant function, that precisely registers facts and views them in the context of what has gone before, is then combined with a relaxed comfortable presence and capacity for joy and delight in the present that contributes both seriousness and pleasure to the situations and people ISTJ leaders meet.

6 Auxiliary Shadow (Critical Parent): Introverted Thinking

For ISTJ leaders, the auxiliary shadow function is introverted thinking. Introverted thinking is a judging function that classifies perceptions based on an internally generated set of logical categories deemed most salient and precise in a particular circumstance. Introverted thinking organizes information according to an internal framework, distilling the formal essence of a phenomenon and giving it a name. For ISTJ leaders, introverted thinking is carried into consciousness through the archetype of the critical parent and is part of the post mid-life journey for most individuals.

The influence of the critical parent archetype is recognized when introverted thinking is deployed protectively to block sensed threats to survival. Introverted thinking often shows up in the *senex* or witch position in a crass power-oriented manner in order to resist change and new developments and is deployed to thwart new energy and demoralize threatening agents of change invoking a protective wisdom that "knows best." The *senex* or witch quality of introverted thinking may show itself in a forceful hostility to innovation and intensify ISTJ leaders' instinctual predilection and reputation for conserving tradition. However, once the playful aspect of introverted thinking emerges from its archetypal casing, and integrated into consciousness, it can add a lighter, cooler facet to the usually serious profile of ISTJ leaders.

The development of introverted thinking within leaders may equip them to lead at a time of crisis. For example, when there are basic changes of scale in a religious group (rapid growth or marked decline in membership), the underlying structure of relationships between important factors change, for instance, the rate of participation and degree of financial generosity. Only introverted thinking naturally orients to such inter-relationships. However, the feeling ethos prevailing in Christian communities orients overwhelmingly to the human impact of such changes. Thinking processes in both their introverted and extraverted modes tend to be marginalized, but are nonetheless required for the development of an effective response to change and its correlates. Introverted thinking will be essential for developing an appropriate set of categories for analyzing the situation or crisis, and extraverted thinking will be essential for determining salient causes and effects. With introverted thinking in the critical parent position, ISTJ leaders are likely to be challenged.

According to Berens and Nardi (2004, p. 31), ISTJ leaders "prefer not to articulate operating principles" or merely refer back to pre-established ones. However, with the differentiation of introverted thinking, they become able to develop flexible strategies based on principles that draw on a grasp of the *current* situation. These kinds of initiatives may be widely welcomed and experience less resistance than those pre-set programs fueled by ISTJ's extraverted thinking and about which no one else had been consulted.

As introverted thinking is made more conscious, so the effect of introverted thinking that is triggered and operating within ISTJ leaders will be more adaptive. For example, congregants, colleagues, and superiors, long familiar with the staid reliability of their ISTJ leader, may be astounded at the elegant articulation of a key discrimination from their leader that cuts through to the core of the crisis, stopping the threat and much else in its tracks. At other times, members may be won over by the way in which their rather traditional leader has developed an enviable intellectual fluidity.

7 Tertiary Shadow (Trickster): Extraverted Feeling

For ISTJ leaders, the tertiary shadow function is extraverted feeling. Extraverted feeling works to harmonize the values of individuals with one another, and with the conventions of the prevailing culture, so that optimally harmonious relationships prevail. For ISTJ leaders, however, this important function for interpersonal relating is seldom integrated into conscious awareness before mid-life and remains under the influence of the trickster archetype for most of their personal and professional life. The function that is in the "trickster position" for any type tends to be inflected (even subverted) by the archetype of the trickster, who plays with truth, often involving some kind of deception.

The activity of trickster energy may be recognized at a subtle level with the occurrence of mistakes, and the observation of unintended awkward results. The trickster tries to get away with this mischief through the distracting use of humor that brings a leavening and lightening quality to an encounter or situation.

Extraverted feeling is used by ISTJ leaders to get out of double binds, but can also get them *into* tricky situations. Often ISTJ leaders may make mistakes in the extraverted feeling domain of social and personal relationships. Moreover, ISTJ leaders in particular do not like making mistakes, and so integrating extraverted feeling presents a moral challenge and a steep learning curve. For example, their intent to charm may not actually charm. Miscalculation may lead to offence. ISTJ leaders may have to resist the temptation to disparage the whole extraverted feeling enterprise, making fun of cultivating harmonious relationships, and deriding it as "trying to be nice." Avoidance of the extraverted feeling function, however, is near impossible because of the strong extraverted feeling element that is inevitably involved in building community, the more so in a Christian context where extraverted feeling may be a preference (as either dominant or auxiliary) for as many as 44 percent of women (Ross, 1995).

Persevering with cultivating harmonious relationships requires the development of courage, patience, and humility. Often their sincere attempts to use extraverted feeling are not viewed as genuine, and their efforts to take care of others frequently seem to backfire. Moreover, when others use extraverted feeling, ISTJ leaders may distrust and misinterpret their purpose. Berens and Nardi (2004) report that ISTJ leaders "usually disregard most others' opinions" (p. 31), preferring to stick exclusively to their own self-evaluated practical approach.

Progress toward balance and stability with extraverted feeling may be gradual. Initially, ISTJ leaders may get too caught up with others' concerns. They may fail to make subtle distinctions regarding authentic and manipulative feeling. They may indeed be deceived or "taken in" by others "sincere" feelings and over-react with a sense of betrayal, rather than merely feeling disappointed by what turned out to be a misunderstood level of closeness.

With conscious awareness of the use of trickery in order to preserve harmony with others, the humor of ISTJ leaders becomes less manipulative, stemming more frequently now from the joy of connection rather than from the intent to distract from the ISTJ leaders' discomfort with learning how to connect. Eventually and more simply, "they may even see the humorous side" of their previously habitual serious relational style (Berens & Nardi, 2004, p. 31). With more conscious knowledge of extraverted feeling comes appreciation of its value, and ISTJ leaders may become more adept in its use, deploying it for fixing or unfixing otherwise tense "impossible" situations. Such predicaments are frequent for religious leaders who often feel pressed by competing commitments and conflicting expectations.

8 Fourth Shadow (Demon/Angel): Introverted Intuition

For ISTJ leaders, the fourth shadow function is introverted intuition. Introverted intuition facilitates awareness of images and abstract ideas, transcending time and space, spanning past and future, and producing insights that arise spontaneously from the unconscious. Such insights transform and re-frame situations. As the last function to be integrated into the conscious, it is carried into consciousness by the archetype of the demon/angel.

The usual effect of the activity of this archetype is to undermine. Introverted intuition is the opposite judging function to the ISTJ leaders' dominant introverted sensing and *directly* clashes with the operations of introverted sensing because it operates in that very same (introverted) world. Accordingly, introverted intuition is often experienced by ISTJ leaders as possessing a destructive flavor, especially in the first half of life. Introverted intuition undermines or even sabotages the operations of dominant introverted sensing. How can the same individual continue to monitor the minute inner response to stimuli drawing on dominant introverted sensing, when introverted intuition resonates to primordial images from the unconscious which "acquire the dignity of things" (Jung, 1971, p. 399)?

When ISTJ leaders are "beastly," negative introverted intuition is often involved. When ISTJ leaders are trying to seek significance and meaning, a quintessential activity of introverted intuition, they may feel beset by hopelessness. When ISTJ leaders do engage with introverted intuition, they are unfamiliar with *how* this contrasting form of inner perceiving works. Having only introverted sensing to go on, they treat what is cognized by introverted intuition (symbols, archetypes, visions) in the same way as they might deal with facts, treating them as actual "guideposts" rather than as impressionistic hints of what may be possible.

ISTJ leaders are often fearful when other people use introverted intuition. This attitude may be in part due to their sole recourse to introverted intuition in desperation, when they have "run out of facts." Consequently, when others use introverted intuition and offer a spiritual insight that has just occurred to them, ISTJ leaders may shut them down. The movement toward acceptance of the offerings of introverted intuition is a life-time's work. The need for tolerance of the *merely possible* in the face of already established facts challenges ISTJ leaders. However, a more realistic goal than actively cherishing the insights and meanings that those with introverted intuition as a dominant or auxiliary function spontaneously offer is to be aware of their own automatic aversion and resistance, and not lash out.

Occasionally, introverted intuition may function for ISTJ leaders like an angel to redeem or transform a situation. Introverted intuition is essential for continued relevance and survival of a community because of the inner prophetic visioning that introverted intuition enables. Because of the huge range of introverted intuition—spanning forwards and backwards across history and continents—a community in effective possession of this capacity is able to remain rooted (with reference to the past), and yet relevant for the future. For this reason, ISTJ leaders should avoid the temptation to shelter with the numerous ISTJs and ISFJs who may make up half of the religious group they lead. Reaching past the discomfort of incorporating their most obscured and usually "beastly" function will enable ISTJ leaders to be more available (and on occasion even angelic) to those with that dominant function in their religious community.

Chapter 10

The Practical Helper

ISFJ Leaders

ISFJ Frequency in the Population

	Male (%)	*Female (%)*
UK	7.0	17.7
USA	6.3	6.2

ISFJ PSYCHOLOGICAL TYPE PROFILE

Leading Functions

Dominant introverted sensing with auxiliary extraverted feeling

Conscious personality
1. Dominant (Hero): Introverted Sensing
2. Auxiliary (Nurturing parent): Extraverted Feeling
3. Tertiary (Eternal child): Introverted Thinking
4. Fourth (Soul-friend): Extraverted Intuition

Shadow personality
5. Dominant shadow (Challenger): Extraverted Sensing
6. Auxiliary shadow (Critical parent): Introverted Feeling
7. Tertiary shadow (Trickster): Extraverted Thinking
8. Fourth shadow (Demon/Angel): Introverted Intuition

CONSCIOUS PERSONALITY

1 Dominant (Hero): Introverted Sensing

The dominant function of ISFJ leaders is introverted sensing. Introverted sensing is an information-gathering function that focuses on particular elements that make up the subjective internal world of present experience. These specific elements are then compared to previous related experiences (Haas & Hunziker, 2006). For ISFJ leaders, introverted sensing is carried into consciousness through the archetypal energy of the hero. The effects of the heroic archetype on how introverted sensing operates in ISFJ leaders are recognized by the qualities of reliability, hard work, and stability. The heroic archetype that manages the dominant function emerges by late childhood and equips the growing individual to cope with the challenges of life by providing a function that is dependable, stable, and competent. Consolidated so early in their life cycle introverted sensing becomes the function on which ISFJ leaders instinctively rely.

ISFJ leaders cope with life by relying on introverted sensing to register details—both the physical and emotional aspects of experience—that are stored for accurate recall when prompted by new but familiar experiences. However, what seems as objective data to them may be affected by the emotional tone of past experiences that have been evoked again in the present, for when perceiving phenomena in the present moment, the past is used as a basis for comparison. ISFJ leaders use introverted sensing reflexively and often. They proceed on the assumption that with enough accurate facts all important problems can be solved, including those encountered by their religious community.

Introverted sensing reliably registers the minutiae of life and finds spiritual worth in dealing with the facts. This makes others feel grounded. ISFJ leaders are "the salt of the earth", ministers who are comfortable with the familiar. Drawing on their deep-rooted memories of the past, ISFJ leaders sacralize what is known and familiar to them, and this is done well through the beliefs and practices of religious traditions. The "tried and true" is commended and trusted, and institutions that protect traditions evoke loyalty and deserve fidelity. Religious leaders, therefore, with introverted sensing as their dominant function rely on and lead with their grasp of detail. Because life is cherished for its vividly experienced and remembered concrete experiences, their sense of community too must be built on a solid basis of commonly agreed facts.

Two implications for ISFJ leaders flow from the high frequency of ISFJs among lay and clergy groups. First, how they approach life, including religious life, will find resonance with a significant group of like-minded quiet, friendly traditionalists in the congregation, especially among female churchgoers, where almost one in three have been found to be ISFJs (Ross, 1995; Bramer & Ross, 2012). Second, ISFJ clergy will constitute a significant subgroup within their own denomination at diocesan, presbytery, or conference level. Thus, they will tend to have significant peer (and very often institutional) support for their restrained, traditional perspectives and priorities. Moreover, they tend to be admired by many in the community for their patience with routine, and their willing application to detail. Community members, however, with intuitive preferences may be frustrated that ISFJ leaders seem to have only one speed which to them feels slow. ISFJ leaders may not impress immediately and so may be under-estimated in an interview situation or at a large meeting. Those other types who are willing to slow down to ISFJ pace may discover an amused acute observer who sees things in a special and unique way.

2 Auxiliary (Nurturing Parent): Extraverted Feeling

The auxiliary helping function of the ISFJ leader is extraverted feeling. Extraverted feeling is an externally focused function that makes judgments and determinations based on systems of shared values (Haas & Hunziker, 2006), that is, on the basis of human relatedness. Extraverted feeling is concerned to affirm and support others, and this quality is enhanced when it develops in the auxiliary position. It is invaluable as the means by which ISFJ leaders reach out to give to those around them. Extraverted feeling in the auxiliary position enables ISFJ leaders to be quiet and careful community builders. Because they are self-effacing, however, others may neglect acknowledgement of their contributions, but which are silently appreciated, and quietly settling for them.

ISFJ leaders naturally focus on how to care for the feelings of others, and the nurturing parental quality of their auxiliary extraverted feeling makes them natural harmonizers, readily smoothing over difficulties. Others often feel deeply touched by their display of care and concern (McAlpine, Shumate, Evers, & Hughey, 2009). Religious ministry provides ISFJs with a sense of place and provides them with a specific role through which to help people in ways that matter to themselves and to those others also drawn to religion as a grounding to human life.

ISFJ leaders may become overextended, however, and forget their own needs in the face of those of others whose needs always seem more pressing and deserving. Generally, ISFJ leaders seem to need little overt recognition—they simply wish to know their efforts make a difference. However, in circumstances when their high level of self-sacrifice is not reciprocated, ISFJ leaders may experience resentment that can sour their relationships.

By the same token, ISFJ leaders may become overprotective of others and not leave enough connective slack for the development of healthy autonomy in the other person, producing dependency and even what has been described as co-dependency. Accordingly, that minority within the community possessing thinking preferences may be less comfortable engaging with them. This is a loss for all involved. For these thinking types are the very ones who can provide a counter-balance to the warm but sometimes overly needy groups that cluster around ISFJ leaders.

Because they only like to manage relationships in a nurturing way, ISFJ leaders tend to avoid problems that involve personal conflict. However, ISFJ leaders' sense of responsibility combines with their introverted sensing powers of observation to prevent them hiding from the practical consequences of their avoidance. As a result, an inner tension develops inside ISFJ leaders.

A second source of stress for ISFJ leaders is their tendency to take on others' feelings and expectations and lose themselves in the process (Berens & Nardi, 2004). However, because of their private ways, and their withdrawal from tough thinking types who might confront them, physical symptoms may be the first indicator of stress that has been accumulating over months and years. Finally under stress, "they may also play favorites and insist on their own very subjective opinions and preferences" (Berens & Nardi, 2004, p. 34).

3 Tertiary (Eternal Child): Introverted Thinking

The tertiary function of ISFJ leaders is introverted thinking. Introverted thinking is the process *par excellence* that organizes information according to an internal framework, distilling the formal essence of phenomena and giving it a name. As the tertiary function for ISFJ leaders, introverted thinking is carried by the archetype of the eternal child. This archetype is recognized by the ways in which introverted thinking shows up in innocent, playful, creative ways, while at the same time carrying a sense of wounding.

Introverted thinking in ISFJ leaders is volatile, having an innocent, exuberant flavor one moment, displaying vulnerability the next, and then succumbing suddenly to the rapid fatigue that we associate with young children. The child-like innocent but unreliable tertiary function of introverted thinking provides relief to the caring, but usually unplayful, ISFJ leaders. It frees them on occasion from the burden of only ever seeing people's needs and feeling that they should be able to respond to those needs. According to Grant, Thompson, and Clarke (1983), with the development of introverted thinking, ISFJ leaders begin "to make decisions in a more logical and analytical way" (p. 223). Introverted thinking helps protect ISFJ leaders from burnout because they "become more protective of their own interests and feel more free to deny requests which made [inordinate] demands on their time" (p. 223).

From introverted thinking, ISFJ leaders can draw on an archetypal critic that is unafraid to think the "dangerous, subversive or heretical" (Beebe, 2006a, p. 135) and so operate with more autonomy. Colleagues and congregants may be baffled by this change of manner. Whereas before they cared little for objective analysis, limiting themselves to sincere and caring words, ISFJ leaders may find they have acquired a rich set of principles to draw on in order to solve problems in which they are interested (Berens & Nardi, 2004). This may give rise to a new-found independence, humor, and assertiveness that may also serve as a liberating model for the many ISFJ (usually female) churchgoers who see how much happier, and less wearied, worn down, and worried their revered leader now seems, even though at first they may have been "shocked" at this shift.

There are ups and downs in the ISFJ leaders' journey of integrating introverted thinking into consciousness. It takes time to find balance, sometimes giving too much time to analysis and classification. They are frequently exhausted when required to focus on abstract systemic issues. When confronting introverted thinking in others, ISFJ leaders fluctuate in their response, sometimes prematurely submitting to others' reasoning instead of first taking time for their own processing. At other times, however, they may simply dismiss the value of listening to others' views.

In their wider church community or beyond, introverted thinking enables ISFJ leaders to speak out with a more independent voice. Others often take note because ISFJ leaders are anything but habitual naysayers, and so their voice is felt to come from a place of integrity that is informed by care. Finally, ISFJ leaders can use their facility with detail to help individuals to sort information of relevance to the harmonious functioning of the community and devise ways of categorizing and analyzing a problematic situation, including drawing on specific precedents that may be discussed for the potential relevance to the present one. When other SJs in the religious community become impatient and self-righteous, they can diffuse the conflict by telling a story from their own journey toward becoming more flexible in the application of principle.

4 Fourth (Soul-Friend): Extraverted Intuition

The fourth function of ISFJ leaders is extraverted intuition. Extraverted intuition is an information-gathering function that seeks connections and relationships between objects, peoples, and events in the external world with a view to generating "real-world possibilities" (Haas & Hunziker, 2006, p. 53). The integration of extraverted intuition into conscious awareness seldom starts before the mid-thirties and does so under the archetypal influence of the soul-friend.

The soul-friend archetype suffuses extraverted intuition with such qualities as mission, intensity, and the capacity for deep connection. Accordingly, the psychological spine of the ISFJ is formed when extraverted intuition is integrated into consciousness along with the dominant function of introverted sensing. Much is to be gained, therefore, both for themselves and for those around them, when ISFJ leaders become more familiar and practiced with intuition. Impetus may come from within the religious community when ISFJ leaders see the utility of, for example, the creative improvisation of committed ENFP church members in dealing with unforeseen circumstances.

If ultra-clear ISFJ leaders can recognize their anxiety of not having "everything worked out and practical", then the magic of their expansive and creative fourth function can act as a gateway to the power, depth, and breadth of their largely unconscious functions. With such courage, ISFJ leaders are able to become patient with brainstorming, more spontaneous, following possibilities to see where they might lead and exploring multiple meanings. ISFJ leaders are aided in this risky process if they are not subjected to premature problem solving by others but taken seriously, and allowed time to ventilate fears and worries, without being patronized (Quenk, 2000). Such patience allows ISFJ leaders to relax, let go of compulsion to conserve at any cost, and empower a deeper realization that everything changes—nothing remains the same. This insight may free them up internally to identify opportunities for change and support others to do the same. They become more comfortable with self-criticism and more open to identifying improvements in past projects.

Before the integration of extraverted intuition into consciousness, when ISFJ leaders are under stress, the "inferior" aspects of the fourth function may erupt in the way that Quenk (1993, 2000) has characterized as "being in the grip." Catastrophizing by stressed ISFJ leaders is but one expression of being "in the grip." Intuition is concerned with the future, and conscious, integrated extraverted intuition is excited by future possibilities, but, for ISFJ leaders, the future is full of foreboding at the best of times, because it has yet to be directly experienced. And so under stress, ISFJ leaders become even more wildly imaginative about disastrous outcomes (Quenk, 2000). Paralysis and procrastination may result, or the other extreme—reckless, impulsive activity. Vigilance regarding early signs of panic, loss of focus, and confusion may avert uncharacteristic rashness.

Harnessing the rich connectivity of extraverted intuition is not a smooth process for ISFJ leaders. Intuitions come too fast for ISFJ leaders to process accurately, since they are so used to the slow, accurate operations of introverted sensing. Early in the process of the integration of the fourth function, ISFJ leaders experience great difficulty attending to the big picture until all the details are accounted for and understood, and when others use extraverted intuition they often feel overwhelmed fearing that the outflow of possibilities will never cease.

SHADOW PERSONALITY

5 Dominant Shadow (Challenger): Extraverted Sensing

For ISFJ leaders, the dominant shadow function is extraverted sensing. Extraverted sensing enjoys scouting the external environment, taking pleasure in the experience of sights, smells, tastes, sounds, and textures through the five senses. There exists a competitive tension between sensing in its introverted and extraverted aspect. ISFJ leaders, whose dominant function is introverted sensing, may be put off by the behavior of extraverted sensing types (ESFPs and ESTPs) and may view them as behaving inappropriately if not downright irresponsibly. When they themselves indulge in the delight of the senses, they may feel that they are "being wasteful" of resources and experience feelings of guilt.

Immediately responding to sensory experience without taking time for reflection may feel to ISFJ leaders to border on the insane and to be an invitation to physical or ethical disaster. They feel that such intense focus on the present without reference to the past will be perceived by others, as well as themselves, as operating without care, and hence without integrity. By the same token, with insufficient opportunity to reflect, ISFJ leaders feel overwhelmed by the need to make rapid responses.

Before extraverted sensing is integrated into consciousness, ISFJ leaders will tend to demand that the present be made relevant by referring back to the past. Shorn of the opportunity for such checking, ISFJ leaders may simply reject or even deny current reality in the moment. This reactivity may disturb other types who had hitherto come to respect and expect reasonable realism of their ISFJ leaders. Such ignoring may lead to division inside the community, with sensing judging types (sometimes constituting two-thirds of the congregation) colluding with the ISFJ leader's denial of or withdrawal from the unfolding situation. Awareness of these type dynamics and of the different character of sensing in its introverted and extraverted aspects (clarity as opposed to delight) can reduce conflict, misunderstanding, minimization, or denial.

The integration of extraverted sensing into a conscious orientation must be undertaken as a personal journey for most ISFJ leaders. There will be little positive encouragement from members of their community to develop this important function since so few have it as a dominant or auxiliary function. However, if ISFJ leaders rise to the personal challenge, because of their commitment to wholeness and balance in themselves, they will make an immense contribution to the viability and the attractiveness of religious community to the wider society, since extraverted sensing types are a middle frequency type group in the general population of both the United Kingdom (Kendall, 1998) and the United States (Hammer & Mitchell, 1996). Conscious integration, therefore, of extraverted sensing by ISFJ leaders constitutes a much needed re-balancing of the religious culture and may aid the restoration of the appeal of religious institutions to the significant cultural matrix of the spiritual-but-not-religious in Western societies (Fuller, 2001).

Integration of extraverted sensing is a significant accomplishment on a personal level for ISFJ leaders: it magnifies their effectiveness, as leaders whose realism and gathered presence cannot be ignored. The grounded reflectiveness of their dominant function that precisely registers facts, viewing them in the context of that which has gone before, is then combined with a relaxed comfortable presence and capacity for joy and delight in the present that contributes both seriousness and pleasure to situations and individuals.

6 Auxiliary Shadow (Critical Parent): Introverted Feeling

For ISFJ leaders, the auxiliary function is introverted feeling. Introverted feeling is an inwardly directed decision-making function of inner valuing, assessing everything on the basis of non-negotiable personal values with a view to optimizing inner harmony. As the auxiliary shadow function, introverted feeling is carried by the archetype of the critical parent. The influence of the critical parent archetype is recognized when introverted feeling is deployed protectively to block sensed threats to survival. It functions to thwart new energy and demoralize threatening agents of change invoking a protective wisdom that knows best.

Introverted feeling lies in the shadow of ISFJ leaders' auxiliary function of extraverted feeling, the means by which they usually nurture others. By contrast, their introverted feeling performs the role of the critical or forbidding parent and is often mobilized in order to thwart threatening forces or intent. Introverted feeling may show itself in an inexplicable but deeply felt forceful hostility to innovation, which only intensifies ISFJ leaders' predilection for conserving tradition.

Introverted feeling is likely to occur when ISFJ leaders sense that their personal values may be violated. They become moralistic and self-righteous, and individuals under their suspicion are decried and made to feel *persona non grata.* This, of course, threatens a sense of community and is shocking to members who may have accepted their ISFJ leaders' conservatism because of their usually restrained and measured style and demeanor. By the same token, however, when this strong reaction is to a *commonly agreed* shared community threat, then members may be amazed, heartened, and grateful for their

ISFJ leaders' vehemence in the face of threat. There is great value, therefore, in ISFJ leaders becoming aware of this hidden strength of introverted feeling that they possess, and its possible deployment in a more conscious and discerning manner.

Another way that introverted feeling shows up under the influence of critical parent energy is in the guise of a brutal perfectionism that neither they nor others can ever attain. This is a special problem for ISFJ leaders in religious roles, since, because of their elevated status, members of their community are unlikely to challenge them or their impossibly high self-expectations.

While the instances may be few that trigger such severe reactions, their intensity argue for pre-emptive education and for the value of introverted feeling being integrated into conscious awareness. The rewards are there and are not solely preventive or remedial. When ISFJ leaders are more in contact with their personally held inner values they have access to the intensity and power that accompanies a resultant *owned sense of self*: whereas before they cared naturally and protectively about tradition and meeting members' tangible needs, now they are empowered to be more active and initiating. An ISFJ once averred that we can "wield the sword of justice on behalf of peace and harmony." ISFJ leaders, however, may "become stubborn about going with the flow of a single impulse, and insist that they have an accurate read on the current situation" (McAlpine, Shumate, Evers, & Hughey, 2009).

With the critical parent energy of their introverted feeling integrated into a conscious orientation, ISFJ leaders become more dynamic and widen their base of support in the community. For example, they begin to affirm more openly those types who naturally speak with the same integrity that they themselves have begun to develop. This will secure their relationship with a quiet but powerful element in any religious community, the introverted feeling types, who were described by Isabel Briggs Myers, herself an INFP, as constituting the moral backbone of a society. By the same token, ISFJ leaders may better understand what drives the vociferous articulations of the important ENFP subgroup found in most liberal Protestant and Catholic congregations.

7 Tertiary Shadow (Trickster): Extraverted Thinking

For ISFJ leaders, the tertiary shadow function is extraverted thinking. Extraverted thinking is an externally directed decision-making function that seeks to establish systems of organization so that phenomena may be compared on the basis of objective criteria (Haas & Hunziker, 2006). For ISFJ leaders, extraverted thinking lays in the shadow of their tertiary function, *introverted* thinking. Accordingly, extraverted thinking finds expression in ISFJ leaders through the archetype of the trickster whose activity and effect is recognized by deception, mistakes, unintended results, abrupt reversal of fortunes, and humor. Trickster energy can be effective in escaping double binds and other seemingly impossible situations.

Extraverted thinking is a prevailing function in Western societies with their deeply embedded technocratic culture. For example, TJs (those types with extraverted thinking as their dominant or auxiliary process) accounted for more than 71 percent of high level corporate executives (Macdaid, McCaulley, & Kainz, 1986). Thus, though religious groups with their prevalence of extraverted feeling rather than extraverted thinking represent an alternative or counter-cultural way of organizing institutions, most religious leaders will feel pressure at times to be efficient and effective, the trademarks of extraverted thinking in our society. When ISFJ leaders yield to this pressure, it may have tricksterish qualities and yield unintended results.

Berens and Nardi (2004) report that ISFJ leaders misguide themselves and others when organizing more efficient operations. ISFJ leaders are prone to treat logic as irrelevant, making fun of logical thinking, and when pressed by situations or TJ community members to be logical, ISFJ leaders "laugh at how they neglect organization until they have to stop and fix everything" (Berens & Nardi, 2004, p. 35). This may provide comic relief to the minority of perceiving types in the congregation, but is likely to annoy and lower their credibility among others members. In particular, their attitude may erode the trust of the STJs who tend to feature prominently on important financial subcommittees of organizations.

When others use extraverted thinking, ISFJ leaders may feel trapped into making decisions too quickly. Under stress, ISFJ leaders may feel pressured to use extraverted thinking and then spend inordinate and sometimes "unnecessary time establishing order" (Berens & Nardi, 2004, p. 35). When others use extraverted thinking to impose a program, ISFJ leaders may set out to undermine its value. This may create a crisis within the community and points to the wisdom and even the necessity of developing conscious awareness around the play of the trickster archetype, in general, and then, in particular, the potential undermining that may be perpetrated by ISFJ leaders in relation to extraverted thinking. Otherwise scarce and valuable resources invested in jeopardized programs may be wasted.

When extraverted thinking is more integrated into a conscious orientation, some ISFJ leaders report enjoying systematizing and planning (Berens & Nardi, 2004). Nevertheless, their trickster extraverted thinking may fruitfully appear in finding rationale and developing arguments for breaking the rules in an otherwise seemingly impossible situation. This may have the side benefit of feeling like a breath of fresh air to members who respect their ISFJ leaders but hitherto had found them all too serious and predictable.

Generally, without conscious commitment to personal growth informed and perhaps even awakened by being "type-wise," the *trickster* aspect of extraverted thinking is seldom consistently developed, but may come in handy in extricating ISFJ leaders from the frequent occasions in which they feel themselves in double-binds on account of the numerous factional forces within the congregation, the wider church, and the local community.

8 Fourth Shadow (Demon/Angel): Introverted Intuition

For ISFJ leaders, the fourth shadow function is introverted intuition and this seldom occurs until after the mid-life passage. Introverted intuition facilitates awareness of images and abstract ideas that span past and future, transcend time and space, and produce insights that arise spontaneously from the unconscious. Such insights transform and re-frame situations. As the fourth shadow function among ISFJ leaders, introverted intuition is carried by the archetype of the demon/angel.

The usual effect of the demonic archetype is to undermine. Introverted intuition is the opposite judging function to that of ISFJ leaders' dominant introverted sensing, and it *directly* clashes with the operations of introverted sensing because it operates in the very same (introverted) world. Introverted intuition, therefore, tends to have a disruptive impact on ISFJ leaders. Introverted intuition undermines or even sabotages the operations of the superior, dominant introverted sensing function.

When ISFJ leaders appear "beastly," negative introverted intuition is often involved. Some ISFJ leaders may feel that when they are trying to employ introverted intuition to seek significance and meaning, they become overwhelmed by hopelessness and loneliness. The activities of introverted intuition are frequently suffused with dysphoria and negative moods, since not only is introverted intuition unfamiliar to ISFJ leaders, there is something foreign about its activities because when it is engaged as noted above, it subverts the functioning of ISFJ leaders' usual way of coping through introverted sensing. When they encounter introverted intuition, ISFJ leaders are unfamiliar with *how* this contrasting form of inner perceiving works. Being familiar with introverted sensing, they treat what is cognized by introverted intuition (symbols, archetypes, visions) in the same way as they might deal with facts, rather than as impressionistic hints of what may be possible.

ISFJ leaders are often fearful when other people use introverted intuition. McAlpine, Shumate, Evers, and Hughey (2009) report that ISFJ leaders may view an intense focus on the abstract as evidence of mental instability. This attitude may be in part due to their own recourse to introverted intuition only in desperation, when they have run out of facts. Consequently, when others use introverted intuition and offer a spiritual insight that has just occurred to them, ISFJ leaders may try to shut them down.

Occasionally, introverted intuition functions like an angel to redeem or transform a situation. One reason for ISFJ leaders to meet the challenge of incorporating their most obscured function is their enhanced availability to those with that dominant function in their religious community. ISFJ leaders should avoid the temptation to shelter with the numerous ISFJs in their congregations and the nearly as numerous ISTJs. By comparison, dominant introverted intuitives (INFJs and INTJs) are in the mid-frequency range of types in Christian churches, and there are similar numbers of ENFJs and ENTJs who have introverted intuition as their auxiliary function. Together all four types with strong introverted intuition are likely to constitute merely a seventh of the total community. However, introverted intuition is essential for continued relevance and survival of a community because of the inner prophetic visioning that introverted intuition enables. For introverted intuition spontaneously orients to archetypes that span backward into the past and forward into the future and range freely across cultures and continents. Because of the huge range of introverted intuition, a community is able to remain rooted (with reference to the past), and yet relevant for the future.

Chapter 11

The Objective Analyst

INTP Leaders

INTP Frequency in the Population

	Male (%)	*Female (%)*
UK	4.1	1.0
USA	6.5	4.0

INTP PSYCHOLOGICAL TYPE PROFILE

Leading Functions

Dominant introverted thinking with auxiliary extraverted intuition

Conscious personality

1. Dominant (Hero): Introverted Thinking
2. Auxiliary (Nurturing parent): Extraverted Intuition
3. Tertiary (Eternal child): Introverted Sensing
4. Fourth (Soul-friend): Extraverted Feeling

Shadow personality

5. Dominant shadow (Challenger): Extraverted Thinking
6. Auxiliary shadow (Critical parent): Introverted Intuition
7. Tertiary shadow (Trickster): Extraverted Sensing
8. Fourth shadow (Demon/Angel): Introverted Feeling

CONSCIOUS PERSONALITY

1 Dominant (Hero): Introverted Thinking

The dominant function of INTP leaders is introverted thinking. Introverted thinking organizes information and ideas into categories on the basis of consistently applied logical principles and develops a framework that sorts what is perceived until a more parsimonious model and appropriate filter for experience is devised (Hartzler & Hartzler, 2005). As the dominant function, introverted thinking provides the foundation for INTP leaders' basic coping with the challenges posed by life, including religious ministry.

Dominant introverted thinking applies an objective approach to most things. INTP leaders approach people and events as dispassionate observers, with the main goal of arriving at the most comprehensible truth for that state of affairs or situation (Quenk, 1993, p. 109). An objective detached approach is used to deal routinely with the slings and arrows encountered at work and in the whole of life. For the most part INTP leaders will let these bounce off, but remain curious about why what is happening is indeed happening now.

According to Berens and Nardi (2004, p. 42), INTP leaders' talents reside in identifying the underlying principles. They focus on the underlying logic of the person or situation encountered and readily change their approach when the underlying logical connections in an unfolding situation change. They tend to assess information experientially, on a case-by-case basis, unlimited by external rules or constraints. To make sense of a problem, they create a mental model that incorporates all aspects of the problem and then they continuously refine it.

Few people in religious settings share the INTP leaders' way of dealing with life, and so INTP leaders will have to deal with being regarded as different, unpredictable, and even strange. INTP leaders naturally improvise, troubleshoot, and problem-solve and need to learn to spell out the practical results of their ingenuity and flexibility. Likewise as a minority type in society, but especially in religious groups, they must learn to resist their propensity for "ruthless argumentation." Church congregations are first and foremost about community and its cultivation, and so it is surprising in view of the skills and interests of INTPs that they are not even rarer than studies have found.

Often INTP leaders within a Christian community will seek out a specialized ministry that plays to their strengths of articulating principles and spotting inconsistencies. They may make an original contribution in the development of new policy or articulate guidelines for the application of established doctrine to ethical issues arising from new cultural developments. Their detachment, cool, whimsical humor may be particularly helpful and refreshing. They must, however, be allowed sufficient time to present their extended reasoning if they are to accept future invitations to be helpful.

INTP leaders in a Christian community are used to being surrounded by a preponderance of people with feeling preferences, especially extraverted feeling. If the INTP leader is an ordained person and male, this may not be a problem especially for the female feeling congregants, since it fits social stereotypes of the male gender, on the one hand, and, on the other, of clergy being a little different. However, if the introverted thinking leader is female, she may encounter antipathy from both women and men in the community for not conforming to the requirement of warmth from women, especially for those in a facilitative role. Whether male or female, INTP leaders will find less resistance to their ingenious solutions if they precede critique with praise (Berens & Nardi, 2004).

2 Auxiliary (Nurturing Parent): Extraverted Intuition

The auxiliary function for INTP leaders is extraverted intuition. Extraverted intuition provides the means to connect with and nurture those around them, especially the feeling majority in Christian community, who otherwise might be at a loss to know how best to connect with leaders who seem mainly to live in their heads. By way of contrast and balance, extraverted intuition tunes into the possibilities in the external world by seeing patterns and interrelationships amidst disparate phenomena. Through their auxiliary function INTP leaders give to others and even to the neglected and vulnerable parts of themselves. The out-turned perceiving function of extraverted intuition enables INTP leaders more fully to "recognize their own outward needs and their responsibilities to others" (Thomson, 1998, p. 293). When ITPs feel related to a situation, they are unfailingly generous. Thus, ITPs can feel like different people in different contexts. Therefore, with INTP leaders, the auxiliary radar-like process of extraverted intuition provides the bridge over which they connect to others in their community and by which they are able make their own formulations have relevance.

By means of extraverted intuition, INTP leaders are enabled to give to others through sharing with them the possibilities they see in a common situation. Such possibilities may take the form of initiatives that reach out to new members. In addition, through one-on-one encounters, INTP leaders are able to learn what is going on very quickly and point out unconsidered possibilities in challenging situations. By reaching out with this nurturing "right arm" of their personality, and through their original tongue-in-cheek humor expressed in talks and sermons, INTP leaders provide different ways of analyzing situations and issues that until then may have seemed so complex that the usually majority sensing types chose not to engage them.

The proposals arising from the extraverted intuition of INTP leaders might seem "a bit sketchy" to sensing judging types in the group but may be welcome as something explicit which they can at least attempt to bring down to earth. Going with the extraverted turn of their auxiliary intuition stops introverted thinking types from following an agenda solely of their own making. Instead of investing the outer world with too much power and using their extraverted auxiliary to get things under control, they start to feel responsible in some way for what is going on "out there" even as it unfolds and changes. With a kind of awakening ITPs realize that what they do and say has meaning for others that they cannot calculate. What started as a silent inner dialogue between the functions of introverted thinking and extraverted intuition develops into one between INTP leaders and others in the community (Thomson, 1998). Developing extraverted intuition is the gateway for INTP leaders to find more satisfaction in relationships. Through extraverted intuition they gradually open up to other people.

3 Tertiary (Eternal Child): Introverted Sensing

The tertiary function for INTP leaders is introverted sensing. Introverted sensing enables INTP leaders to establish an anchor within them that rests on registered details and facts. Introverted sensing is the perceiving function that precisely registers specific details, and selectively records them, favoring those that relate to previously stored details. Under the archetypal influence of the eternal child, both the development and use of introverted sensing is frequently uneven, having a charming playful innocence at times but proving unreliable at other times. Introverted sensing shows up in creative ways, while at the same time carrying a sense of wounding. The operations of introverted sensing are volatile, possessing an exuberant idealistic naive flavor one moment, vulnerability the next, and then, lacking stamina, succumb suddenly to the rapid fatigue that we associate with young children.

Nonetheless, the development into consciousness of introverted sensing within INTP leaders brings diversity to the functions available for conscious deployment in themselves and for building community in a Christian context. For instance, as INTP leaders develop they become "excited about dealing with the world of the senses" while "facts assume more importance" (Grant, Thompson, & Clarke, 1983, p. 231). INTP leaders come to recognize and take comfort in familiar and subtle sensory experiences, preferring "new experiences [that] match old ones that were enjoyable" (Berens & Nardi, 2004, p. 43). The development of introverted sensing grounds INTP leaders and enables hitherto abstract whimsical INTP leaders to connect more easily and directly with the large number of people in the congregation that have introverted sensing as a dominant or auxiliary function. These SJs will appreciate their INTP leaders' seemingly new respect for and interest in accurate detail, together with a *penchant* for drawing on a rich storehouse of memories to review the past and to draw out the lessons for today (Berens & Nardi, 2004).

The path to conscious integration may be uneven. In these early stages of integration, INTP leaders may become fixated on specifics. INTP leaders may still feel drained and exhausted when their responsibilities require sustained engagement with details. Staying with the process of conscious integration, however, brings new sources of satisfaction such as "revisiting places they have been, ideas that they have explored" and exploring the history of their tradition in its surrounding culture (Berens & Nardi, 2004, p. 42). This will endear them to the SJs in the congregation, but also engage such tradition-oriented members in a wider ranging exploration than otherwise.

Balanced judgment about the right amount of detail may take time to achieve, with enthusiastic INTP leaders going "over the top" on the specifics of a plan. On the other hand, the increased tolerance for details may suddenly hit a limit with the old vagueness and impatience for detail supervening, and thus arousing the SJs' suspicion that their INTP leader's apparent conversion to *their* way of doing things was mere "window dressing."

4 Fourth (Soul-Friend): Extraverted Feeling

The fourth function to develop for INTP leaders is extraverted feeling. Extraverted feeling is an externally focused function that makes judgments and determinations based on systems of shared values (Haas & Hunziker, 2006). Extraverted feeling is the foundation of human relatedness and works whenever possible to maximize harmony: "The extravert's feeling is always in harmony with objective values" (Jung, 1971, p. 354). For INTP leaders, the integration of extraverted feeling into conscious awareness seldom commences before the mid-thirties. It is carried by the archetype of the soul-friend. The influence of the soul-friend archetype is expressed, when fully integrated into consciousness, by suffusing extraverted feeling with the qualities of mission, intensity, and capacity for deep connection. When extraverted feeling is integrated into consciousness it forms, along with the dominant function of introverted thinking, the spine of the personality (Beebe, 2016).

Until such time as extraverted feeling is integrated into consciousness, the "inferior" aspects of the function may erupt when INTP leaders are under stress, an occurrence that Quenk (1993, 2000) characterizes as "being in the grip." The triggering stress usually takes one of four forms: (1) expression of strong emotion by others, particularly when this involves criticism of INTP leaders' personal features, (2) emotional crises, (3) perceived disconfirmation of INTP leaders' own values and feelings, or (4) ignoring INTP leaders' need for "alone" time.

With extraverted feeling being the second most prevalent function in the modal Christian group, it is likely that INTP leaders will be frequently exposed to three of these triggers in the course of weekly ministry: strong emotions, pastoral crises, and multiple intrusions on personal time. Developing type awareness of this fourth function can prevent challenges in the early days of new ministry from turning into disasters.

In order to offset the fear of being overwhelmed by their own or others' emotions, INTP leaders may insist on their "logical" approach even when it has already proved unproductive. Their energy is redirected to controlling their own feelings, and their usual conceptual precision dissolves into vague distracting comments. Other members can help by *not* asking how their INTP leaders feel, but working instead to engage their helpful auxiliary process of extraverted intuition whereby a new idea or perspective interrupts such exaggerated sensitivity. Members further help INTP leaders in this situation by tactfully shouldering some of the responsibilities that leadership is carrying at the time (Quenk, 1993).

At first, social networking feels uncomfortable for INTP leaders. However, with patience and some creativity, it is possible for public demonstrations of relationality that are part of the warp and weave of Christian community, to become even tolerable for INTP leaders, especially when these can be ritualized into a role. INTP leaders then need to go on to educate members about how they as INTPs understand their role, so that the sensing and feeling majority in the congregation can adjust their expectations. Resistance to the social aspect of their role and reliance on others as facilitators in this regard may only gradually decrease over the long-term developmental project of individuation.

The rewards and satisfaction of mutual accommodation to each other's magically connective fourth "inferior" function are real, and at times INTP leaders can be the perfect host. With more awareness and appreciation of extraverted feeling, INTP leaders may come to enjoy the company of those many in their community who are consistently inhabited by extraverted feeling and they may feel more at ease networking and taking care of others.

SHADOW PERSONALITY

5 Dominant Shadow (Challenger): Extraverted Thinking

For INTP leaders, the dominant shadow function is extraverted thinking. Extraverted thinking is an externally focused organizing function concerned with practical logic—the application of principles in the external world.

Extraverted thinking applies principles, and segments processes into a sequence of elements that are in turn systematized (Berens & Nardi, 2004) and then organized into a program judged most efficient for a particular situation.

In Beebe's refinement of Jung's approach to personality typology (Beebe, 2007a), a competitive tension exists between thinking in its introverted and extraverted aspect. For INTP leaders, extraverted thinking is put in shadow by the habitual exercise of their dominant introverted thinking. For example, INTP leaders may be offended by the behavior of extraverted thinking types (ESTJs and ENTJs) and their exterior logical structuring ways which INTP leaders may view as domineering. INTP leaders tend to dislike being told what to do. This attitude has implications for those in religious groups that are usually hierarchically organized. INTPs possess a critical spirit that precipitates conflict with and distrust from senior clerics who often have extraverted thinking as their dominant or auxiliary function. This same critical spirit also creates dissonance on the local level within their own community where the numerous Js in their congregation will expect direction from their leader, which they equate with "leadership." However, INTP leaders may actually feel relieved and be appreciative when someone else seems at ease with telling others what should be done, while they themselves are released to go about re-writing the rules or criteria. Most of the time, it simply feels unnatural to INTP leaders to step into visible public leadership roles, a quirk that is hard for the structuring judging types to understand let alone accept.

The struggle to integrate any aspect of the shadow personality is a challenge. The tendency to project onto others our own "disowned" negativity is irresistible, even among those schooled in the spiritual disciplines of self-reflection and self-examination. This same temptation applies to our relationship to those functions that lie in the shadow of our conscious personality. By the same token, INTP leaders, early on in their journey toward the conscious integration of extraverted thinking, may feel bored and frustrated when focusing on established rules and policies. At times, however, they may become stubborn about how things should be organized and insist on systematic approaches that fail to take into account the opinions and feelings of members. This can in turn lead to chagrin and even fury among the majority feeling types.

Ambivalence on the part of INTP leaders about any programmatic proposals, however, may be welcomed by the minority who have a perceiving preference, most numerously the ENFPs, INFPs, and ISFPs, who often feel railroaded and even stifled by the controlled and controlling culture of the majority who have judging preferences. Furthermore, many members, tired of previous rivalries and power struggles, will be relieved at INTP leaders' rejection of overt competition. INTP leaders who succeed in religious organizations learn to be more selective about their fights realizing that feeling types dislike conflict, and that judging types need some structure in order to feel secure and less stressed. Integration of extraverted thinking empowers their worldly effectiveness as leaders, whose intellectual acuity will seldom be in doubt, but whose ability to play on the team may have come into question. If INTP leaders rise to the personal growth challenge through their commitment to wholeness and balance in themselves, they will make an immense contribution to the vitality and intellectual robustness of the religious tradition of which they are a part.

6 Auxiliary Shadow (Critical Parent): Introverted Intuition

For INTP leaders, the auxiliary shadow function is introverted intuition. Introverted intuition is the function that facilitates awareness of images and abstract ideas that transcend time and space, span past and future, and produce insights that arise spontaneously from the unconscious (Ross, 2015). Such insights transform and re-frame situations. Introverted intuition focuses on the subjective internal world of the unconscious and superficially may seem to resemble introverted thinking, the INTP leaders' dominant function. However, introverted intuition shows up very differently from the INTP leaders' critically clear dominant function. Indeed introverted intuition is a form of perceiving, not of judging, and so can survey and "see" in the inward turned mind's eye a whole array of phenomena ranging from the past and into the future in terms of possibilities. Furthermore, introverted intuition is hot and passionate, whereas introverted thinking is cool and analytical.

Introverted intuition lies in the shadow of INTP leaders' auxiliary function of extraverted intuition, the expansive and connective means by which INTP leaders usually nurture and offer assistance to others under the archetypal influence of the nurturing parent. By contrast, the influence of the critical parent archetype is engaged when introverted intuition is deployed protectively to block sensed threats to survival. Introverted intuition often shows up in a crass power-oriented manner in order to resist change and is deployed to thwart new energy and to demoralize threatening agents of change by invoking a protective wisdom that "knows best."

In the early stage of conscious differentiation, introverted intuition may be used more for such defensive purposes. INTP leaders deploy introverted intuition in order to block or immobilize what is experienced sometimes accurately, sometimes mistakenly, as dangerous. Introverted intuition first emerges into the consciousness of INTPs with a distinctly negative aura and may be directed against themselves and take the form of self-criticism for knowing too little or for grasping the point too slowly. By the same token, when others use their introverted intuition, or when a certain vision is expressed for the community, INTP leaders may have to struggle hard to restrain themselves from ridicule on the grounds of being based upon beliefs that lack empirical data.

The integration of any part of the shadow personality requires significant moral effort and a capacity to face what is negative within oneself. The triggering of introverted intuition in congregational work is likely to be rare, however, because only a few members have introverted intuition as their dominant or auxiliary function. However, dominant introverted intuitive types often gravitate into policy development positions at a national or regional level, especially the INTJs, while INFJs often gravitate into spiritual direction positions. These types may help INTP leaders validate, accept, and harness this introverted intuitive aspect of themselves.

As introverted intuition is made more conscious, so its effects within INTP leaders become more adaptive. For example, congregants, colleagues, and superiors, long familiar with the dry wit and clarity of INTP leaders, may be surprised by but sympathetic toward that troubled complexity that peeks through on occasion as introverted intuition emerges into their consciousness. The development of introverted intuition, therefore, within INTP leaders may equip them to lead at a time of crisis when a new vision of what it means to be part of that religious tradition is needed.

7 Tertiary Shadow (Trickster): Extraverted Sensing

For INTP leaders, the tertiary shadow function is extraverted sensing. Delighting in the senses as it does, extraverted sensing enables INTP leaders to gather specific information from their external environment, taking in the surrounding sights, sounds, smells, textures, and tastes. Extraverted sensing is the only function rooted solely in the present moment. For the INTP leaders, extraverted sensing is the function infused with trickster qualities such as playing with reality, deception, and mistaken truths.

INTP leaders may be simply unaware that they frequently miss out on what is happening in the moment because they are attending to the external environment for future possibilities that may then be subjected to logical analysis by their dominant introverted thinking. With extraverted sensing in trickster position, INTP leaders are often deceived in terms of extraverted sensing's reliability for them. Berens and Nardi (2004) report: "They can fool themselves and others by a misguided focus on the perceived 'realities' of a situation" (p. 43).

Their "trickster" extraverted sensing can literally and figuratively trip up INTP leaders in their ministries. Attendance at important events, for example, may be impaired because of difficulties with travel directions. Under stress, some INTPs may get confused by their physical environment, misjudge the space, and bump into things. Under stress, other INTPs may suddenly take impulsive action. The unintended negative results of INTP leaders' unreliable grasp of external realities are compounded by their unpredictable reaction to the use of extraverted sensing by others. INTP leaders are unlikely to have their extraverted sensing triggered in a religious setting, because few extraverted sensing types are motivated to affiliate with religious groups or spend time in religious settings: ESTPs and ESFPs prefer active pursuits and nature as sources of refreshment. However, there is a significant group of ISFPs in both Catholic and liberal and evangelical Protestant congregations and these may softly chuckle at their INTP leaders' misfortune or temporary disorientation, even while helping them off the floor on which they slipped.

For most of their life and work, INTP leaders will tend to discount the pleasurable side of a sensing life. However, with more awareness, they may come to laugh at their lack of comfort in this accident-prone domain. Physical dangers and stress recede. Accordingly, as INTP leaders integrate extraverted sensing into their conscious orientation, parents of adolescents in the youth program may be more confident about the safe return of the INTP leaders who volunteered to lead a weekend camping trip for youth.

Trickster extraverted sensing, when integrated into an expanded self instead of shoring up ego defenses, may be used to wriggle out of the double bind that builders of community encounter. Extraverted sensing becomes a spontaneous resource for dealing with otherwise impossible situations. With this comes a sense of liberation and greater personal freedom as INTP leaders experience the unexpected from a new and more concrete realm of experience than they could have imagined or analyzed.

8 Fourth Shadow (Demon/Angel): Introverted Feeling

For INTP leaders, the fourth shadow function is introverted feeling. This seldom develops until after the mid-life passage. Introverted feeling is an inwardly directed decision-making function of inner valuing. It assesses everything on the basis of non-negotiable personal values with a view to optimizing inner harmony.

As the fourth shadow function introverted feeling is carried into consciousness under the influence of the demon/angel archetype, whose effect usually is to undermine. Introverted feeling is the opposite judging function to that of INTP leaders' dominant introverted thinking and *directly* clashes with it because introverted feeling operates in the same (introverted) world: it is impossible to reflect with thinking and feeling at the same time, for feeling requires consciousness to move close and engage with objects of reflection for appraisal, whereas thinking needs "critical" distance for objective scrutiny. Introverted feeling, therefore, has a disruptive, even destructive impact, on

INTP leaders, especially in early provisional adulthood before the differentiation of introverted feeling from the unconscious where archetypes hold sway. In the first half of life, mobilization of introverted feeling is infused with negative mood, because not only is introverted feeling unfamiliar to INTP leaders, there is something foreign about its activities: it prevents the functioning of INTP leaders' usual way of coping through introverted thinking. When INTP leaders are "beastly," negative introverted feeling is often involved.

INTP leaders are rare in religious environments, and acting out shadow impulses may devastate the development of community, undermining years of perseverance by the INTP leaders whereby trust had been slowly consolidated among the feeling majority within most congregations. INTP leaders do well to be aware of their "demons," especially those arising in association with introverted feeling, their least conscious function. Furthermore, they may project out their own ungainly introverted feeling when others use that function, which will be often among those with introverted feeling as a dominant or auxiliary function (INFPs or ISFPS and ENFPs or ESFPs, respectively). INTP leaders may view reactions from these types as irrational—based on "misplaced sentimentality." Only through mindful awareness and restraint requiring considerable moral effort may the intellectually stringent INTP refrain from direct disparagement, put-downs, or the innuendo of subtle sarcasm.

The path of conscious integration of the fourth shadow function is long and never complete. A shadow aspect remains and requires vigilance. One step toward integration for INTP leaders is merely noticing *how slow* they are in matters involving *their* feelings. They do well to accept the slower speed rather than employ thinking judgment that will often be out of place in dealing with the emotion of relationships in a religious community. A further step is developing awareness of their own self-disparagement when facing the slower more ambling pace of the delicate layering of values that comprises introverted feeling.

There is also the redemptive angelic aspect to introverted feeling, but this appears more frequently when extraverted feeling, their soul function, is better integrated into consciousness. For INTP leaders, engagement with their fourth shadow function will be less daunting with a developed solid connection to their fourth function of extraverted feeling with its concern for external harmony and relatedness. Profound connection accompanies the sense of affinity, even closeness with others, giving rise to a warmth that extraverted feeling brings to consciousness. Nevertheless, extravert feeling moves at a different pace—swiftly filling a room with smiles, or with displeasure—and so even INTP leaders who have befriended extraverted feeling as their soulfriend require further patience because of introverted feeling's slower pace.

Chapter 12

The Logical Pragmatist

ISTP Leaders

ISTP Frequency in the Population

	Male (%)	*Female (%)*
UK	10.8	2.5
USA	8.7	4.3

ISTP PSYCHOLOGICAL TYPE PROFILE

Leading Functions

Dominant introverted thinking with auxiliary extraverted sensing

Conscious personality

1. Dominant (Hero): Introverted Thinking
2. Auxiliary (Nurturing parent): Extraverted Sensing
3. Tertiary (Eternal child): Introverted Intuition
4. Fourth (Soul-friend): Extraverted Feeling

Shadow personality

5. Dominant shadow (Challenger): Extraverted Thinking
6. Auxiliary shadow (Critical parent): Introverted Sensing
7. Tertiary shadow (Trickster): Extraverted Intuition
8. Fourth shadow (Demon/Angel): Introverted Feeling

CONSCIOUS PERSONALITY

1 Dominant (Hero): Introverted Thinking

The dominant function of ISTP leaders is introverted thinking. This is their heroic function that they use to steer their lives and which they instinctively apply to serve their religious community—for in their view, a community of which they are a part deserves objective analysis that will enable it to survive in a changing environment. ISTP leaders like to apply an objective approach to most things. They are energized by problems to look swiftly for expedient and effective action (Berens & Nardi, 2004, p. 22). They take pains not to react emotionally as it interferes with their way of solving problems: finding clear definitions, clarifying relevant principles, and noting consistencies or their absence. It is frustrating when other more extraverted or more feeling members of their community seem to over-react.

When encountering introverted thinking in others, ISTP leaders should be aware of a tendency to engage in ruthless argument. They will tend to respond by asking many questions which may seem excessive to some external judging types or intrusive to introverted feeling types. On the other hand, they may respond by clarifying ideas, rather than starting with the facts which may come as a surprise to the larger number of members with strong introverted sensing.

Because they are such a rarity among clergy and in Christian congregations, ISTP leaders must be prepared to deal with surprised reactions from many when they do not conform to the feeling culture cherished and even held sacred by many in their community. However, taking time to establish solid relationships with a few key members will pay dividends, as these members may act as interlocutors with the wider community. Over time the cool relaxed playful detachment of ISTP leaders may be seen as an asset, especially in times of crisis, and more routinely simply refreshing as a way to deal with problems, especially those problems arising from change as experienced by the judging types who form the majority in religious groups.

ISTP leaders naturally focus on the logic of the process that they see unfolding before them, and respond readily to improvise, to trouble shoot, and to problem solve. They assess information experientially on a case-by-case basis, unlimited by external rules or constraints. This perceiving adaptable style may conflict with the more structured culture formed by the preponderance of judging types in almost all religious groups and the rule orientation of sensing-judging types in particular. As a consequence, ISTP leaders may frustrate the judging types within the congregation.

The pattern of adaptation between leader and community will vary with the circumstances that gave rise to the ISTP being in a leadership position. If the appointment was in response to a crisis then, when the crisis is past, the majority may take *longer* to adjust to the ISTP leader's habitual style, than if the rare ISTP candidate was more knowingly selected for his or her rare combination of talents. Much too will depend on the ISTP leader's awareness of being "rare fish" in the religious pond. With this insight they can re-balance from a tendency to insist on accuracy and consistency and be sensitive to leaping to critique before praise, realizing that most in their community cannot detach from an issue in the way that is natural for them. ISTP leaders will need to be aware too of a kind of grandiosity whereby the heroic energy surrounding their introverted thinking may make them feel flawless.

2 Auxiliary (Nurturing Parent): Extraverted Sensing

The auxiliary function of ISTP leaders is extraverted sensing. This function takes pleasure in sights, smells, tastes, sounds, and textures as these are experienced in the moment. ISTP leaders enjoy "scouting" the external environment for these experiences (Hartzler & Hartzler, 2005). Extraverted sensing supplies the direct perceptual experience that their introverted thinking needs to guide their actions. "Unless they experience this kind of contact, they're likely to be bored and restless" (Thomson, 1998, p. 306). ISTP leaders need to develop their auxiliary extraverted sensing for it serves as an essential bridge to the external world. This can save them from being trapped in an inner world of their subjective logic and abstract reasoning.

For ISTP leaders, drawing on extraverted sensing is under the guiding influence of the archetype of the nurturing parent: practical problem solving is the way by which they *give* to others, and ISTP leaders work hard to offer concrete solutions to assist them. In turn, helping others in this way helps them to feel needed and satisfied with *their* work.

More generally, it is through shared activity that ISTP leaders connect to others. Consequently, when other community members use extraverted sensing, ISTP leaders feel a close bond with them as they dwell together in the joy of the present moment. There are a modest number of ISFPs in most religious groups who would quietly affirm the tactical realism that comes naturally to ISTP leaders. However, there are very few extraverted sensing types (ESTPs and ESFPs), and so sharing "the simple joy in doing" is a rare experience in most religious communities. For affirmation of this important aspect of their personality, it is important for ISTP leaders and all sensing perceiving types (SPs) in religious leadership roles to take the time to seek sensing perceiving company in the wider community in order to avoid resentment, burnout, and fatigue and to continue to feel nurtured and be nurturing as leaders in their own faith group.

A few more types, the NJs, will have extraverted sensing as part of their conscious personality, through their tertiary or fourth function, but this type group (while less scarce than the SPs) are not that numerous especially compared to the large proportion of SFJs. Hence, pleasure in details (introverted sensing) and warm agreement (extraverted feeling) are far more likely to be available as mirrored experiences in a religious setting as compared to extraverted sensing beloved by ISTPs.

It is really helpful for ISTP leaders when they realize that they are such a rare fish in the world of organized religion. ISTPs will usually be too remote from their feelings—or else fail to consider their feelings relevant to the situation at hand—to experience hurt when their best efforts go unacknowledged. Rather realizing their minority status may help ISTP leaders control their irritation when others do not seem so inclined to leap to action, want involved discussions instead, or seem immobilized by complex reservations. Such realization of the uniqueness of their combination of functions and gifts can help ISTP leaders accept that others simply take longer to see the practical details requiring action.

Brownsword (1988) writes (himself an INTP) "They [ISTPs] want to deal with and collect details that can be judged logically and analytically" (p. 29). This poses a real problem for ISTP leaders in a religious context, for logical analysis is not what most folk are looking for when it comes to religion. Brownsword continues, "their sensing ability does not naturally extend to people's feelings and values" (p. 29). Therefore, since introverted thinking and extraverted sensing are in such short supply in the conscious personalities of individuals attracted to religious groups, in order to connect with the vast majority of their congregation, ISTP leaders need to develop the two remaining functions that form part of their conscious personality, introverted intuition and extraverted feeling.

3 Tertiary (Eternal Child): Introverted Intuition

The tertiary function of ISTP leaders is introverted intuition. This function enables insight into a situation by imagining possibilities hitherto hidden in the unconscious. Introverted intuition enlivens through its capacity to scan backwards and forwards in time, recognizing and accessing the power of symbols to resonate to underlying archetypal patterns. Under the influence of the archetype of the eternal child, this function within ISTP leaders frequently has an innocent, playful quality, but also sometimes proves unreliable and lacking maturity.

The development of introverted intuition may also presage an inward turning on the part of ISTP leaders, so that on occasion, outward engagement yields to readiness to explore the imagination and future possibilities

(Grant, Thompson, & Clarke, 1983). ISTP leaders may discover that they enjoy spending time alone in order to allow their imaginations to give flight to future courses of action. It may, however, take a while for them to learn to trust their new insights.

Introverted intuition broadens the focus of ISTP leaders from the specifics of the here and now to a visionary concentration. Berens and Nardi (2004, p. 2) argue that as they develop, ISTP leaders focus their vision into creating more long-term strategies. This represents a shift in social style from the trouble-shooting mode arising from the pragmatic partnership of their first two functions. The change may bring them into easier rapport with that small but significant group within many religious groups, the intuitive judging types (INFJs, ENFJs, INTJs, and ENTJs) who have introverted intuition as their dominant or auxiliary function.

ISTP leaders' new-found tolerance for complexity may prove confusing and even perplexing to the large subgroup of SJs with strong preference for introverted sensing. Hitherto this latter subgroup may have put up with their ISTP leader's quirky independence, occasional irreverent comments, and impatience for their own cherished predilection for rules and routines, because at least they seemed clear, quick-witted, and practical, enabling this SJ phalanx to relax occasionally because their leader seemed to have a finger on the pulse of the present moment. But then things may change with the advent of a seemingly "childish" idealism as introverted intuition is borne into consciousness on the unreliable wings of eternal child energy.

The ISTP leader's integration of introverted intuition is a clear instance of how internal development within a leader may be disruptive to a delicate equilibrium within the religious community. ISTP leaders' strengthening introverted intuition increases orientation to religious and spiritual perspectives and practices that "cannot be reconciled with prevailing social norms" (Thomson, 1998, p. 303). This aspect of the development of introverted intuition may increase their disconnect from the many socially conventional SFJs in their congregation, while in their sermons and public speaking profile ISTP leaders are even more likely to focus on social or institutional hypocrisy. Furthermore, until introverted intuition is fully integrated into consciousness, when other community members use introverted intuition, ISTP leaders may feel uncertain, uncomfortable, or suspicious.

In conclusion, although the development of introverted intuition can bring a refreshing capacity to foresee implications, and the effects of transformation, its volatility can feel unsettling, not just for ISTP leaders themselves but for the communities they lead. Berens and Nardi (2004) elaborate: "They can lock into a vision ignoring their usual need for . . . tangible data" (p. 23). These disjunctions may be softened, however, with the development of extraverted feeling that is the soulful bedrock of ISTP leaders' conscious personality and usually the next function to differentiate into consciousness.

4 Fourth (Soul-Friend): Extraverted Feeling

The fourth function to develop for ISTP leaders is extraverted feeling. This is an externally focused function that makes judgments and determinations based on systems of shared values (Haas & Hunziker, 2006). Extraverted feeling is the foundation of human relatedness, and works whenever possible to maximize harmony: "The extravert's feeling is always in harmony with objective values" (Jung, 1971, p. 354). For ISTP leaders, the integration of extraverted feeling into conscious awareness seldom commences before the mid-thirties and does so under the archetypal influence of the soul-friend that forms the base of their psychological spine connecting to the dominant introverted thinking and providing magical depth to their conscious personality.

Before the integration of extraverted feeling into consciousness, when ISTP leaders are under stress the "inferior" aspects of the fourth function may erupt, a predicament that Quenk (1993, 2000) has characterized as "being in the grip." The trigger for stress usually takes one of four forms: (1) expression of strong emotion by others, particularly when this involves criticism of ISTP leaders' personal features, (2) emotional crises, (3) ignoring ISTP leaders' need for "alone" time, or (4) perceived disconfirmation of ISTP leaders' own values and feelings.

With extraverted feeling being the second most prevalent function in the typical Christian group, it is likely that ISTP leaders will be frequently exposed to the first three of these triggers in the course of weekly ministry in the form of (1) strong emotions, though usually of a positive caring nature, (2) pastoral crises, and (3) multiple intrusions on personal time. Developing type-awareness particularly of this fourth function can prevent challenges in the early days of beginning a new ministry from morphing into disasters. At first, ISTP leaders may tend to imagine that people who inquire about their needs are being patronizing, and they become "vexed by what they see as illogical emotional behavior, making relationships difficult to navigate" (Berens & Nardi, 2004, p. 23).

Resistance to the social aspect of their role—and compensatory reliance on others as facilitators in this regard—may only gradually decrease over the individual's life-long project of individuation. However, community members may adjust to ISTP leaders' teasing jokes and challenges as everyone realizes and accepts that there are many ways to do ministry. With this "type wise" perspective, members may find it easier to appreciate ISTP leaders for their incisive, refreshing, playful, and detached way of dealing with life, one that is in short supply in religious communities, and a helpful balance to the sometimes cloying intensity of fidelity to a particular way of doing things that predominates because of the prevailing number of SFJs in most religious groups.

The rewards and satisfaction of mutual accommodation to each other's magically connective fourth "inferior" function are real, and at times ISTP leaders can be the perfect host. As they develop their soulful fourth function of extraverted feeling, ISTP leaders can come to enjoy the company of people who display extraverted feeling. With commitment to their own growth in this regard, and to that of the community, they can begin to feel responsible for and to take care of others' feelings. When this unfamiliar side is witnessed, many community members are more disposed to forgive their ISTP leader's lapses into insensitivity every now and again.

SHADOW PERSONALITY

5 Dominant Shadow (Challenger): Extraverted Thinking

For ISTP leaders, the dominant shadow function is extraverted thinking. This externally focused organizing function concerned with practical logic applies principles—the application of principles in the external world. For ISTP leaders, extraverted thinking seldom emerges into conscious awareness before mid-life and does so under the archetypal influence of the challenger.

Extraverted thinking is constantly put in shadow by the habitual exercise by ISTP leaders of their dominant function of introverted thinking. For example, ISTP leaders may be offended by the decisive behavior of extraverted thinking types (ESTJs and ENTJs) and their exterior logical structuring ways which they may experience as domineering. ISTP leaders' spontaneous anti-programmatic attitude will be frequently evoked in religious groups that tend to be organized hierarchically, and ISTP leaders may have to struggle hard against a tendency to feel on a perpetual crusade against the establishment.

First, their critical spirit brings them into conflict with—and to being distrusted by—senior clerics who often have extraverted thinking as their dominant or auxiliary function. Second, their critical spirit may create dissonance on the local level within their own community where the numerous judging types in their congregation will expect direction from their leader, which they equate with "leadership." However, it does not fit with ISTP leaders' style to lead in a programmatic fashion. The judging majority within most congregations find it hard to believe that their ISTP leaders may actually feel relieved and be appreciative when someone else seems at ease with telling others what should be done, allowing them meanwhile to shelter in the shade of their own cool reflection as they go about re-writing the rules or criteria. Third, they have to resist the wish to rewrite all rules in the light of what they know to be more relevant and clearer criteria. Similarly, they need to overcome their aversion to programmatic approaches and to suppress clear signs of boredom in planning and administrative meetings.

Ambivalence on the part of ISTP leaders about any programmatic proposals, however, may be welcomed by the minority who have a perceiving preference, most numerously the ENFPs, INFPs, and ISFPs, who often feel railroaded and even stifled by the controlled and controlling culture of the majority who have judging preferences. Furthermore, many members, tired of previous rivalries and power struggles, will be relieved at ISTP leaders' rejection of overt competition. ISTP leaders who succeed in religious organizations learn to pick their fights realizing that feeling types dislike conflict and that judging types need some structure in order to feel secure and less stressed. Integration of extraverted thinking empowers their worldly effectiveness as leaders, whose intellectual acuity had never been in doubt, but whose ability to play in the team had been in question. If ISTP leaders rise to the personal growth challenge, through their commitment to wholeness and balance in themselves, they will make an immense contribution to the vitality and intellectual robustness of the religious tradition of which they are a part.

6 Auxiliary Shadow (Critical Parent): Introverted Sensing

For ISTP leaders, the auxiliary shadow function is introverted sensing. Introverted sensing registers, reviews, and recalls minute detailed impressions, including the subjective affective response to those details (Hartzler & Hartzler, 2005). Introverted sensing naturally remembers details of a situation and considers these to be objective facts (Berens & Nardi, 2004). For ISTP leaders, introverted sensing is carried into consciousness by the archetype of the critical parent that is concerned with threats to the ego's survival and acts to immobilize such threats.

As the auxiliary shadow function, introverted sensing does not usually become more conscious until well into the mid-life passage (Sheehy, 1995), and so early in ISTP leaders' careers this detail-oriented function, remains in the shadow of the nurturing parental function of their auxiliary extraverted sensing, that expansive grounded orientation to and delight in the senses, which ISTPs use to nurture themselves and others. *Introverted* sensing, however, forming part of their shadow personality, is filtered through the archetype of the critical parent that is negative and forbidding, often using clumsy, misguided, and morally questionable means such as shaming and blaming to protect their fragile inner child. Therefore, introverted sensing is often deployed in a crass power-oriented way to resist change—thwarting new energy, demoralizing threatening agents of innovation, and invoking a protective wisdom that "knows best."

Before its conscious differentiation, introverted sensing is used for defensive purposes. Past recorded facts, accessed and facilitated by introverted sensing, have a negative aura: *old* details are felt to be stale and dead, overshadowed by the excitement of extraverted sensing delights and by ISTPs' swift elegant responses to them. When threatened, ISTP leaders may refer to the past (Berens & Nardi, 2004), defensively displaying "factual mastery" in order to deflect criticism. In their view, past performances lack the live energy of the moment, and so ISTP leaders negatively regard them. Contrary to their usual openness to the present, "negative" instances fuel objections to trying something different. Holding this murky lens to the past drains energy in the present and thwarts innovation. Under stress, ISTP leaders may refuse to try something again if it has failed in the past. People experienced as threatening are blocked by misrepresenting certain facts or disavowing the experience of these individuals.

The gains are clear for community-oriented ISFP leaders becoming more mindful of their uncharacteristically critical reaction to past experience. Related problems arise frequently in religious communities because so many have introverted sensing as their dominant or auxiliary. On the conservative wing, SJs will regard ISTP leaders' disparaging use of past experience as inaccurate. Likewise, change-oriented intuitive Ns are put off by the selective use of the past to block change. However, conscious familiarity with introverted sensing and how it operates takes time for ISTPs. For their part, ISTP leaders might profitably befriend, on an individual basis, ISTJs in the lay leadership, with their shared introversion and thinking preferences, for frank friendly feedback.

When introverted sensing becomes more conscious and familiar to ISTP leaders, Berens and Nardi (2004) report that "they magically . . . tune in to past mistakes [in order] to improve tactical maneuvers" (p. 23) and in so doing help others progress beyond ideas that have not worked in the past. Before consolidation of this post mid-life aspect of personal growth, ISTP leaders deploy introverted sensing in order to block or immobilize what was mistakenly apprehended as dangerous. After consolidation with the introverted sensing function being more conscious, perceptions and memories of ISTP leaders are more often accurate, and their new proficiency with sensing details can be strategically employed in times of crisis to deal with real threats to survival.

7 Tertiary Shadow (Trickster): Extraverted Intuition

For ISTP leaders, the tertiary shadow function is extraverted intuition. This is the perceiving function that makes ISTP leaders aware of the patterns, connections, and inter-relationships in the external world, including situations in their religious community. Through extraverted intuition they interpret situations, assign meanings, and make connections to other supposedly related contexts (Berens & Nardi, 2004). For ISTP leaders, extraverted intuition is seldom integrated into conscious awareness before mid-life. It does so under the influence of the trickster archetype, and is therefore the function most infused with such qualities as playing with reality, deception, and mistaken truths. The activity of trickster energy is recognized in the occurrence of mistakes, acts of deception, and unintended results.

Before mid-life, in those rare instances in which ISTP leaders draw on extraverted intuition, they are prone to mistakes, for instance when they link the present situation to other seemingly unrelated contexts and situations. The trickster element also emerges in ISTP leaders' lack of awareness of their own limitations regarding this aspect of themselves. More specifically ISTP leaders are often deceived in terms of extraverted intuition's *reliability* for them. They may, for example, be unaware that they frequently fail to consider the future implications and wider impact of their actions. Furthermore, subtleties not tied to concrete experience are ignored or given erroneous, idiosyncratic, or malevolent interpretations.

Ripples of tension may arise within a religious community, especially among the ENFPs and INFPs (a moderately large and significant group in many liberal Protestant and Catholic congregations) who play an important role in offering a spontaneous counterbalance to the rule-bound sensing judging majority. Thus, there is significant incentive for ISTP leaders to be aware of the unreliable "tricksterish" quality of their capacity to interpret situations, since the NFP groups, who have extraverted intuition as a dominant or auxiliary function, are potential allies who are likely to enjoy the more free-wheeling style of ISTP leaders and would be happy to be a sounding-board for them regarding, for example, the emotional undercurrents of community meetings which ISTPs might otherwise miss or pass over.

ISTP leaders may use extraverted intuition in a tricky, even deceitful, fashion. By the same token their use of extraverted intuition may be playful and produce unanticipated good results as well as misadventures. At other times, however, they may produce multiple possibilities simply to confuse others. When others use extraverted intuition, however, ISTP leaders themselves often feel tricked, for instance, when others change future plans or introduce new sets of alternatives.

When extraverted intuition is more integrated into the conscious psychological life of ISTP leaders, they may begin to enjoy exploring unlikely scenarios. With extraverted intuition familiar to them inside themselves as a conscious function, they will be more likely to develop communities where those with well-developed extraverted intuition (ENFPs, ENTPs, INFPs, and INTPs) are respected and feel invited to contribute their imaginative talents.

8 Fourth Shadow (Demon/Angel): Introverted Feeling

For ISTP leaders, the fourth shadow function is introverted feeling which seldom develops until after the mid-life passage. Introverted feeling is an inwardly directed decision-making function of inner valuing: it assesses everything on the basis of non-negotiable personal values with a view to optimizing inner harmony. For ISTP leaders, however, introverted feeling is carried into consciousness under the influence of the demon/angel archetype, whose effect is to undermine.

Introverted feeling is the opposite judging function to that of ISTP leaders' dominant introverted thinking function and clashes *directly* with it, as both operate in the same (introverted) world: it is impossible to think and feel at the same time, for feeling moves close to engage the objects for appraisal, whereas thinking requires "critical" distance. Introverted feeling has a disruptive impact for ISTP leaders, especially in early adulthood while still undifferentiated within the unconscious where archetypes hold sway.

At the early stage of integration, the activities of introverted feeling, whether engaged by chance, trauma, or necessity are often suffused with negative mood. Not only is introverted feeling unfamiliar to ISTP leaders, there is also something alien about its activities, because ISTP leaders' habitual cool detached introverted thinking way of coping is sabotaged when introverted feeling demands deep resonance to, and engagement and reconciliation with, heart-felt inner values. When ISTP leaders are "beastly," negative introverted feeling is often involved.

ISTP leaders are rare personality types in religious environments, and enacted shadow impulses may devastate a community, undermining years of ISTP leaders' perseverance whereby trust has been slowly consolidated among the feeling type majority. ISTP leaders do well to be aware of their "demons," especially those associated with their least conscious function, introverted feeling. ISTP leaders are prone to make errors of judgment, according insufficient priority to considerations that matter to the majority in their charge. They may project their ungainly introverted feeling onto others when others use this function, which will often be by those with introverted feeling as their dominant or auxiliary function (INFPs or ISFPs and ENFPs or ESFPs, respectively). ISTP leaders may view reactions from them as irrational and based on "misplaced sentimentality." Only through mindful awareness and restraint requiring moral effort may the stringent ISTP refrain from direct disparagement, put-downs, or the innuendo of subtle sarcasm.

The process of conscious integration of the fourth shadow function is a long one and never complete. A shadow aspect always remains that requires vigilance. One step toward integration for ISTP leaders is merely noticing *how slow* they are in regard to matters involving *their* feelings. A further step is developing awareness of their own self-disparagement when facing the slower more ambling pace of the delicate layering of values that comprises introverted feeling.

There is the redemptive angelic aspect to introverted feeling but this appears more frequently when extraverted feeling is better integrated into consciousness. For ISTP leaders, engagement with their fourth shadow function will be less daunting with a developed solid connection to their fourth and soul-function of extraverted feeling. Profound connection accompanies the sense of affinity, even closeness with others, giving rise to a warmth that extraverted feeling brings to consciousness. Nevertheless, extravert feeling moves at a different pace—swiftly filling a room with smiles or with displeasure—and so even ISTP leaders who have befriended extraverted feeling as their soul-friend require further patience because of introverted feeling's slower pace. The journey toward integration bears rich rewards that add to the pragmatics of disaster control that is a special gift of the ISTP leader.

Chapter 13

The Compassionate Facilitator

ENFJ Leaders

ENFJ Frequency in the Population

	Male (%)	*Female (%)*
UK	2.0	3.4
USA	1.5	3.4

ENFJ PSYCHOLOGICAL TYPE PROFILE

Leading Functions

Dominant extraverted feeling with auxiliary introverted intuition

Conscious personality
1. Dominant (Hero): Extraverted Feeling
2. Auxiliary (Nurturing parent): Introverted Intuition
3. Tertiary (Eternal child): Extraverted Sensing
4. Fourth (Soul-friend): Introverted Thinking

Shadow personality
5. Dominant shadow (Challenger): Introverted Feeling
6. Auxiliary shadow (Critical parent): Extraverted Intuition
7. Tertiary shadow (Trickster): Introverted Sensing
8. Fourth shadow (Demon/Angel): Extraverted Thinking

CONSCIOUS PERSONALITY

1 Dominant (Hero): Extraverted Feeling

The dominant function of ENFJ leaders is extraverted feeling. Extraverted feeling is a function that naturally orients to harmonizing with the values of the external environment. At its core, extraverted feeling serves to maintain relationships and social networks, seeking to co-ordinate people and material resources with a view to "harmoniously achieve group and individual goals" (Hartzler & Hartzler, 2005, p. 45). A religious community is very much an extraverted feeling affair, with up to 65 percent of female congregants having extraverted feeling as their dominant or auxiliary process (Bramer & Ross, 2012).

When extraverted feeling is the first and so the dominant process to develop into consciousness, its operations have the archetypal aura of the hero. Thus, for ENFJ leaders extraverted feeling is reliable and dependable and provides the foundation for ENFJ leaders' basic coping with the challenges posed by life and work, including religious ministry. In fact maintaining relationships is so much part of the "warp and weave" of their life that they may be unaware of its operations. Extraverted feeling for ENFJ leaders is so permeating that it is invisible and, like water to a fish, mainly thrust into awareness only with threatened absence. When extraverted feeling plays out the heroic role in individuals' personality, they become naturals for leadership in building community in a religious context, since they connect effortlessly with others singly or in a group.

When conflict arises, however, they may suffer dreadfully if the conflict cannot be readily resolved. For their part ENFJ leaders provide many chances for the "difficult" party to make amends, merely wanting their own needs acknowledged, and a genuine apology is readily accepted. However, when their efforts and openness are insufficient and fail to produce the ready restoration of harmony that they seek, ENFJ leaders may feel torn apart and become vociferously personal and even vindictive, feeling and often expressing their indignation that, while *they* have given praise, recognition, and respect, this has not been reciprocated.

With extraverted feeling in its heroic aspect as the dominant function, ENFJ leaders rely on their natural harmonizing capacity to connect with congregants and probably assume that this is how all good people really cope or should cope with the challenges of life, since it seems to work so well for them. Religion with the near universality of the golden rule—do to others as you would have them do to you—is attractive to extraverted feeling types as it celebrates and sacralizes their core heroic principle of harmonic connection.

ENFJ leaders may overlook the fact that the need to be helpful in others may not be as strong as theirs. They may become overbearing regarding what they think others need, so that others may feel smothered. This may be an issue when an ENFJ senior leader tries to mentor a younger leader who has not asked for mentoring. Regular community members may be shocked at the tensions generated for someone whom they regard as usually very warm and friendly. The more independent junior colleague may be further alienated, resenting other members feeling that s/he has been cast in the role of the ungrateful one.

The dominant function is often invisible to an individual, and so extraverted feeling dominant leaders feel that everyone is really like they are, but being obtuse. Therefore, development and awareness of the introverted auxiliary function can provide a very useful perspective from which to reflect, gain insight, and slow things down sufficiently for conflicts not to escalate.

2 Auxiliary (Nurturing Parent): Introverted Intuition

The auxiliary function of ENFJ leaders is introverted intuition. Introverted intuition, being a form of inward perceiving, provides balance to their externally oriented, powerful harmony-seeking dominant function. Furthermore, under the archetypal influence of nurturing parent, introverted intuition is the primary way that ENFJ leaders nurture themselves and others. Introverted intuition in the nurturing parent auxiliary position both softens and deepens ENFJ leaders and can provide them with an inner compass.

Introverted intuition brings an inner vision of what may be possible. Introverted intuition has a long range perspective and so frees ENFJ leaders from the tyranny of always requiring approval. Introverted intuition ranges backwards and forwards across time and resonates to deep themes or archetypes that span human culture and civilizations. By drawing on this resource, ENFJ leaders generate a vision or visions that sustain them, and in turn they are able to provide a rich variety of alternative perspectives that they can offer other members of their community.

Introverted intuition is a form of perceiving that is vast and deep, and that compensates for the continual other-orientation of dominant extraverted feeling. The rich perspectives that introverted intuition derives from the background processes of consciousness provide psycho-spiritual nourishment to leaders in ministry which they can then pass on to others. For through contact with ENFJ leaders who have access to introverted intuition (with its capacity to transcend time and space to envision what is possible), community members obtain a sense of their own potential from inspiring leaders who are resourceful and committed to developing potential in themselves and in others.

To access this introverted function, however, ENFJ leaders need time alone, away from continually having to make decisions that optimize the welfare of those around. They need the permission from their community to take the time to step back and see the bigger picture. Without this support, they may feel too obligated to others to take this time to renew themselves. However, if they are given and take the time and space, new insights about people and about working with people occur to them in those valuable solitary moments. "Alone they generate the new ideas that support or modify their decisions and plans" (Brownsword, 1988, p. 32). ENFJ leaders may not, however, receive much encouragement for such reflective visioning from the SJs, who often form the majority in the congregation. However, if they receive such encouragement, tangible benefits will come from such time-out and, if these can be documented, they may be eventually accepted by the SJ community.

With time-out for reflection, ENFJ leaders discover they "just know" things—how events may turn out or what may be going on with someone. This is really helpful, both in planning new projects in the community and in individual pastoral care and counseling. The dominant function (heroic extraverted feeling) needs to cede center stage for a while to allow introverted intuition to work its disconcerting magic. It is disconcerting because introversion may require facing loneliness. Comfort with their own non-rational introverted intuition provides ENFJ leaders with a well of deep perspectives that they can use to nurture others without feeling the drain and strain of always having to be agreeable and of always having to quash their own needs and point of view. In short, developing a strong and viable auxiliary function is the first and best antidote to burnout, and to compassion fatigue, for ENFJ leaders.

A grasp and relish for the dirty details of life, though, may be lacking from both the heroic dominant and nurturing auxiliary until the tertiary function comes onto the open stage of consciousness in the form of extraverted sensing.

3 Tertiary (Eternal Child): Extraverted Sensing

The tertiary function of ENFJ leaders is extraverted sensing. Extraverted sensing orients to and enjoys the external sensory world. For ENFJ leaders, this process is carried into consciousness by the archetype of the eternal child. Because of the bi-polar aspect of this archetype, where charm alternates with unreliability, the emergence and integration of extraverted sensing brings unexpected jolts to lives of the usually warm and dependable ENFJ leaders and those around them. Nonetheless, the bumpy ride is worth it, because with the integration of the third function into the conscious personality, leaders accomplish real diversity and discover a refreshing flexibility. The risk of suppression is far greater, with sporadic eruption of physical acting out that can spell disaster for a delicate spiritual community.

Other aspects of more conscious development of extraverted sensing are: (1) increased use of and reliance on the five senses, (2) taking in information just as it is, without evaluation, (3) absorbing details and registering differences between sensation, for example, knowing that the scent of a red "strawberry" candle is in fact different from the last time you smelt actual strawberries, (4) focus on the here and now and allowing one's body to adjust spontaneously to what is discovered and staying aware of what is happening in each moment, (5) merging with what absorbs the attention.

Extraverted sensing is usually in short supply in Christian communities and so only ENFJ leaders own commitment to personal and spiritual growth will encourage emergence of this valuable source of human pleasure and satisfaction. As the tertiary or third process to develop into consciousness for ENFJ leaders, extraverted sensing is managed by the archetype of the eternal child. Thus, extraverted sensing often manifests with a playful innocence in ENFJ leaders. This may be greeted with relief by those with well-developed extraverted sensing, but few extraverted sensing types darken the doors of organized religion, although there may be a few more ISFPs with extraverted sensing as their auxiliary function.

Starting in their twenties, ENFJ leaders may feel more comfortable in the *habitus* of their body. They may enjoy the temporary release from the responsibility of having to make accurate feeling judgments about their social situation, and with the development of extraverted sensing, simply delight in the sounds, sights, touch, smell, and taste of life: "Often they enjoy the tangible pleasures in life . . . . [a keener] appreciation of how things look, feel, smell and taste" (Berens & Nardi, 2004, p. 44). ENFJ leaders' increased relaxation and casualness may be disconcerting to the *introverted* sensing majority (the SJs) for whom extraverted sensing is their dominant shadow function carried by the archetype of the challenger. Their leaders' increased casualness, which comes with the development of extraverted sensing, rather than the decisiveness of extraverted judging, may make SJs nervous and feel that their warm dependable ENFJ leaders were somehow less reliable. While extraverted sensing is becoming stabilized, ENFJ leaders may suddenly stiffen up and revert to a more structured demeanor, perhaps feeling guilty for being so indulgent and not thinking of others enough. Thus, it is the turn of perceiving types to become confused by their ENFJ leaders. Awareness of type dynamics in the community may reduce this kind of conflict and confusion.

In summary, extraverted sensing in the tertiary position of the *eternal child* archetype equips the minister with an occasional playful innocence, which may, however, become easily fatigued and disappear much to the disappointment of few extraverted sensing congregants who welcomed seeing their minister's more easygoing side.

4 Fourth (Soul-Friend): Introverted Thinking

The fourth function of ENFJ leaders is introverted thinking. Introverted thinking is concerned with reaching truth by discerning underlying structures and principles through precise internally consistent application of logical analysis, epitomized by the questions "What's going on here?" or "How does this work?" Critique and criticism is accepted as an inevitable part of inquiry, but not so for ENFJ leaders at the beginning of this phase of development that seldom commences much before mid-life. At first, "Detached analysis strikes them as heartless" (Berens & Nardi, 2004, p. 45). Later through awareness of the variety of functions, each with its own "way of being human," ENFJ leaders may become able to stand back and analyze and classify problems. Gradually and with experience they may "see the value in having logical consistency" (Berens & Nardi, 2004, p. 45) at least when it comes to running a large organization which may be the consequence of successful religious community that their drive and inspiration has helped create. Becoming familiar with the function of introverted thinking will involve dealing with feelings of inferiority such as "feeling dumb" as they struggle to understand principles that are spelt out too quickly from the "management types" in their community.

There are few introverted thinking types in religious communities and so ENFJ leaders' "descent" into introverted thinking is usually triggered either by their own stress and fatigue, or lack of appreciation, manifested in distrust of their intentions, or in discounting their ability (Quenk, 2000), and it in turn shows in their sensitivity to the assessment by others of their intellectual competence (Quenk, 1993). Pressure to conform at the price of their cherished values is another trigger, as is conflict that cannot be discussed and resolved quickly into harmony. Thus, when the church is growing, conflicts are more readily resolvable, but the EFJ may become oppressed with inward-turning negative thoughts when there is no win-win solution for both sides in conflict. In this circumstance, ENFJ leaders' usual enthusiasm and concern with others gives way to withdrawal and pessimism, and introverted thinking manifests in a negative way as: (1) excessive criticism and global condemnation; (2) convoluted logic including rigid all or none categorizations, and making up stories that explain peoples' "bad" behavior; (3) compulsive search for truth, for example, hunting down the right expert or looking for the "truth" in books.

Integration of this logical function is worth the effort involved. A depth of flexibility and stability becomes possible for ENFJ leaders who develop a capacity to make judgments based not solely on harmony, with prevailing values and ongoing relationships, but also on clear distinctions through inner critical reflection deriving from introverted thinking. For "introverted thinking involves naming things in fresh ways, in relation less to outer definitions already agreed upon than to an archetypal sense of the things unconscious resonance" (Beebe, 2007a, p. 4). This capacity is likely to come as a surprise to colleagues and congregants, but is a significant development in the psycho-spiritual development of a spiritual community because few individuals in the Christian context have introverted thinking, either as a dominant or auxiliary function. Occurring as a development within a warm friendly extraverted feeling type and facilitated through the connective quality of the contra-gender energy within the individual, the terse critical reflection of introverted thinking may be less intimidating to the prevailing extraverted harmony at all cost that suffuses and sometimes suffocates Christian communities. Using the insights of shadow type theory in particular enables community members to take preventive measures and to see crises as a spur to inner and community development rather than a sign of a terminal condition.

SHADOW PERSONALITY

5 Dominant Shadow (Challenger): Introverted Feeling

For ENFJ leaders, the dominant shadow function to develop is introverted feeling. Introverted feeling is a function essential for complete psychological functioning. It enables us to use our emotions to identify what is important to us. Through introverted feeling we organize our values so that we can maintain our personal identity and structure our life around these deeply held values (Hartzler & Hartzler, 2005).

Introverted feeling for ENFJ leaders is positioned at their blind-spot in the center of the long shadow cast by their dominant extraverted feeling. Being the same function as the dominant function, but directed in the opposite attitude, introverted feeling bears the archetypal character of the challenger. Lying in the shadow of extraverted feeling, introverted feeling is often experienced as an adversary to the heroic dominant function, and frequently embarrassing it. Introverted feeling is likely to find expression in avoidant, passive aggressive ways. Until it becomes more fully integrated into a conscious orientation in mid-life, introverted feeling is only recognized by ENFJ leaders in their reactions to other people's intense moods that seem far too deep and frustratingly impervious to the "good cheer" that ENFJ leaders like to employ.

The antagonism between feeling in its introverted and extraverted forms is the most marked of all the four functions of thinking feeling, intuition, and sensing. The challenger archetype may be triggered when the function it carries, in this case introverted feeling, is required in a situation. Such triggering is likely when the extraverted feeling minister intersects with introverted feeling types who form a significant subgroup in liberal Protestant and Catholic churches. Unwitting confrontation between extraverted and introverted feeling may evoke intense negativity producing noxious countertransference reactions in the pastoral counseling situation or in contentious church committees. Sharp remarks will be remembered or may be repressed by extraverted feeling leaders causing resentment and brooding on the part of this usually vibrant personality, who then becomes a negative caricature of the introverted feeling type. Another conflictual scenario may occur between ministry leaders. Relational dynamics between extraverted feeling leaders and their introverted feeling assistants may become quite troublesome, and also when the power hierarchy is reversed. The embrace of introverted feeling by ENFJ leaders requires facing what they most abhor—antagonism.

If ENFJ leaders come to respect the introverted feeling person and that same aspect within themselves, they may discover a new resilience and become able to sweep aside the feelings of horror and anxiety when their beloved project meets disapproval. Moreover, they may discover the courage to be stubborn in essential matters, even though they cannot fully articulate the basis for their intransigence. This may dismay some members of the community, who have been accustomed to the tireless and upfront consultative style of ENFJ leaders. The introverted feeling group in the church, of course, is relieved and impressed that their ENFJ leaders can quietly stand ground, have the courage of their convictions, and risk unpopularity. Introverted feeling types may be impressed too at their ENFJ leaders' surer sense of what causes to champion, that may run contrary to prevailing convention, but which are worth standing up for despite strong opposition (Berens & Nardi, 2004).

6 Auxiliary Shadow (Critical Parent): Extraverted Intuition

For ENFJ leaders, the auxiliary shadow function is extraverted intuition. Extraverted intuition is the function that discerns patterns, connections, and relationships in the external world and uses this knowledge to generate possibilities of how things could be. Extraverted intuition, therefore, frequently is a catalyst for change in the external world and is also used to tune into what is "going on" in other people. As the auxiliary shadow function in ENFJ leaders, extraverted intuition is influenced by the archetype of the critical parent. It functions to immobilize what are experienced as threatening forces, nailing the heralds of such threat in their tracks. It is often brought into play in response to an influx of new and youthful energy that threatens to bring change that requires adaptation or accommodation.

Extraverted intuition for ENFJ leaders feels frequently like a bulldozer and evokes a reciprocal and resistant response. The radar antennae of extraverted intuition are used by ENFJ leaders at best to protect what they hold precious by blocking perceived threats, pulling rank if necessary. At worst, it stultifies new energy and developments in the congregation. ENFJ leaders may use their own extraverted intuition to disarm threatening forces in a more subtle way by demoralizing those who represent this force.

Before the integration of extraverted intuition, ENFJ leaders often miss the mark with their extraverted intuition, on some occasions, reading into a situation or exchange "inferences about others that are off base" or which, when shared, leave others unable to respond, and close down the communication (Berens & Nardi, 2004, p. 45). By the same token, ENFJ leaders may threaten others with the possibilities of untoward consequences, and when things go wrong may criticize themselves and others for not having thought through all the possible consequences.

ENFJ leaders may feel uncharacteristically threatened by extraverted intuitive dominants (ENFPs and ENTPs): feeling overwhelmed by ENFPs' energy, they push back with their own negative energy. Complicated dynamics producing chronic conflict may arise since ENFPs constitute an important group in many liberal Protestant and Catholic congregations: they are vociferous, articulate, and often inspire. To the many quieter and generally more conservative ISJs in the congregation, ENFJs and ENFPs probably appear quite similarly expressive and forceful, and the ISJs may be confused and intimidated by sporadic conflictual exchanges between these two extraverted type groups.

The influence of the archetype of the critical parent, on extraverted intuition, sometimes shows up in ENFJ leaders when certain inferences and interpretations are read into the words and actions of others that seem "off," and put others on the spot, leaving them unable to respond or to use profitably what ENFJ leaders offered through their extraverted intuition.

When extraverted intuition is better integrated into consciousness, or when ENFJ leaders are not under threat, they may use their extraverted intuition to "magically tune-in to what is really going on in a situation and catalyze change" (Berens & Nardi, 2004, p. 45). Indeed the struggle to integrate this contrasting extraverted energy is worthwhile not least because extraverted intuition is a powerful catalyst for change and, if harnessed, can excite others as well as bring "onside" the ENFP subgroup as a significant progressive group in Catholic and liberal Protestant congregations. Furthermore, extraverted intuition is used to tune into what is "going on" in other people, and added to ENFJs' natural expressive warmth can work miracles in establishing a welcoming and vibrant community.

7 Tertiary Shadow (Trickster): Introverted Sensing

For ENFJ leaders, the tertiary shadow function is introverted sensing. Introverted sensing is the function that "recalls how thing were in detail and what it felt like when they were that way" (Hartzler & Hartzler, 2005, p. 15). Introverted sensing amasses a detailed array of stored facts, which are passed through a subjective filter where present impressions are selected for resemblance to past impressions. Present impressions then trigger a vivid recall of similar past impressions which are relived with visceral accuracy. Introverted sensing "skillfully compares current situations with past situations and readily discerns any differences" (Hartzler & Hartzler, 2005, p. 15).

Since for ENFJ leaders introverted sensing is the tertiary shadow function, the deployment and experience of using introverted sensing is influenced by the energy deriving from the trickster archetype. It is the same function as the eternally childlike tertiary function, but in the shadow attitude. Thus, under the influence of the trickster archetype, the atmosphere around the deployment and receptive experience of introverted sensing is that of error, mistake, and deception. Introverted sensing may get ENFJ leaders into trouble, but also sometimes out of trouble.

ENFJ leaders' use of introverted sensing may be inaccurate. They may, however, *imagine* that they have a grasp of the facts of a situation or an accurate recollection of a past event in the community or personal exchange with someone. In fact they may often be mistaken regarding the details. If this remains a blind spot, the credibility of otherwise inspiring and well-organized ENFJ leaders may be compromised in the eyes of the large number of SJs in the congregation. This lack of a natural memory for detail may be compensated for by ENFJ leaders taking the time in their preparations of talks and sermons to include vivid and accurate details that will engage SJs and increase their trust and loyalty. ENFJ leaders may be willing to conduct this extra research if through their extraverted feeling they can see it not only as a way of pleasing people but also value the introverted time spent in research because it is part of their transcendent vision for the community that satisfies their introverted intuition as well.

As ENFJ leaders become more aware of the value and prevalence of introverted sensing, this function will be less likely to trip them up and less likely to land them in awkward situations. By the same token, they may discover that an accurate grasp of facts on a topic, event, or issue, whether past or present, can in fact get them out of double binds. In particular, ENFJ leaders may find that a command of the facts may reframe many situations in which they feel torn between their extraverted feeling that requires them to seek approval and the call of their introverted intuition that transcends (and disregards) social custom and even nicety. Humor is a characteristic of the trickster and ENFJ leaders may be willing to get the exact words of a joke right (especially the "punch" line) in order to share in the mirth with everybody in the room when everyone enjoys the relaxation that laughter brings.

8 Fourth Shadow (Demon/Angel): Extraverted Thinking

For ENFJ leaders, the fourth shadow function is extraverted thinking, and this seldom develops until after the mid-life passage. Extraverted thinking is an organizing function that relishes ordering external realities in a logically consistent way. Through the operations of extraverted thinking, problems are dealt with by first analyzing their causes, determining priorities, defining goals and then sequencing activities, and applying resources, both people and materials, in the service of these goals. Extraverted thinking naturally evaluates the present situations in terms of its proximity to these goals. For this reason, standards and rules are valued. Extraverted thinking, however, in ENFJ leaders occupies the same external world as their dominant function and, consequently, directly clashes with it. Accordingly, extraverted thinking is usually the last of the eight functions to develop.

Because extraverted thinking is the opposite function that operates in the same (extraverted) world as the dominant extraverted feeling, it is in the position that is most unconscious and troublesome. Because extraverted thinking can seldom be tolerated as part of self by ENFJ leaders, it is experienced as "beastly," and is most often projected onto others, reflected, for example, in the comment "That person behaved just like an animal, don't you think?". As Beebe (2007a, p. 6) aptly states: Aspects of the demonic personality form "the *realistic* basis of the 'unfair' judgments we sometimes receive from others." The tough, objective causal analysis of a situation, the brutally frank assessment that is natural to extraverted thinking seems antithetical to the ENFJ leaders' natural response to a situation which is to appreciate.

Consequently, for ENFJ leaders, the effect of extraverted thinking is radically to undermine the operations of their dominant extraverted feeling. Whereas extraverted feeling establishes external structures based on relational agreement, extraverted thinking does the same, but based on logic and consistency. Herein lies the problem. It is as if two architects with different architectural plans are assigned to supervise the building of the same dwelling, turning up on alternate days. The building must inevitably collapse. Certainly, the architects will fight when they both turn up at the building site on the same day. Since ESTJs may constitute up to 15 percent of males in a congregation (Ross, 1995), this least conscious part of the ENFJ leaders' personality may be triggered quite often. Both protagonists are likely to experience each other as so "over the top" as to be barely recognizable as human, making power struggles hard to avoid, and the right kind of mediator, informal or formal, should be made available, perhaps an introverted feeling type, if they can withstand the heat.

Furthermore, Beebe assures us that the "beast" of our demonic personality is easier to handle if we have been able to incorporate into consciousness the "beauty" of our fourth function, which for this type is introverted thinking, with its attendant soulful energy from the *anima* or *animus*. With this work in progress, it is easier to transform the demon into an angel that can redeem even the worst situation. If extraverted thinking can be brought into a degree of consciousness, the gains for ENFJ leaders are formidable. Not only will ENFJ leaders be their usual charming, warm well-organized selves, they will also be able to be efficient and systematic in sticking to their program goals, even when at times these goals are seen as irrelevant or undesirable to key players in the church community.

Chapter 14

The Supportive Contributor

ESFJ Leaders

ESFJ Frequency in the Population

	Male (%)	*Female (%)*
UK	6.0	18.5
USA	4.7	14.1

ESFJ PSYCHOLOGICAL TYPE PROFILE

Leading Functions

Dominant extraverted feeling with auxiliary introverted sensing

Conscious personality
1. Dominant (Hero): Extraverted Feeling
2. Auxiliary (Nurturing parent): Introverted Sensing
3. Tertiary (Eternal child): Extraverted Intuition
4. Fourth (Soul-friend): Introverted Thinking

Shadow personality
5. Dominant shadow (Challenger): Introverted Feeling
6. Auxiliary shadow (Critical parent): Extraverted Sensing
7. Tertiary shadow (Trickster): Introverted Intuition
8. Fourth shadow (Demon/Angel): Extraverted Thinking

CONSCIOUS PERSONALITY

1 Dominant (Hero): Extraverted Feeling

The dominant function of ESFJ leaders is extraverted feeling. Extraverted feeling is a function that naturally orients to harmonizing with the values of the external environment. At its core extraverted feeling functions to maintain relationships and social networks, seeking to co-ordinate people and material resources with a view to "harmoniously achieve group and individual goals" (Hartzler & Hartzler, 2005, p. 45).

When extraverted feeling is the first and so the dominant process to develop into consciousness, its operations have the archetypal aura of the hero. Thus, for ESFJ leaders, extraverted feeling is reliable and dependable and provides the foundation for ESFJ leaders' basic coping with the challenges posed by life, including religious ministry. In fact maintaining relationships is so much part of the "warp and weave" of their life they may be unaware of its operations. Extraverted feeling for ESFJ leaders is so permeating that it is invisible and, like water to a fish, mainly thrust into awareness only with threatened absence.

Religious community is very much an extraverted feeling affair with up to two-thirds of female congregants having extraverted feeling as their dominant or auxiliary process (Bramer & Ross, 2012). When extraverted feeling plays out the heroic role in individuals' personality, they become naturals for leadership in building community in a religious context. ESFJ leaders effortlessly connect to others either singly or in a group.

However, when conflict does arise, as surely it does in any human community, ESFJ leaders suffer dreadfully if the conflict cannot be readily resolved. For their part, ESFJ leaders provide many chances for the "difficult" party to make amends, merely wanting their own needs acknowledged, and a genuine apology is readily accepted. However, when this is not enough they may feel torn apart, and get vociferously personal and even vindictive, feeling and often expressing their indignation that, while they have given praise, recognition, and respect this has not been reciprocated.

With extraverted feeling in its heroic aspect as the dominant function, ESFJ leaders rely on their natural harmonizing capacity to connect with congregants and probably assume that this is how all good people really cope or should cope with the challenges of life, since it seems to work so well for them. Religion with the near universality of the golden rule—do to others as you would have them do to you—is attractive to extraverted feeling types as it celebrates and sacralizes their core heroic principle of harmonic connection.

Nevertheless, the dominant function is often invisible to that individual, and so extraverted feeling dominant leaders may feel that everyone is really like they are, but just being obtuse. Therefore, development and awareness of the introverted auxiliary function can provide a very useful perspective from which to reflect, gather facts, and slow things down sufficiently for conflicts not to escalate.

2 Auxiliary (Nurturing Parent): Introverted Sensing

The auxiliary function for ESFJ leaders is introverted sensing. Introverted sensing is a perceiving function that precisely registers specific details, and selectively records them, favoring those that relate to previously stored details. By the same token, clear memories are triggered by similar present impressions together with their associated visceral reactions. When introverted sensing is the second function developed into a conscious orientation, it is infused with energy from the archetype of the nurturing parent. The introverted sensing of ESFJ leaders enables them to focus on the details of the individuals whom they serve so that they give to them in ways that are relevant to their particular situation. Development of their introverted sensing enables ESFJ leaders to realize their extraverted wish for harmony by focusing on the specific needs of community members.

Development of introverted sensing further enables ESFJ leaders to find balance, for whereas extraverted feeling is an extraverted form of judgment, introverted sensing is an introverted form of perceiving. Introverted sensing frees ESFJ leaders from relying too heavily on their extraverted feeling, so that they can deal better with aspects of life that cannot be dealt with adequately by rational judgment. Through introverted sensing, ESFJ leaders become able to get in touch with their own condition and needs. This entitles them to say "No" on occasion, in spite of their wish never to let anyone down. Often ESFJ leaders carry resentment because others fail to see that they are overextended. The self-awareness of their own needs that introverted sensing brings reduces the resentment that builds as ESFJ leaders realize that other types do not make the same sacrifices for other people that they do.

Introverted sensing is the means by which ESFJ leaders ground their connective principle, through which they precisely register the detailed circumstances of their lives and respond warmly in a timely and practical way to the needs of others. Congregants come to rely on and to trust their practical help and supportive advice.

Berens and Nardi (2004) have summarized how ESFJs use introverted sensing to nourish their community. By means of introverted sensing, ESFJ leaders are able to ground the expectations of the community in a realistic assessment of the present situation and by an accurate recall of what was done before in a comparable situation or setting. They calm heated discussions at meetings by providing precise information in support of decisions made in the past or present. They readily recognize familiar patterns that might count as precedents, and so clarify what further information may be needed. Their trust of and satisfaction in common experiences and the energy that they derive from tradition inspire trust and win the confidence of the many SJs that congregate in Christian groups.

ESFJ leaders use their introverted sensing to review the past so that they plan for the future. While this is a sound strategy in many situations, if ESFJ leaders rely on introverted sensing and extraverted feeling alone, many non-SJs may become weary or bored with sticking to the "tried and true." However, because of the prevalence of feeling in most religious communities, the disaffection may not be articulated through open criticism. Instead gossip and discontent may undermine and de-energize the ministry of ESFJ leaders. Many intuitive types may simply stay away or cease active involvement. Development, therefore, of the third and fourth functions may help mitigate reliance on feeling and sensing in isolation, and instead bring real diversity to ESFJ leaders' ways of operating, increasing their psychological flexibility.

3 Tertiary (Eternal Child): Extraverted Intuition

The tertiary function of ESFJ leaders is extraverted intuition. Extraverted intuition is the function that is aware of patterns, connections, and interrelationships in the external world. For ESFJ leaders, extraverted intuition is the third function to develop into consciousness. As the tertiary function is carried into consciousness by the archetype of the eternal child, much of its activity has the flavor of innocence mixed with vulnerability and the rapid fatigue that we associate with young children.

A number of features that characterize extraverted intuition may help ESFJ leaders build community in a religious context. The development of extraverted intuition will enable ESFJ leaders to appeal to a wider range of community members, especially to ENFPs and INFPs who have extraverted intuition as their dominant and auxiliary function, respectively, and who may form a significant subgroup among women in Catholic and liberal Protestant congregations. They, along with other types with intuitive preferences, enjoy their leaders' enhanced capacity to see possibilities in people and situations (Grant, Thompson, & Clarke, 1983) which were previously missed or passed over or simply dismissed as impractical or too risky. Moreover, a greater openness to more imaginative learning and teaching methods, such as brainstorming, may be welcomed by these types. All intuitive types in the community may feel relieved to find that their hitherto overly "realistic" minister is more responsive to creative ideas and matters close to their heart, such as spirituality and symbolic innovations in liturgy and ritual.

ESFJ leaders in this phase of their development may enjoy spending more time exploring new ideas and even hidden meanings. They may feel energized by conversations in which they are able to connect "the details of their wealth of data and experience" to new possibilities and projects (Berens & Nardi, 2004, p. 33). Their sense of humor and the range of things that make them laugh may increase, enabling them to relax for a while from the responsibility of being so caring all the time.

Regarding their own spirituality, whereas before ESFJ leaders may have been fearful or suspicious of new interpretation of religious life and theological innovation, in later life they may gain confidence and learn to take comfort in being able to use their intuition to look beyond the immediate appearance of things to a hidden world full of magic and potential.

Extraverted intuition for ESFJ leaders, however, is exercised under the *aegis* of the eternal child, and may, like a child, quickly fatigue. Openness to intuition may not be sustained under stress, especially following protest from the SJs who form the largest type-alike group in most Christian churches. Indeed deviance from complete reliability, that community members have come to expect from their ESFJ leaders, may shock many community members. At the same time, ENFPs and INFPs may feel betrayed when ESFJ leaders seem to retreat from their bold proposals before salvos of criticism from more conservative elements within the community, many of whom may be SJs who wondered what had happened to their practical down-to-earth minister.

In summary, since the tertiary function of ESFJ leaders is the opposite of the "good" parental auxiliary function, extraverted intuition takes the form of the eternal child—charming but disappointing when tired. Accordingly the life stage, provisional adulthood (Sheehy, 1995), in which leaders usually incorporate their volatile third function is one of ups and downs, but the foundation for real diversity within the leaders' psyche makes the bumpy journey worthwhile not only for the leader but for the tolerance and openness of the whole community.

4 Fourth (Soul-Friend): Introverted Thinking

The fourth function of ESFJ leaders is introverted thinking. Introverted thinking organizes both information and ideas into logical categories (Hartzler & Hartzler, 2005). Introverted thinking is concerned with reaching truth by discerning underlying structures and principles through precise internally consistent application of logical analysis, epitomized by the questions, "What's going on here?" or "How does this work?" Critique and criticism is accepted by introverted thinking as an inevitable part of inquiry, but not so for ESFJ leaders, at least not at the beginning of this phase of development that seldom commences much before mid-life. However, when introverted thinking does find expression, it does so under the influence of the soul-friend archetype.

Accordingly, introverted thinking's emergence into consciousness at mid-life contributes to a sense of mission, intensity, and capacity for deep connection. At first though, "Detached analysis . . . strikes them as heartless" (Berens & Nardi, 2004, p. 33). Later through awareness of the variety of functions and personality types, each with their own way of being human, ESFJ leaders may become able to stand back and analyze and classify problems. Gradually, and with experience, they may appreciate the value of logical consistency at least when it comes to running a large organization, which a successful religious community may become given ESFJ leaders' warmth, industry, and organization (Berens & Nardi, 2004). The process will involve dealing with feelings of inferiority such as "feeling dumb" as they struggle to understand principles as spelt out quickly from the "management types" in their community. However, patient respect from other more analytical types, especially from a member of the opposite sex, may help ESFJ leaders stay with the challenging process.

ESFJ leaders' "descent" into introverted thinking is usually triggered either by their own stress and fatigue, or lack of appreciation, manifested in distrust of their intentions, or in discounting their ability (Quenk, 2000), and it in turn shows in their sensitivity to the assessment by others of their intellectual competence (Quenk, 1993). Pressure to conform at the expense of their cherished values is another trigger, as is conflict that cannot be discussed and resolved quickly into harmony. In such circumstances, the habitual enthusiasm of the ESFJ leader along with their concern with others falls into pessimism and withdrawal.

Nevertheless, ESFJ leaders have many potential resources. If the triggering conflict is in the community, then ESFJ leaders will usually benefit from being able to talk about the issue with someone who is less involved. They can obtain relief through their auxiliary function of sensing and with time alone "put things in perspective" through a thorough review of the facts or through their tertiary of extraverted intuition take time out to enjoy some fun projects or new ventures.

A depth of flexibility and stability becomes possible for ESFJ leaders who develop a capacity to make judgments based not solely on harmony with prevailing values and ongoing relationships but also on clear distinctions through inner critical reflection deriving from introverted thinking. For "introverted thinking involves naming things in fresh ways, in relation less to outer definitions already agreed upon than to an archetypal sense of the things' unconscious resonance" (Beebe, 2007a, p. 4).

The capacity for detached analytic judgment is likely to come as a surprise to colleagues and congregants but is significant in the psycho-spiritual development of a spiritual community because few individuals in the Christian context have introverted thinking either as a dominant or auxiliary function.

Occurring as a development within a warm friendly extraverted feeling type and facilitated through the connective quality of the contra-gender energy within the individual, the terse critical reflection of introverted thinking may be less intimidating to the prevailing extraverted harmony at all cost that suffuses and sometimes suffocates Christian communities. Using the insights of shadow type theory in particular enables community members to take preventive measures and see crises as a spur to inner and community development rather than a sign of a terminal condition.

SHADOW PERSONALITY

5 Dominant Shadow (Challenger): Introverted Feeling

For ESFJ leaders, the dominant shadow function is introverted feeling. Introverted feeling is a function essential for complete psychological functioning. It enables us to use our emotions to identify what is important to us. Through introverted feeling we organize our values so that we can maintain our personal identity and structure our life around these deeply held values (Hartzler & Hartzler, 2005).

Introverted feeling is positioned for ESFJ leaders at their blind spot in the center of the long shadow cast by their dominant extraverted feeling. Being the same function as the dominant function but directed in the opposite attitude, introverted feeling bears the archetypal character of the challenger. Lying in the shadow of extraverted feeling, introverted feeling is often experienced as an adversary to the heroic dominant function, and as frequently embarrassing it. Introverted feeling is likely to find expression in avoidant, passive aggressive ways. Until it becomes more fully integrated into a conscious orientation in mid-life, introverted feeling is only recognized by ESFJ leaders in their reactions to other people's intense moods that seem far too deep and frustratingly impervious to the "good cheer" that ESFJ leaders like to employ. ESFJ leaders often misrecognize their own introverted feeling in the projections they place on others whom they regard as avoidant—"Why don't you just tell me what you are feeling?" "How do you expect me to know, if you won't tell me?"

The antagonism between feeling in its introverted and extraverted forms is the most marked of all the four functions. Such antagonism is legendary and makes for high drama, which Beebe (1988) documents from *King Lear* the tragedy by Shakespeare epitomized in the portentous utterance of Cordelia: "I cannot heave my heart into my mouth." Cordelia is the quintessential introverted feeling type who cannot declare her heart-felt feelings even at the risk of great cost to herself and her potential "subjects" who might prosper under her rule. Hers is the introverted feeling type's dilemma—being moved and governed by what is unspeakable, and yet being coerced to give voice to this depth by close and even discerning extraverts who know that their lives are most certainly affected by their beloved's priorities. To the *extraverted* feeling type in particular, this dilemma makes no sense at all, for them feeling is the lifeblood of relationships that are sustained by open communication.

The challenger archetype may be triggered when the function it carries, in this case introverted feeling, is required in a situation. Such triggering is likely when the extraverted feeling minister intersects with introverted feeling types who form a significant subgroup in liberal Protestant and Catholic churches. Unwitting confrontation between extraverted and introverted feeling may evoke intense negativity producing noxious counter-transference reactions in the pastoral counseling situation or in contentious church committees. Sharp remarks will be remembered or may be repressed by the extraverted feeling minister causing resentment and brooding on the part of this usually vibrant personality, who then becomes a negative caricature of the introverted feeling type.

The ESFJ leaders' embrace of introverted feeling requires facing what they most abhor—antagonism. If ESFJ leaders come to respect the introverted feeling person and that same aspect within themselves, they may discover a new resilience and become able to sweep aside the feelings of horror and anxiety when their beloved project meets disapproval. Moreover, they may discover the courage to be stubborn in essential matters, even though they cannot fully articulate the basis for their intransigence. This may dismay some members of the community, who have been accustomed to the tireless and upfront consultative style of ESFJ leaders. The introverted feeling group in the church of course is relieved and impressed that their ESFJ leaders can quietly stand ground and have the courage of their convictions.

6 Auxiliary Shadow (Critical Parent): Extraverted Sensing

For ESFJ leaders, the auxiliary shadow function is extraverted sensing. There is a "scout" in all of us. This is the term that Hartzler and Hartzler (2005) use to describe extraverted sensing, the process that "focusses on the tangible reality around us" (p. 9), directly accessing in a largely unfiltered way the sensory information that pours in through our five senses and that guides us through the external physical world. Extraverted sensing centers us in the present moment and orients to the strongest source of stimulation, which usually yields pleasure.

For ESFJ leaders, this "scout" function of extraverted sensing lies in the shadow of the ESFJ leaders' auxiliary function of introverted sensing, which is the means by which ESFJ leaders usually nurture. However, their extraverted sensing, being the same function but in the shadow attitude, is managed by the archetype of the critical parent. Accordingly, extraverted sensing performs the role of the forbidding parent and is often mobilized in order to block what is experienced as a threat to survival.

Berens and Nardi (2004, p. 33) describe how ESFJ leaders are prone to use their extraverted sensing: "They can go on about 'facts' blocking others' proposed actions." Beebe (2006b) cautions that ESFJ leaders will especially bring extraverted sensing into play in this defensive way when they are threatened with disconnection from their magical soul-friend function of introverted thinking. The facts that root ESFJ leaders in the present immediate situation are used to blockade anything that may separate ESFJ leaders from the sense of mission provided by their introverted thinking, with its abstract principles that float free from the requirement of approval imposed by their dominant extraverted feeling.

By the same token, when confronted with extraverted sensing themselves, ESFJ leaders may feel immobilized. They may feel stuck and may not know what to do in a physical emergency. They may feel at a loss in terms of knowing how to respond to extraverted sensing personality types (ESFPs and ESTPs) with their affinity for and immediate orientation to strong sensory experience in the moment. This may not retard ESFJ leaders in making progress with their religious community as very few extraverted sensing types are drawn to religious groups. However, if extraverted sensing remains undeveloped, ESFJ leaders, like most religious leaders, remain out of contact with the extraverted sensing world that prevails in society at large.

This function position is evoked in order to deal with perceived threats to the ESFJ leaders' own existence or to values or institutions like the church with which they identify. They may resort to pulling rank, laying great emphasis on "What is" and "The tried and true" with a view to discouraging innovators and disabling their innovations. When extraverted sensing appears it will be seen by congregants, colleagues, and superiors as "out of character" which it is. Others may occasionally be grateful for the self-preserving results it produced depending on whether they evaluated the situation as an opportunity or a threat. Nevertheless, the resort to power on the part of the minister will likely be remembered by those on either side of the issue.

The benefits of making extraverted sensing a more conscious orientation are significant. By bringing extraverted sensing into their own awareness and making room for it in their lives and in their theology, ESFJ leaders will honor the function that is in shortest supply in Christian communities and provide the basis for a connection to those in society at large who feel that the church is remote from them and their vital concerns of everyday living.

7 Tertiary Shadow (Trickster): Introverted Intuition

For ESFJ leaders, the tertiary shadow function is introverted intuition. Introverted intuition is the function that facilitates awareness of images and abstract ideas that span past and future transcending both time and space. These insights arise spontaneously from the unconscious and transform and re-frame situations.

For ESFJ leaders, introverted intuition, as the tertiary shadow function falls in the shadow attitude of the up-and-down, bipolar tertiary function which for ESFJ leaders is extraverted intuition. The function in the tertiary shadow position in the psyche is managed by the archetype of the trickster: introverted intuition in ESFJ leaders functions to get them into and out of "tricky" situations, where they feel trapped. A trap or double bind for ESFJ leaders occurs when the realities of the situation dictate a course of action which will displease one section of the religious community. Frequently, ESFJ leaders do not know what to do in this situation. They suffer. Their extraverted feeling dominant dictates that they do the most popular thing or at least something that will displease as few people as possible, while their grasp of the facts provided by their auxiliary introverted sensing dictates another course of action. The trick of introverted intuition is that it does not care necessarily to please anyone nor is it limited by the tangible facts. Introverted intuition allows ensnared ESFJ leaders to see the situation in a stunningly novel way that ignores both conventional morality and factual reality.

At first their introverted intuition is likely to get ESFJ leaders into trouble. Berens and Nardi (2004) illustrate how the process of integration of introverted intuition is slow and troublesome. ESFJ leaders' "vision" will play tricks on them. They envision how a situation will play out and ignore signs that what they are doing is not working out. They imagine an action "has to please" and feel crestfallen when it fails to do so.

Often ESFJ leaders are limited in foreseeing more remote implications or causative factors that nonetheless impact their ministry and work. They may misread the *Zeitgeist*, or the spirit of the times, and make unnecessarily personal attributions of success and failure. However, with openness to and awareness of this troublesome and mistake-prone side of themselves, they can become more forgiving, less perfectionistic, less guilty about their own shortcomings, and less burdened by hostile feelings they bear toward others who do not like them enough. Mistakes and failures are stripped of their oppressively moral overtone. Eventually, "they may laugh at their own fears of the future" (Berens & Nardi, 2004, p. 33).

In summary introverted intuition, as the shadow of the tertiary function, operates as a *trickster* to extricate ESFJ leaders from double binds—traps where they and others may be "taken." Though unlikely to be well integrated for conscious use except in the unusually individuated religious leader, on occasion the capacity of introverted intuition to contact and directly cognize images from the unconscious may be triggered by the requirements of the situation. Congregants, superiors, and colleagues may be surprised at the ESFJ leaders' imaginative response, because it was unbound by the conventions that usually constrain ESFJ leaders. However, introverted intuition in its trickster aspect enabled those involved to escape the consequences of what seemed to be an "impossible situation."

8 Fourth Shadow (Demon/Angel): Extraverted Thinking

For ESFJ leaders, the fourth shadow function is extraverted thinking, and this seldom develops until after the mid-life passage. Extraverted thinking is an organizing function that relishes ordering external realities in a logically consistent way. Through the operations of extraverted thinking, problems are dealt with by analyzing their causes, determining priorities, defining goals, and then sequencing activities and applying resources, both people and materials, in the service of these goals. Extraverted thinking naturally evaluates the present situations in terms of its proximity to these goals. For this reason, standards and rules are valued. Extraverted thinking, however, in ESFJ leaders occupies the same (extraverted) world as their dominant function and, therefore, directly clashes with it.

Because extraverted thinking is the opposite function that operates in the same attitude as the dominant extraverted feeling, extraverted thinking is in the position that is most unconscious and troublesome, under the archetype of the demon/angel. Because extraverted thinking can seldom be tolerated as part of self by ESFJ leaders, it is experienced as "beastly" and is most often projected onto others, reflected, for example, in the comment "That person behaved just like an animal, don't you think?". Beebe (2007a, p. 6) aptly states that aspects of the demon/angel personality form "the *realistic* basis of the 'unfair' judgments we sometimes receive from others. It would be wiser for someone receiving such a judgment to say to him or herself, 'that person has just seen my shadow.'" The tough, objective causal analysis of a situation and the brutally frank assessment that are *natural* to extraverted thinking are deeply undermining of the ESFJ leaders' *natural* response to a situation which is to appreciate.

Consequently for ESFJ leaders, the effect of extraverted thinking is to invalidate radically the operations of their dominant extraverted feeling. Whereas extraverted feeling establishes external structures based on relational agreement, extraverted thinking does the same but based on logic and consistency. Herein lies the problem. It is as if two architects with different architectural plans are assigned to supervise building the same dwelling, turning up on alternate days. The building must inevitably collapse. Certainly, the architects will fight when they both turn up at the building site on the same day. Since ESTJs may constitute up to 15 percent of males in a congregation (Ross, 1995), quite often this least conscious part of ESFJ leaders' personality may be triggered. Both protagonists are likely to experience each other as so "over the top" as to be barely recognizable as human, making power struggles hard to avoid, and the right kind of mediator, informal or formal, should be made available, perhaps an introverted feeling type, if they can withstand the heat.

Furthermore, Beebe assures us that the "beast" of our demonic personality is easier to handle if we have been able to incorporate into consciousness the "beauty" of our fourth function, which for this type is introverted thinking, with its attendant soulful energy from the *anima* or *animus*. With this work in progress, it is easier to transform the demon into an angel that can redeem even the worst situation. If extraverted thinking can be brought into a degree of consciousness, the gains for ESFJ leaders are formidable. Not only will ESFJ leaders be their usual charming, warm well-organized selves, they will also be able to be efficient and systematic in sticking to their program goals, even when at times the goals are seen as irrelevant or undesirable to key players in the church community.

Chapter 15

The Decisive Strategist

ENTJ Leaders

ENTJ Frequency in the Population

	Male (%)	*Female (%)*
UK	4.3	1.7
USA	3.5	2.1

ENTJ PSYCHOLOGICAL TYPE PROFILE

Leading Functions

Dominant extraverted thinking with auxiliary introverted intuition

Conscious personality

1. Dominant (Hero): Extraverted Thinking
2. Auxiliary (Nurturing parent): Introverted Intuition
3. Tertiary (Eternal child): Extraverted Sensing
4. Fourth (Soul-friend): Introverted Feeling

Shadow personality

5. Dominant shadow (Challenger): Introverted Thinking
6. Auxiliary shadow (Critical parent): Extraverted Intuition
7. Tertiary shadow (Trickster): Introverted Sensing
8. Fourth shadow (Demon/Angel): Extraverted Feeling

CONSCIOUS PERSONALITY

1 Dominant (Hero): Extraverted thinking

The dominant function of ENTJ leaders is extraverted thinking. ENTJ leaders cope with their life by coming to rely on the capability of their extraverted thinking to analyze situations objectively and then to organize resources toward a goal. Extraverted thinking is so familiar to this type that it becomes invisible to those who use it reflexively and so often. ENTJ leaders automatically assume that knowledge and expertise, together with an objective viewpoint, will solve all important problems, including those encountered by their religious community.

Those who share the goals of ENTJ leaders will feel empowered by the sense of purpose, direction, and confidence that ENTJ leaders tend to exude. Those, however, who do not share their goals, may feel they get less time, attention, and respect. This may become a significant barrier to community building in a religious context, since the majority of those drawn to religious groups have a feeling rather than a thinking preference, especially among female members who form the majority in most religious groups (Francis, Robbins, & Craig, 2011). Such members with a feeling preference may feel hurt and offended when ENTJ leaders put achieving a goal, however laudable, above maintaining harmonious relationships. This may be particularly noticeable at meetings when ENTJ leaders gravitate toward a formal, and some might say, officious style. Furthermore, following the meeting ENTJ leaders may compound the problem because they tend not to spare the time, or even see the need, to mend fences through brief "pleasant" one-on-one encounters or through follow-up telephone calls or emails. Such relational diligence will not spontaneously occur to ENTJ leaders because they always put the cause before their own personal feelings and assume others will do likewise. Difficulties may compound since feeling types may be less likely to identify with the ENTJ leaders' all important goals that naturally occur to thinking types. Such chafing may go undetected for a long time since ENTJ leaders seldom go out of their way to consult, for they assume that others are like themselves and would readily speak up if they did not like a course of action or procedure.

When ENTJ leaders become self-aware and realize that extraverted thinking is their heroic function, they can both embrace it as their basic way of coping with life's challenges, and continue to resort to it in crises, while recognizing that it is in the nature of heroes to see themselves as the most competent and most important. Blindness to this one-sided view is more likely in the case of heroic extraverted thinking because the pervading contemporary Western technocratic culture values problem solving and achievement above all else.

Wise ENTJ leaders, therefore, are aware of their bias and do well to learn to listen to the feeling majority that is found in most religious groups. ENTJ leaders are enabled to cast their reliable heroic, but sometimes unyielding, extraverted thinking in a wider context, by their next most consciously available function—introverted intuition that is influenced by the archetype of the nurturing parent.

2 Auxiliary (Nurturing Parent): Introverted Intuition

The auxiliary function of ENTJ leaders is introverted intuition. Introverted intuition ranges backwards and forwards across time and resonates to deep themes or archetypes that span human culture and civilizations. By drawing on this resource, ENTJ leaders generate visions that sustain them, and in turn they are able to provide a rich variety of alternative perspectives that they can offer to other members of their community.

Introverted intuition is a form of perceiving that is vast and deep and balances the pragmatic pre-occupation of dominant extraverted thinking. The rich perspectives that introverted intuition derives "from the background processes of consciousness" (Jung, 1971, p. 399) provide psycho-spiritual nourishment to leaders in ministry that they in turn can pass on to others. Through contact with ENTJ leaders, who have access to introverted intuition with its capacity to transcend time and space and to envision what is possible, community members obtain a sense of their own personal potential within that rich community inspired by their leader.

Introverted intuition, being a form of inward perceiving, provides balance to ENTJ leaders' externally oriented, sometimes intimidating, logical, and structuring dominant function. Introverted intuition in the nurturing parent auxiliary position both softens and deepens ENTJ leaders and provides them with an inner compass. Introverted intuition brings an inner vision of what may be possible. Introverted intuition always has a long range perspective and so frees ENTJ leaders from the tyranny of always planning and strategizing in the perpetual search for efficiency.

To access this introverted function, however, ENTJ leaders need time alone, away from continually having to make strategic decisions that optimize the programmatic fulfillment of complex and numerous goals. Without the development of their nurturing introverted intuition, ENTJ leaders barely keep exhaustion at bay. They need permission from themselves to take the time to step back and see just what they have already accomplished, before further draining themselves by adopting an additional set of objectives.

ENTJ leaders need to share their vision with several others, not just those they deem competent. Without others' support they may feel too obligated to take the time to renew themselves. However, if they are given and take the time and space, "New insights, particularly about people and working with people occur to them" in those valuable solitary moments. "Alone they generate the new ideas that support or modify their decisions and plans" (Brownsword, 1988, p. 28). ENTJ leaders may not, however, receive much encouragement to do this from the SJ types who often form the majority in the congregation. Yet if tangible benefits are realized, they can be documented and eventually accepted by the SJ community.

With time out for reflection, ENTJ leaders discover that they "just know" things, such as "how events may turn out" or "what may be going on with someone." This really is helpful both when participating in planning new projects in the community and engaging in individual pastoral care and counseling. The dominant function (heroic extraverted thinking) needs to cede center stage for a while for introverted intuition to work its disconcerting nurturing magic.

Nevertheless, a grasp of, and relish for, the bothersome and dirty details of life may be lacking for ENTJ leaders with only the perspectives provided by the heroic dominant and the nurturing auxiliary functions. That is until the tertiary function is allowed to come onto the open stage of consciousness in the form of extraverted sensing.

3 Tertiary (Eternal Child): Extraverted Sensing

The tertiary function of ENTJ leaders is extraverted sensing. Extraverted sensing, carried by the eternal child archetype, lightens up the intensely focused and complex ENTJ leader. Extraverted sensing takes delight in the five senses: (1) enjoying the external sensory world, (2) taking in information just as it is, without evaluation, (3) simply merging with whatever absorbs the attention, (4) registering differences between sensations, (5) providing future-oriented ENTJ leaders with a means to focus on the here and now. Starting in their twenties, ENTJ leaders may feel more comfortable in the *habitus* of their body. They may enjoy the temporary release from the dictates of their plans, and with the development of extraverted perceiving through the senses, simply delight in the sounds, sights, touch, smell, and taste of life.

Under the archetype of the eternal child, extraverted sensing often manifests with a playful innocence in ENTJ leaders. Under the youthful tutelage of this out-turned delighting function, leaders enjoy taking charge at social events that have no business agenda, bringing energy and gusto to them. This may be greeted with relief by those precious few members with well-developed extraverted sensing, since few extraverted sensing types darken the doors of organized religion.

There are indeed some cross-currents in this passage toward greater spontaneity and wholeness, in part because of the bi-polar, double-edged character of the archetype of the eternal child that carries this function in ENTJ leaders. The development of the tertiary function of any type tends to follow a fluctuating course: the use of the tertiary function is charming, even seductive, but tires easily and is not so reliable. As with a tired child, innocent charm can yield to over-sensitivity and a disconcerting fragility. The emergence and integration of extraverted sensing brings unexpected jolts to the lives of usually robust and reliable ENTJ leaders and also affects those around them. Berens and Nardi (2004, p. 37) report that ENTJs "can become distracted by irrelevant happenings" that are going on around them and allow these to disrupt their usually ordered conversation. They may also waste "time and resources on indulging their senses."

ENTJ leaders' increased relaxation and easygoingness may be particularly disconcerting to the introverted sensing majority (the SJs), for whom extraverted sensing is their dominant shadow function and shows up under the challenger archetype. Their ENTJ leaders' increased casualness, which comes with the development of extraverted sensing, rather than the decisiveness of extraverted judging, may make SJs nervous and feel that their complicated but dependable ENTJ leaders are now less reliable for some unknown reason.

While extraverted sensing is not yet stabilized, ENTJ leaders may suddenly stiffen up and revert to a more structured demeanor and become narrowly focused on goals once again, afflicted by guilt for being so indulgent. Such back paddling may confuse the minority perceiving types in the group, who had thought that their ENTJ leaders' shift to a more spontaneous way of being was genuine and permanent.

Awareness of type dynamics in the community may reduce this kind of conflict and confusion. Nonetheless, the bumpy ride of integrating the third function into consciousness is worth it. ENTJ leaders become more rounded and discover a refreshing flexibility. In comparison, complete suppression of extraverted sensing—and the ensuing compartmentalization—carries greater danger with sporadic eruption of physical acting out that can spell disaster for the delicate dynamics of a spiritual community.

In summary, extraverted sensing in the tertiary position of the eternal child archetype equips the minister with an occasional playful innocence, which may, however, become easily fatigued and disappear much to the disappointment of those few extraverted sensing and perceiving congregants who welcomed seeing their minister's more easygoing side.

4 Fourth (Soul-Friend): Introverted Feeling

For ENTJ leaders, the fourth function to develop is introverted feeling. Introverted feeling is an inwardly directed decision-making function of inner valuing that assesses everything on the basis of non-negotiable personal values with a view to optimizing inner harmony. The integration of introverted feeling into conscious awareness seldom starts before the mid-thirties, and it does so under the archetypal influence of the soul-friend. The archetype of the soul-friend is recognized by its capacity to forge profound and deep connection, providing a sense of mission, on the one hand, and a bridge to the unconscious, on the other.

In the case of ENTJ leaders, the soul-friend archetype adds a mysterious air to the already heavily subjective tone of introverted feeling and contrasts with the articulate and focused persona of ENTJ leaders. Undergirding the programs and objectives around which ENTJ leaders energetically rally themselves and others, there lies a strong, yet inchoate, value system, an intensely held but dimly perceived network of beliefs. These in turn empower unconscious motivations that are kept in the shadows by ENTJ leaders. Von Franz and Hillman state: "They will consist in a childlike belief in peace, charity and justice." Such "high ideals remain in the realm of the inferior feeling function." "The subjective element remains in the background" but fuels "a mystical feeling attachment to their ideal" (von Franz & Hillman, 1971, p. 38). Intense introverted feeling then attaches to certain ideals or to people producing very strong loyalty in ENTJ leaders, one that is unswayed by reason.

While as yet unintegrated into consciousness, this introverted feeling domain is associated with fears of incompetence and melancholy. Only slowly and over a long period of time, as ENTJ leaders become comfortable with their own company for sustained periods of time, does the inner world of introverted feeling become less threatening and more accessible to consciousness. At first, ENTJ leaders may feel overwhelmed when others express strong feelings, since they are "unable to deal with [such an emotional] situation in their typical direct and logical way" (Quenk, 2000, p. 12). ENTJ leaders cannot help but feel and display their discomfort. At the same time, they may feel overwhelmed by their own feelings, especially when one of their cherished values is disregarded (Quenk, 2000), giving rise to particular feelings of being ignored or unappreciated. They become hyper-sensitive to their negative inner feelings, misrepresenting mere comments as criticism. Unacceptable feelings of incompetence may also arise within, and they become uncharacteristically defensive. Emotional outbursts may result, followed by strong feelings of remorse when they learn of the hurt others have felt at their harsh insensitive remarks.

Their un-nuanced display of emotion may surprise some and forfeit the respect of others in the community. These eruptions of inferior introverted feeling are usually brief and infrequent, but for someone in a leadership role in a community, they can cause resentment in others that may play out later at a critical time for the success of ENTJ leaders within that community.

Those with a feeling preference form a majority in most religious groups, and so ENTJ leaders' lack of facility with this engaged and subjective way of coming to decisions, based on appreciation rather than analysis and critique, may be a handicap in building trusting relationships with many group members. The integration of introverted feeling is likely to take time, but yields rich dividends. Trusted friends or family members are invaluable for this process, as is anyone with whom competent ENTJ leaders do not feel obliged to "have it altogether." At critical times, ENTJ leaders need to be listened to and the depth of their feeling held and accepted. ENTJ leaders are then able to return quickly to their functioning capable selves. As they allow feeling values as a basis for their enthusiasms, ENTJ leaders will feel less pressure to buttress everything by evidence and reason.

SHADOW PERSONALITY

5 Dominant Shadow (Challenger): Introverted Thinking

For ENTJ leaders, the dominant shadow function to develop is introverted thinking. Introverted thinking enables us to "sort and re-sort ideas" and information into systems of categories according to the changing requirements of a situation (Hartzler & Hartzler, 2005, p. 39). Introverted thinking is concerned with the precision and economy of thinking and with the process rather than the outcome of decision-making. Integration of introverted thinking into conscious awareness seldom starts for ENTJ leaders before mid-life and does so under the archetypal influence of the challenger.

Because introverted thinking comprises a part of the shadow personality, before such time as introverted thinking is "owned" in consciousness, it is "disowned" by ENTJ leaders, projected onto other people and experienced more frequently in the problematic and oppositional behavior of others, particularly those who have introverted thinking as a dominant function. Thus, in the earlier stages of integration, introverted thinking finds expression in ENTJ leaders tinged with challenge that often has a passive aggressive flavor.

Introverted thinking is put in shadow by the habitual exercise of dominant extraverted thinking. There exists a competitive tension between thinking in its introverted and extraverted aspect. For example, ENTJ leaders: (1) may feel anxious faced with having to explain their ideas to others. They may (2) make nihilistic assessments of situations and people as lacking worth. They may (3) contradict others, while (4) stubbornly adhering to the models and principles they think are relevant, seemingly (5) "categorizing everything simplistically and robotically" according to *their* principles (Berens & Nardi, 2004, p. 37). Their oppositional use of introverted thinking can also manifest in (6) an intolerance for inefficiencies and requests to repeat something for another's benefit. They may also (7) singularly concentrate upon results, the purview of extraverted thinking, and resist any focus on the *process* of a decision that relates more closely to how introverted thinking operates.

ENTJ leaders are often "put off" by the operations of introverted thinking types, who are ignored or criticized for being too abstract, impractical, and "into their heads." ENTJ leaders may feel that introverted thinking is finicky and precious, and so preoccupied with the rationale for "how we get there" that no fuel is left for "delivery." Nevertheless, the playful creative aspect to introverted thinking may sometimes win out. The most important challenge for ENTJ leaders is to accept this playful aspect of introverted thinking, to be open to it in others, and to recognize it as a capacity within themselves that others may welcome as softening the sharp shadow of their sometimes oppressive extraverted thinking. Such awareness of shadow cast by their extraverted thinking will enable ENTJ leaders to accept defensive responses by introverted thinkers to their firm proposals, and so prevent a negative interactive spiral. Introverted thinking should have a place in a religious setting. Giving free rein to abstract thought, questioning for the sake of questioning, can engender excitement and delight into an otherwise overly business-like church meeting.

The struggle to integrate introverted thinking is likely to be an internal personal process for ENTJ leaders in view of the scarcity of introverted thinking in most religious communities. Nevertheless, the struggle by ENTJ leaders to see the value of and harness the resources of this function is an important one that can be part of their contribution to the community. Playing the devil's advocate can be informative and fun. Much may be learned in the process of the debate, even if the outcome is a foregone conclusion. Development of introverted thinking within the religious community will also help outreach to the wider political and intellectual communities where religious groups are often passed over because of the lack of intellectual rigor displayed by those representing religious perspectives.

6 Auxiliary Shadow (Critical Parent): Extraverted Intuition

For ENTJ leaders, the auxiliary shadow function to develop is extraverted intuition. Extraverted intuition is the function that discerns patterns, connections, and relationships in the external world and uses this knowledge to generate possibilities of how things might be. For ENTJ leaders, extraverted intuition is influenced by the archetype of the critical parent. The critical parent blocks threats to survival. Its role is to immobilize what are experienced as threatening forces. In ENTJ leaders, extraverted intuition exists in the shadow of introverted intuition which as the third function operates under the influence of the archetype of the nurturing parent. In contrast, extraverted intuition is often brought into play in order to block the influx of new and youthful energy that threatens to bring change requiring adaptation.

Before the integration of extraverted intuition, ENTJ leaders may seem, on the one hand, oblivious to "unspoken potentials", while on the other, themselves "getting off track with other inferences and interconnections" (Berens & Nardi, 2004, p. 37). ENTJ leaders may threaten others with the possibilities of untoward consequences, and when things go wrong may criticize self and others for not having thought through all the possible consequences.

Because of the unconscious association of this function with the critical parent archetype, extraverted intuitive dominants (ENFPs and ENTPs) may be experienced by ENTJ leaders as threatening. In many liberal Protestant and Catholic congregations, ENFPs constitute an important group: they are vociferous, articulate, and often inspire, while ENTPs are few and far between in most religious groups. To the many quieter and generally more conservative ISJs in the congregation, ENTJs, ENTPs, and ENFPs probably appear quite similarly "heady" and "headstrong." All three extraverted types with intuition will appear as expressive and forceful to the ISJs, who are therefore marginalized and mystified by the sporadic conflictual exchanges that flare up between these type groups.

ENTJ leaders may feel bulldozed by extraverted intuition energy and push back with their own negative energy. Accordingly, ENTJ leaders' own extraverted intuition may itself be used to disarm threatening forces—by demoralizing those who represent this force, by cutting them off from their sense of mission. The radar antennae of extraverted intuition are used by ENTJ leaders at best to protect what they hold precious by blocking perceived threats, pulling rank if necessary. At worst, it stultifies new energy and developments.

The critical parent aspect of extraverted intuition sometimes shows up in ENTJ leaders in the form of reading negative inferences and interpretations into the words and actions of others. They may then put others on the spot, leaving these members unable to respond or utilize what ENTJ leaders have to offer through their extraverted intuition. At such time as extraverted intuition is better integrated into consciousness, or when they are not under threat, ENTJ leaders may use their extraverted intuition to "magically tune in to what is really going on in a situation and catalyze change" (Berens & Nardi, 2004, p. 37).

The struggle to integrate this contrasting extraverted energy is worthwhile because extraverted intuition is a powerful catalyst for change and, if harnessed, can excite others, as well as bring "onside" the ENFP subgroup that is a significant progressive group in Catholic (Ross, 1995) and liberal Protestant (Ross, 1993) congregations. Furthermore, extraverted intuition is used in order to tune into what is "going on" in other people, something that is essential for ENTJ leaders' long-term survival.

7 Tertiary Shadow (Trickster): Introverted Sensing

For ENTJ leaders, the tertiary shadow function is introverted sensing. Introverted sensing focuses on details and reviews present experiences in the light of finely calibrated, but selectively recalled arrays of details of past experiences. For ENTJ leaders, introverted sensing operates under the influence of the archetype of the trickster. The function managed by the trickster is the same function as is managed by the eternal child archetype (the tertiary function), but in the opposite attitude. Thus, in the case of ENTJ leaders, introverted sensing operates in the shadow of innocent child-like extraverted sensing. Under the influence of the trickster archetype, introverted sensing may get ENTJ leaders into—and out of—a lot of trouble.

ENTJ leaders may recognize the play of introverted sensing in their life and world when plans go wrong. For ENTJ leaders, the devil, or at least the trickster, is indeed in the details. Introverted sensing for ENTJ leaders is prone to mistakes, to unintended consequences, and to deception of self and of others. Often "omni-competent" ENTJ leaders seem curiously oblivious to the fact that details are a problem for them. Not only can they not be bothered with minutiae, but worse still, they can't be bothered either to anticipate or to compensate for this limitation.

Trickster introverted sensing may also have unintended positive consequences, especially when ENTJ leaders find themselves in a tricky situation that they did not anticipate and from which they cannot escape. This may feel like a double bind (damned if you do, dammed if you don't) situation, and yet—unable to think their way out of the situation—they may manage to "massage" the facts to good effect. For example, they may use "selective recall" in order to maintain the illusion of control in an encounter defined by power rather than knowledge and logic. In another kind of tricky scenario, such as being confronted with detailed evidence that they have made a poor decision, they may deceive themselves into believing that it was someone else's fault.

Introverted sensing naturally not only recalls in seemingly exact detail "how things were" but also involuntarily reexperiences what it felt like when they were that way. Introverted sensing amasses a detailed array of stored facts, which are passed through a subjective filter where present impressions are selected for resemblance to past impressions. Present impressions then trigger a vivid recall of similar past impressions which are relived in visceral detail.

ENTJ leaders' grasp on detail is often loose, their introverted sensing, often inaccurate. They may in fact *imagine* that they have a grasp of the facts of a situation or an accurate recollection of a past event in the community or of a personal exchange with someone. In fact, they may often be mistaken regarding the details. If this remains a blind spot, the credibility of otherwise competent and well-organized ENTJ leaders may be compromised in the eyes of the large number of SJs in the congregation.

The lack of a natural memory for detail may be compensated for by ENTJ leaders by taking the time in their preparations of talks and sermons to include vivid and accurate details that will engage SJs and increase their trust and loyalty. At first, ENTJ leaders may be willing to conduct such painstaking research only if they can remember that the engagement of sensing types will make it more likely that their programs will be supported and successful. The introverted time spent in research is more likely to be accepted when they can see it as part of their transcendent vision for the community, something that also satisfies and inspires their introverted intuition.

8 Fourth Shadow (Demon/Angel): Extraverted Feeling

For ENTJ leaders, the fourth shadow function is extraverted feeling and this seldom occurs until after the mid-life passage. Extraverted feeling contributes to consciousness by cognizing and gathering values through interacting with the external world and evaluates ideas and events in accordance with these prevailing values, especially those that foster harmony and positive and caring relationships (Hartzler, McAlpine, & Haas, 2005). It does so for ENTJ leaders under the influence of the archetype of the demon/angel. The essential effect of the demonic archetype is felt through a dynamic of undermining: extraverted feeling is the opposite judging function to that of extraverted thinking (the dominant function for ENTJ leaders), and it *directly* clashes with the operations of extraverted thinking because it operates in the same (extraverted) world. Extraverted feeling, therefore, tends to have a disruptive or undermining impact on ENTJ leaders.

The expression of extraverted feeling by ENTJ leaders often possesses a destructive quality, especially in the first half of life when the process of integrating its operations into a conscious orientation has barely begun. When ENTJ leaders are "beastly," negative extraverted feeling is often involved. According to Beebe (2007a, p. 5), it is "usually the locus of our most unyielding and unconscious flaws of character." While extraverted feeling remains undeveloped, ENTJ leaders remain unconcerned with how others feel about them. Because they do not acknowledge their need for appreciation from others they tend not to express feeling appreciation toward others. Under stress, ENTJ leaders' reliance on extraverted thinking may result in deprecating comments to others.

When others express strong feeling, ENTJ leaders may attempt to control or suppress the expression of strong emotion in order to avoid the arousal of powerful, hard to control, feelings inside themselves. Those who observe such attempts at control by those in a leadership position may feel alienated, because they are seen as wielding power by virtue of their role in the community. ENTJ leaders may accept that they have earned a reputation for being harsh, but suffer at the thought they are seen as unfair, and this can encourage them to give more attention to their feelings. Meanwhile, their mortification at such a discovery may further be uncomfortable for others to witness. Furthermore, in the face of florid positive extraverted feeling, they may succumb to flattery, as their own undifferentiated extraverted feeling is unable to discriminate sincere emotional expressions from manipulative ones (McAlpine, Schumate, Evers, & Hughey, 2009).

The lack of nuance with extraverted feeling may be a challenge for ENTJ leaders in a religious community because extraverted feeling is the second most frequent function in religious groups. Many church members have extraverted feeling as their strongest way of coping (dominant) or caring (auxiliary). Thus, ENTJ leaders' least conscious function will be called upon on a regular basis, leading to them experiencing church ministry as being "heavy-going," feeling themselves as misunderstood and others as "difficult." It takes ENTJ leaders time and patience to calibrate their external emotional responses and to remain relaxed in the face of strongly expressed emotion by other people. However, with increased conscious awareness, extraverted feeling is associated more frequently with angelic moments of unexpected and surprising transformation. They can be capable of great altruism for a higher cause that is inspiring and emboldening to others. On a more personal level, they can also "make personal connections and adjust to other people in ways that transform their daily lives" (Berens & Nardi, 2004, p. 37).

Chapter 16

The Efficient Organizer

ESTJ Leaders

ESTJ Frequency in the Population

	Male (%)	*Female (%)*
UK	11.6	9.5
USA	12.9	7.3

ESTJ PSYCHOLOGICAL TYPE PROFILE

Leading Functions

Dominant extraverted thinking with auxiliary introverted sensing

Conscious personality

1. Dominant (Hero): Extraverted Thinking
2. Auxiliary (Nurturing parent): Introverted Sensing
3. Tertiary (Eternal child): Extraverted Intuition
4. Fourth (Soul-friend): Introverted Feeling

Shadow personality

5. Dominant shadow (Challenger): Introverted Thinking
6. Auxiliary shadow (Critical parent): Extraverted Sensing
7. Tertiary shadow (Trickster): Introverted Intuition
8. Fourth shadow (Demon/Angel): Extraverted Feeling

CONSCIOUS PERSONALITY

1 Dominant (Hero): Extraverted Thinking

The dominant function of ESTJ leaders is extraverted thinking. ESTJ leaders cope with their life by coming to rely on the capability of their extraverted thinking to analyze situations objectively and then to organize resources toward a goal. ESTJ leaders use extraverted thinking reflexively and so often that its operations become invisible to them. ESTJ leaders automatically assume that knowledge, expertise and an objective viewpoint will solve all important problems, including those encountered by their religious community.

Those who share the goals of ESTJ leaders will feel empowered by the sense of purpose, direction, and confidence that ESTJ leaders tend to exude. Those, however, who do not share their goals, may feel they get less time, attention, and respect. Such a goal-oriented focus may become a significant barrier to community building in a religious context, since the majority of those drawn to religious groups have a feeling rather than a thinking preference. This is especially the case for female members who form the majority in most religious groups. Members with a feeling preference may feel hurt and offended when ESTJ leaders put achieving a goal, however laudable, above maintaining harmonious relationships. Lack of emotional responsiveness may be particularly noticeable at meetings when ESTJ leaders gravitate toward a formal, and some would say, officious style. Furthermore, following the meeting ESTJ leaders may compound their problems because they tend not to spare the time, or even see the need, to mend fences with brief "pleasant" one-on-one encounters, follow-up telephone calls, or emails. Such relational diligence will not spontaneously occur to ESTJ leaders because they always put the goal ahead of their own personal feelings and assume others do likewise. Difficulties may compound since the feeling types may be less likely to identify with the sort of goals that are all important to ESTJ leaders. The resulting emotional chafing may go undetected for a long time, since ESTJ leaders seldom go out of their way to consult, for they mistakenly assume that others are like themselves and would readily speak up if they did not like a course of action or procedure.

When ESTJ leaders become more self-aware, they may realize that their extraverted thinking function is only one of eight functions. They further realize that they can continue to embrace extraverted thinking as their heroic function, their basic way of coping with life's challenges, and continue to resort to it in crises, while at the same time recognizing that it is in the nature of heroes to see themselves as the most competent and most important. Blindness to this one-sided view is more likely in the case of heroic extraverted thinking because of the pervading contemporary culture in Western societies that values problem solving and goal achievement above all else. Wise ESTJ leaders, therefore, are aware of their bias and do well to learn to listen to the feeling majority that is found in most religious groups. ESTJ leaders are enabled to cast their reliable heroic, but sometimes unyielding, extraverted thinking in a more informed context, by their next most consciously available function, introverted sensing, that is influenced by the archetype of the nurturing parent.

2 Auxiliary (Nurturing Parent): Introverted Sensing

The auxiliary function of ESTJ leaders is introverted sensing. Development of introverted sensing frees ESTJ leaders from relying too heavily on their extraverted thinking, so that they can perceive "the messy, irrational side of life" that cannot be addressed by rational judgment (Thomson, 1998, p. 273). Introverted sensing makes for a more balanced rounded personality.

Introverted sensing precisely registers specific details, and selectively records them, favoring those that relate to previously stored details. ESTJ leaders often carry strong visual memories of incidents forming the history of the community and so make it a shared history including those who were not present at the actual time and place. They may be aware of emotions associated with such clear visualizations, but can be skilled about when to share these. Introverted sensing makes ESTJ leaders practical and dependable (Grant, Thompson, & Clarke, 1983, p. 225) giving the religious community a secure environment for its members. The introverted sensing of ESTJ leaders enables them to focus on the details of the individuals whom they serve so that they give to them in ways that are relevant to their particular situation.

Introverted sensing is the means by which ESTJ leaders ground their organizing principles, through precisely registering the detailed circumstances of their own and others' lives and responding in a practical way to the needs of others and the present situation. Congregants come to rely on and to trust their practical help and supportive advice. By means of introverted sensing, ESTJ leaders are able to ground the expectations of the community in a realistic assessment of the present situation and in an accurate recall of what was done before in a comparable situation or setting. They calm heated discussions at meetings by providing precise information in support of decisions made in the past or present. They readily recognize familiar patterns that might count as precedents, and so clarify what further information may be needed.

Berens and Nardi (2004, p. 28) state that ESTJ leaders "trust common experiences and feel energized by participating in traditions or customary activities, knowing that these common activities will solidify the group." This trust of and satisfaction in common experiences and the energy that they derive from tradition inspires trust and wins the confidence of the many SJs that congregate in Christian groups. Their willingness and ability to share stories that illustrate how others have handled situations is of particular solace to the many in the congregation with an SJ temperament.

ESTJ leaders use their introverted sensing to review the past so that they plan for the future. While this is a sound strategy in many situations, if ESTJ leaders rely on introverted sensing and extraverted thinking alone, many non-SJs may become weary or bored with sticking to the "tried and true." However, because of the prevalence of feeling in most religious communities, the disaffection may not be articulated in the form of open criticism. Instead gossip and discontent may undermine and de-energize the ministry of ESTJ leaders. Intuitives may simply stay away or cease active involvement. Development, therefore, of the third and fourth functions may help to mitigate reliance on thinking and sensing in isolation, and instead bring real diversity to ESTJ leaders' ways of operating, increasing their psychological flexibility.

3 Tertiary (Eternal Child): Extraverted Intuition

The tertiary function of ESTJ leaders is extraverted intuition. Extraverted intuition orients to possibilities in the environment by being aware of patterns, connections, and inter-relationships in the external world. For ESTJ leaders, extraverted intuition is under the influence of the archetype of the eternal child. The eternal-child archetype is recognized by the ways in which extraverted sensing shows up for ESTJ leaders in innocent, playful, creative ways, while at the same time carrying a sense of wounding. Accordingly, much extraverted intuition in ESTJ leaders is volatile, having an innocent, exuberant flavor one moment, vulnerability the next, and then succumbing suddenly to the rapid fatigue that we associate with young children.

ESTJ leaders in this phase of their development may enjoy spending more time exploring new ideas and even hidden meanings. They may feel energized by conversations in which they are able to connect "the details of their wealth of data and experience" to new possibilities and projects (Berens & Nardi, 2004, p. 29). Their sense of humor and the range of things that make them laugh may increase, enabling them to relax for a while from the responsibility of having to keep everything and everyone "on track" all the time. On occasion ESTJ leaders can be comfortable with others using extraverted intuition as in brainstorming as long as a decision is made within a reasonable amount of time. Of course what counts as a "reasonable amount of time" may be different for judging and for perceiving types.

The development of extraverted intuition enables ESTJ leaders to appeal to a wider range of community members, especially to ENFPs and INFPs who have extraverted intuition as their dominant and auxiliary function respectively and who may form a significant subgroup among women in Catholic and liberal Protestant congregations. As extraverted intuition becomes a more conscious orientation, all intuitive types in the community may feel relieved to find that their previously overly "realistic" minister is now more responsive to creative ideas and matters close to their heart, such as spirituality and symbolic innovations in liturgy and ritual.

The process of integrating extraverted intuition is seldom smooth for ESTJ leaders, especially when done within a religious community. ESTJ leaders may, like a child, quickly fatigue when using extraverted intuition. Under stress, openness to intuition may not be sustained, for example, following protest from the SJs who form the largest type-alike group in most Christian churches. Indeed, deviance from complete reliability that the SJ members have come to expect from their fellow SJ leader may shock many of them. For when ESTJ leaders start to develop extraverted intuition, SJ churchgoers may wonder what had happened to their practical down-to-earth minister. However, it is important that ESTJ leaders persevere with their nascent extraverted intuition, because this is an important facet of spirituality and one with which the numerous SJs in religious communities are more likely to engage when this is pioneered by such trusted SJ leaders as ESTJs.

4 Fourth (Soul-Friend): Introverted Feeling

The fourth function of ESTJ leaders is introverted feeling. Introverted feeling is an inwardly directed decision-making function of inner valuing that assesses everything on the basis of non-negotiable personal values with a view to optimizing inner harmony (Haas & Hunziker, 2006). The integration of introverted feeling into conscious awareness seldom starts before the mid-thirties, and it does so under the archetypal influence of the soul-friend. The archetype of the soul-friend is recognized by its capacity to forge profound and deep connection, providing a sense of mission, on the one hand, and a bridge to the unconscious, on the other.

In the case of ESTJ leaders, the soul-friend archetype adds a mysterious air to the already heavily subjective tone of introverted feeling and contrasts with ESTJ leaders' sharp and focused persona. Undergirding the programs and objectives around which ESTJ leaders energetically rally themselves and others, there lies a strong yet inchoate value system, an intensely held but dimly perceived network of beliefs. Intense introverted feeling then attaches to certain ideals or to people producing very strong loyalty in ESTJ leaders, one that is unswayed by reason.

While yet unintegrated into consciousness, introverted feeling is associated with fears of incompetence and melancholy. Only slowly, as ESTJ leaders become comfortable with their own company for sustained periods of time, does the inner world of introverted feeling become less threatening to them, and more accessible to consciousness. At first, ESTJ leaders may feel overwhelmed when others express strong feelings. They also tend to feel overwhelmed by their own feelings. For example, when one of their cherished values is disregarded, feelings of being ignored or unappreciated rush unpredictably to the surface. They become hyper-sensitive to their negative inner feelings that are projected outward onto other people whose mere neutral comments are misinterpreted as criticism (Quenk, 1993). Unacceptable feelings of incompetence may arise inside them, and they become uncharacteristically defensive. Emotional outbursts may result, followed by strong feelings of remorse when they learn that others have felt them to be harsh or insensitive.

These eruptions of inferior introverted feeling are infrequent and usually brief, but such un-nuanced displays of emotion may shock some members of the community and forfeit the respect of others. Moreover, for someone in a leadership role in a community, they may be the occasion for resentment on the part of other members that only plays out later, perhaps at a critical time for the success of ESTJ leaders' programs in that community.

Those with a feeling preference form a majority in most religious groups, and so religious leaders' lack of facility with this subjectively engaged way of coming to decisions, based on appreciation rather than analysis and critique, may be a handicap in building trusting relationships with many of these members. As introverted feeling emerges into consciousness, the values that drive the passions and programs of ESTJ leaders will become more differentiated and they will be able to calibrate more finely the priority and vigor with which their passions and programs are pursued.

The integration of introverted feeling is likely to take time, but will yield rich dividends. Trusted friends or family members are invaluable for this process, as is anyone with whom tough ESTJ leaders do not feel obliged to "have it altogether." At critical times, ESTJ leaders need to be listened to and the depth of their feeling held and accepted by another. ESTJ leaders are then able to return quickly to their functioning capable selves. As they allow feeling values as a basis for their enthusiasms, they will feel less pressure to buttress *everything* by evidence and reason.

SHADOW PERSONALITY

5 Dominant Shadow (Challenger): Introverted Thinking

For ESTJ leaders, the dominant shadow function is introverted thinking. Introverted thinking enables us to "sort and re-sort ideas" and information into systems of categories according to the changing requirements of a situation (Hartzler & Hartzler, 2005, p. 39). Integration of introverted thinking into conscious awareness seldom starts for ESTJ leaders before mid-life and does so under the archetypal influence of the challenger. Because introverted thinking for ESTJ leaders comprises part of the shadow personality, before it is "owned" in consciousness, this function is "disowned" and projected onto other people experienced as "bad" characters who display oppositional attitudes and generally problematic behavior. Those who have introverted thinking as their dominant function are particularly liable to fall victim to such projections.

Introverted thinking is put in shadow by the habitual exercise by ESTJ leaders of their dominant extraverted thinking. There exists a competitive tension between thinking in its introverted and extraverted aspect. For example, ESTJ leaders (1) may feel anxious faced with having to explain their ideas to others in their community. They may (2) make nihilistic assessments of situations and people as lacking worth. They may (3) contradict others, while (4) stubbornly adhering to models and principles *they* think are relevant, seemingly (5) "categorizing everything simplistically and robotically" according to *their* principles (Berens & Nardi, 2004, p. 29). Their oppositional use of introverted thinking can also manifest in (6) an intolerance for inefficiencies and having to repeat something for another's benefit. They may also (7) concentrate solely upon results, the purview of extraverted thinking, and resist any focus on the *process* of a decision that is the purview of introverted thinking.

ESTJ leaders are often "put off" by the operations of introverted thinking types, whom they either ignore or criticize for being too abstract, impractical, and "into their heads." ESTJ leaders may feel that introverted thinking is finicky and precious, and so preoccupied with the rationale for "how we should get there" that they leave no fuel for "delivery." There is, however, a playful creative aspect to introverted thinking. The most important challenge for ESTJ leaders is to accept this playful aspect of introverted thinking, to be open to it in others and to recognize it as a capacity within themselves that others may welcome as lightening the sharp shadow of their sometimes oppressive goal-oriented style.

Awareness of the shadow cast by their extraverted thinking will enable ESTJ leaders to accept the sometimes critical response of introverted thinking to their own firm propositions and proposals, and so prevent a defensive spiral. This will become easier for ESTJ leaders as they relax and enjoy the mental activity of analyzing, categorizing, and evaluating according to abstract principles without a set agenda that requires pre-ordained productivity. ESTJ leaders may eventually embrace and relish stimulating energy that arises from the sheer originality of introverted thinking.

The struggle to integrate introverted thinking is likely to be an internal personal process for ESTJ leaders in view of the scarcity of introverted thinking in most religious communities. Nevertheless, ESTJ leaders' struggle to see the value of and harness the resources of this function is an important one that can be part of the leader's contribution to the community. Playing the devil's advocate can be informative and fun. Much is learned in the unfolding of the debate, even when the outcome is a foregone conclusion. Development of introverted thinking within the religious community will also ferment outreach into the wider political and intellectual communities where religious groups are often passed over because of the lack of intellectual rigor when presenting their religious perspectives.

6 Auxiliary Shadow (Critical Parent): Extraverted Sensing

For ESTJ leaders, the sixth function to develop is extraverted sensing. Extraverted sensing "focuses on the tangible reality around us" directly accessing in a largely unfiltered way the sensory information that pours in through our five senses and which guides us through the external physical world. Extraverted sensing centers us in the present moment and orients to the strongest source of stimulation, because it usually yields the most pleasure. Extraverted sensing lies in the shadow of ESTJ leaders' auxiliary process of introverted sensing, the means by which ESTJ leaders usually extend themselves to care for others under the archetypal influence of the nurturing parent. By contrast, their extraverted sensing, being the same function but in the shadow attitude, is managed by the archetype of the critical parent. Accordingly, extraverted sensing is often mobilized in order to block what is experienced as a threat to survival.

Berens and Nardi (2004) describe how ESTJ leaders are prone to use their extraverted sensing: "They can go on about 'facts' blocking others' proposed actions" (p. 29). The facts that root ESTJ leaders in the present immediate situation are used to blockade anything that may separate ESTJ leaders from the sense of mission provided by their introverted feeling, their soul function. When others respond with extraverted sensing, ESTJ leaders may feel distrustful.

By the same token, when confronted with extraverted sensing themselves, ESTJ leaders may feel immobilized. They may feel stuck and may not know what to do in a physical emergency. They may feel at a loss in terms of knowing how to respond to extraverted sensing types (ESFPs and ESTPs) with their affinity for and immediate orientation to strong sensory experience in the moment. This may not retard ESTJ leaders in making progress with their religious community as very few extraverted sensing types are drawn to religious groups. However, if extraverted sensing remains undeveloped, ESTJ leaders (like most religious leaders) remain out of contact with the extraverted sensing world that prevails as a strong current in society at large.

Extraverted sensing is invoked in order to deal with perceived threats to ESTJ leaders' own existence or to values or institutions with which they identify. ESTJ leaders use extraverted sensing to pull rank, laying great emphasis on "what is," and "the tried and true," with a view to disable or discourage innovators and their "newfangled ideas." The sheer irrationality of their obstructiveness will appear as "out of character" (which it is as part of their shadow personality rather than their conscious personality). Usually ESTJ leaders will couch their objections with an appeal to facts and inductive reasoning from these facts. On other occasions, church members may be grateful for the self-preserving results it produced depending on whether they too evaluated the situation as a threat. Nevertheless, the resort to power on the part of the minister will likely be remembered by those on either sides of the issue, and hopefully by ESTJ leaders themselves to sobering effect. However, this is unlikely in the absence of wise counsel or sophisticated psycho-spiritual direction. At other times, extraverted sensing may manifest in ESTJ leaders getting caught up in the immediate moment or indulging in impulsive behavior.

The benefits of making extraverted sensing a more conscious orientation are significant. By bringing extraverted sensing into their own awareness and making room for it in their lives and in their theology and presentations, ESTJ leaders will honor the function that is in shortest supply in Christian communities and provide the basis for a connection to those in society at large who feel that the church is remote from them and from concerns of everyday living.

7 Tertiary Shadow (Trickster): Introverted Intuition

For ESTJ leaders, the tertiary shadow function is introverted intuition. Introverted intuition facilitates awareness of images and abstract ideas that span past and future, transcending both time and space. These insights arise spontaneously for they are unconscious and transform and re-frame situations. For ESTJ leaders, introverted intuition lies in the shadow attitude of the tertiary function, extraverted intuition. As such it finds expression through the archetype of the trickster whose activity and effect is recognized by deception, mistakes, unintended results, abrupt reversal of fortunes, and humor. Trickster energy can be effective in escaping double binds and other seemingly "impossible" situations.

While introverted intuition has yet to come into consciousness, ESTJ leaders may not be able to reflect in an insightful way on the situation that they or their community experience, especially if it is an unusual one, precipitated by new cultural forces and developments. Under stress, in particular, they "foresee disaster or nothing at all" (Berens & Nardi, 2004, p. 29). When others use their introverted intuition, ESTJ leaders may feel themselves put at a disadvantage. However, as introverted intuition permeates into a more conscious orientation, they may struggle to explain from where a sudden thought came. ESTJ leaders may sometimes make a spiritual connection that makes them feel uncomfortable.

Introverted intuition in ESTJ leaders serves to get them into and out of "tricky" situations, where they feel trapped. A trap or double bind for ESTJ leaders occurs when the realities of the situation dictate a course of action that is not consistent with their chosen goal and objectives. Frequently ESTJ leaders do not know what to do in this situation. Their dominant extraverted thinking dictates that firmness and consistency require staying the course, while their grasp of the facts provided by their auxiliary introverted sensing dictates another course of action. The trick of introverted intuition is that it does not care about consistency and is oblivious or indifferent to the constraining facts of the situation. Introverted intuition allows ensnared ESTJ leaders to see the situation in a stunningly novel way that reconfigures the original objectives, enabling the facts to be reinterpreted or to be legitimately disregarded as now irrelevant.

At first, introverted intuition is likely to get ESTJ leaders into trouble. ESTJ leaders' "vision" will play tricks on them. They envision how a situation will play out and ignore signs that what they are doing is not working. Often ESTJ leaders are limited in foreseeing more remote implications or somewhat remote causative factors that, nonetheless, impact their ministry and work. However, with openness to and awareness of this troublesome and mistake-prone side of themselves, they can become more forgiving, less driven, rigid, and perfectionistic. Delays and changes of course can be grasped, comprehended in a wider vision, held in a wider context. Eventually, according to Berens and Nardi (2004, p. 29), "they may laugh at their own fears about the future," as well as the inaccurate perception of or blindness to subtle but pervading contexts. They may increasingly "delight in wise foresight" and come to appreciate the role and value of the symbolic in human life and religious community (Berens & Nardi, 2004, p. 29).

8 Fourth Shadow (Demon/Angel): Extraverted Feeling

For ESTJ leaders, the fourth shadow function is extraverted feeling. Extraverted feeling contributes to consciousness by cognizing and gathering values through interacting with the external world. It evaluates ideas and events in accordance with these prevailing values, especially those that foster harmony and positive and caring relationships (Hartzler, McAlpine, & Haas, 2005). Extraverted feeling usually assigns positive value to ideas and events that accord with these values, while negatively evaluating those that do not.

For ESTJ leaders, extraverted feeling is carried by the archetype of the demon/angel. The effect of the demonic archetype is to undermine.

Extraverted feeling is the opposite judging function to that of ESTJ leaders' dominant extraverted thinking, and it *directly* clashes with the operations of extraverted thinking because it operates in the same (extraverted) world. Extraverted feeling, therefore, tends to have a disruptive impact on ESTJ leaders. Accordingly, the expression of extraverted feeling by ESTJ leaders often possesses an undermining destructive flavor, especially in the first half of life when the process of integrating its operations into a conscious orientation has barely begun.

When ESTJ leaders are "beastly" negative extraverted feeling is often involved. While extraverted feeling remains undeveloped, ESTJ leaders appear to be unconcerned about how others feel about them. Because they do not acknowledge their own need for appreciation from others they may fail to express appreciation to others. Under stress, ESTJ leaders' reliance on extraverted thinking may result in deprecating comments to others.

When others express strong feeling, ESTJ leaders may attempt to control or suppress this expression of strong emotion in order to avoid the arousal of powerful, hard-to-control feelings inside themselves. Those who observe such attempts at control may feel alienated, especially when noted in those regarded as wielding power by virtue of their role as leaders in the community. ESTJ leaders may earn a reputation for being harsh. Their mortification at such a discovery may further be uncomfortable for others to witness. By the same token, in the face of florid positive extraverted feeling, they may succumb to flattery.

The lack of nuance with extraverted feeling may be a challenge for ESTJ leaders in a religious community, because extraverted feeling is the second most frequent function in religious groups. Thus, ESTJ leaders will frequently be dealing with church members who have this as their strongest way of coping (dominant) or caring (auxiliary). By the same token, ESTJ leaders' least conscious process will be called upon on a regular basis. This may account for ESTJ leaders experiencing church ministry as being "heavy-going" with themselves often feeling misunderstood and others being "difficult."

ESTJ leaders tend to be sturdy believers in and outspoken champions of institutional solidarity and committed to its survival. They may be relied upon to defend it boldly at times of crisis and may be prepared to be ruthless toward those who seem disloyal and thereby threaten its cohesion, welfare, and survival. With increased conscious awareness extraverted feeling is associated more frequently with angelic moments of unexpected and surprising transformation. They can be capable of great altruism for a higher cause that is inspiring and emboldening to others. On a more personal level, they can also make better personal connections to other people.

Chapter 17

The Imaginative Motivator

ENFP Leaders

ENFP Frequency in the Population

	Male (%)	*Female (%)*
UK	5.1	7.5
USA	6.0	6.6

ENFP PSYCHOLOGICAL TYPE PROFILE

Leading Functions

Dominant extraverted intuition with auxiliary introverted feeling

Conscious personality
1. Dominant (Hero): Extraverted Intuition
2. Auxiliary (Nurturing parent): Introverted Feeling
3. Tertiary (Eternal child): Extraverted Thinking
4. Fourth (Soul-friend): Introverted Sensing

Shadow personality
5. Dominant shadow (Challenger): Introverted Intuition
6. Auxiliary shadow (Critical parent): Extraverted Feeling
7. Tertiary shadow (Trickster): Introverted Thinking
8. Fourth shadow (Demon/Angel): Extraverted Sensing

CONSCIOUS PERSONALITY

1 Dominant (Hero): Extraverted Intuition

The dominant function of ENFP leaders is extraverted intuition. Extraverted intuition instantly sees "patterns, connections and inter-relationships in the external world" (Hartzler & Hartzler, 2005, p. 21), and, grasping "the sensory data as a pattern of changing relationships" (Thomson, 1998, p. 197), uses this awareness to envision new possibilities. Extraverted intuition "strives to apprehend the widest range of possibilities in the objective situation" (Sharpe, 1987, p. 60) and "with an attitude of expectancy" (Jung, 1971, p. 366) senses "what is going on behind the scenes, under the surface" (Sharpe, 1987, p. 59).

Under the guidance of the heroic archetype, extraverted intuition may equip ENFPs to make ideal leaders for building community in a religious context, especially in changing circumstances. Like ESFPs, "ENFPs are in the moment" (Thomson, 1998, p. 215). But they are not guardians of the *status quo* and serve as a natural foil to the perspectives and priorities of the SJ type group that is often the largest type cluster in Christian communities or in any religious community. Quenk describes ENFP leaders as people who have:

> a passion for new ideas and especially enjoy the pursuit of possibilities in the external world. They prefer what might be over what is, approach the outer world with trust and optimism, and see environments as welcoming, safe, and exhilarating. (Quenk, 1993, pp. 191–192)

Leaders with dominant extraverted intuition will automatically see the "big picture" for their church and community, but miss some of the details of administration, much to the frustration of the many with SJ preferences, especially the STJs who may think them irresponsible, a sentiment that may be shared at times by those in the church hierarchy, like presbytery chairpersons and bishops who tend to be STJs. However, ENFP leaders may well feel like a "breath of fresh air" to NFs, the next largest temperament subgroup in liberal Protestant and Catholic congregations. ENFP leaders may be particularly appreciated by church members who are themselves ENFPs, and also by INFPs.

For ENFP leaders, using imagination to handle the world is habitual and reliable and there is often unconscious pride, or even arrogance, that this is the one natural way to face life's challenges: to look beyond the immediate facts of a situation and to anticipate the implications. Berens and Nardi (2004, p. 48) warn that "they may overdo interpretations and read other people's minds without checking" for accuracy. They may "get too fragmented with flights of ideas or want continuously to make changes [in order] to incorporate *their* latest insights not settling on any long enough to see their ideas brought to fruition." They seem to exhibit a lack of realism to other types because they underestimate the time, patience, and attention to detail required for lasting change. Because of this, they may come in conflict with the ecclesiastical hierarchy.

Lenore Thomson (1998, p. 207) argues that ENFPs need to draw on their auxiliary introverted judgment to remain centered even as they use their dominant extraverted intuition to give them "an unrivalled ability to adapt and roll with the punches of life."

2 Auxiliary (Nurturing Parent): Introverted Feeling

The auxiliary function of ENFP leaders is introverted feeling. Introverted feeling allows us to use our emotions to identify what matters to us (Berens & Nardi, 2004). Jung wrote: "The depth of this feeling can only be guessed—it can never be clearly grasped. It makes people silent and difficult to access; it shrinks back like a violet from the brute nature of the object in order to fill the depths of the subject" (Jung, 1971, p. 387). Through using their introverted feeling, ENFP leaders are able to hone in on their own deeply held values and those of others in their community and to connect these to some universally held values that transcend external conventions. Introverted feeling helps ENFP leaders to develop and maintain a firm inner integrity whereby their values are used to guide their decisions. Attuned to their own inner moral compass, ENFP leaders are able to support others in maintaining their own integrity. They possess a keen sense of authenticity and its eclipse and can tune in easily to others' emotional states and incongruence.

As these leaders' auxiliary function, that is the function carried by the archetype of the nurturing parent, introverted feeling is the right arm of their personality. Through this function of deep sensitivity, ENFP leaders give to others and also to themselves. Many congregants will be grateful for the deep caring of a quiet presence that they feel one-on-one with ENFP leaders who are usually so charged with extraverted enthusiasm. At times community members, especially those with dominant introverted feeling (INFPs and ISFPs), may feel disconcerted when the intense feeling focus is jerked away by ENFP leaders' extraverted intuitive radar at the periphery of their vision.

Berens and Nardi (2004) discuss the nurturing role of introverted feeling in ENFP leaders in these terms: "Like a supportive parent, they are helpful when they key in on their values and stay with what's important to themselves and other individuals" (p. 48). Indeed, without this inner compass of introverted feeling, their heroic intuition can go astray into the sky-blue yonder or inner city social project with insufficient financial or political backing. Hence, ENFP leaders need to maintain a good trusting relationship with the SJs who have the necessary facts and details to inform them.

When introverted feeling feels bad, extraverted intuition exaggerates this down turn in ENFP leaders. A senior colleague or confidante, who is permitted to be in touch with the subtle but decisive peregrinations of this private aspect of ENFP leaders, plays an important role in mitigating their energetic fluctuations and increasing their predictability.

Bringing introverted feeling into full consciousness is an important process for ENFP leaders. Berens and Nardi (2004, p. 48) warn that before auxiliary introverted feeling is integrated into consciousness, they may be overprotective of their own values. The integrative journey is worthwhile. In summary, Lenore Thomson (1998) describes the balancing role that auxiliary introverted feeling can play in the life and work of ENFP leaders. It enables them to reflect on a situation from an introverted standpoint—to recognize that *their* responsibility to a situation outweighs some of the options available to them.

3 Tertiary (Eternal Child): Extraverted Thinking

The tertiary function of ENFP leaders is extraverted thinking. Extraverted thinking empowers an administrative capacity within ENFP leaders: it is the function concerned with organizing the external world in a logically consistent way. There is enjoyment in making decisions, especially those related to goals that have been selected and chosen, on the basis of explicit guiding principles. On this same logical basis, priorities are determined, and activities segmented and sequenced in pursuit of noble goals. The need for objective analysis and relevant evidence is accepted and provided accordingly with less protest and resistance to the relevant committee or ecclesiastical structure. Appropriate standards, rules, and regulations are applied, against which performance is evaluated, with a particular value placed on efficiency.

As the tertiary function for ENFP leaders, extraverted thinking is carried by the archetype of the eternal child. The mark of children is their winning energy that is often compromised by rapid fading, resulting in sometimes "unforgivable" behavior. Extraverted thinking in this position is quite charming, but subject to rapid fatigue. Volatility therefore may characterize the use of extraverted thinking by ENFP leaders, at least until it becomes more fully integrated into consciousness. This archetypal energy means that the use of extraverted thinking by ENFP leaders often has a disarming, even endearing innocence.

Berens and Nardi (2004, p. 48) describe how extraverted thinking emerges in ENFP leaders. Sometime in their twenties or thirties they may start to "enjoy organizing data, space or clutter to make life flow better." They show a renewed respect for testing their ideas and accept the needs of others to have evidence and explanations for even small decisions.

Such patience for discursive reasoning will be particularly welcomed by community members with TJ type preferences, who have extraverted thinking as their dominant or auxiliary function. This type subgroup may form up to a third of the general church community. TJs in the church will likely appreciate ENFP leaders for a newfound concern for order and consistency regarding some projects and be impressed at the written plan that inspirational ENFP leaders have put together. However, because tertiary extraverted thinking is under the bi-polar influence of child-like archetypal energy, these same TJ parishioners may be dismayed at the sudden wane of interest on the part of their ENFP leaders when the time comes for revisions to the plan, budget submissions, details of implementation, or requests for periodic review and accountability. TJs' trust is not deepened when they sense or actually hear from ENFP leaders the impatient reaction, "Why don't you trust me?" However, when deployed non-defensively, extraverted thinking allows ENFP leaders to bring more of their community members along with them on their new project. When integrated, extraverted thinking provides a second string to their assertiveness, one based on reason as well as inspiration.

4 Fourth (Soul-Friend): Introverted Sensing

The fourth function of ENFP leaders is introverted sensing. Introverted sensing registers and recalls details, relying on "the subjective psychological impressions made by our concrete sensory experiences" (Hartzler & Hartzler, 2005, p. 15). Precisely registered present impressions trigger recall of similar past impressions that in turn determine which present impressions will remain registered in consciousness long enough for storage. Recall is extremely vivid and accompanied by the physical and emotional reactions associated with the original experience. Hartzler and Hartzler (2005) label this process as the "conservator" in the human *psyche*, because of the continuity it provides between the past and present.

For ENFP leaders, introverted sensing is the mirror opposite of their dominant function of extraverted intuition. Before it is integrated into consciousness, introverted sensing is usually experienced as a reaction to stress. For example, usually positive and flexible ENFP leaders may become a caricature of an ISFJ or ISTJ exhibiting an uncharacteristic pessimism, narrow focus, and "tunnel vision", once described by an ENFP as "A sense of feeling numb and frozen with no way out" (Quenk, 2000, p. 43). Other signs of ENFP leaders being "in the grip" of unintegrated "inferior" introverted sensing are: (1) an obsession with a few unrelated facts which are catastrophized as blocking all future developments, and (2) "vacillation between over activity and withdrawal" (Quenk, 2000, p. 43). Furthermore, ENFP leaders may become so pre-occupied with their projects that they neglect their physical health. They may then veer to the other extreme of hypochondriasis, imagining any physical ache or pain as a sign of a fatal disease.

While change may be stressful to judging types, it is stimulating to ENFP leaders. By contrast, ENFP leaders find too much routine and too much attention to detail stressful, along with over-close supervision and rules that stifle intuition. Unintegrated introverted sensing comes into play as a compensation for the overuse of intuition in mid-life, giving rise to un-realistic yearning for absolute stability and security on the part of ENFP leaders (Thomson, 1998).

Changes occur as introverted sensing becomes more conscious and less shameful to the dominant extraverted intuitive. For example, whereas before ENFP leaders may have neglected detailed work like record keeping, they may gradually develop more patience for careful data gathering. They may also start to see some value in tradition, including using "the work, ideas and examples of others who have come before" (Berens & Nardi, 2004, p. 49). They may start to develop a nostalgia for certain previously passed-over customs or objects from their past that may now be suffused with attractive mystery.

The intensity involved in the integration of introverted sensing is worthwhile. In particular, it will increase the trust that SJ types in the community have for their inspiring and often activist ENFP leaders. When extraverted intuitive leaders are able to access the contribution of introverted sensing, they become grounded and rooted in facts and less stressed by details. The capacity for profound connection opens up even with congregants, colleagues, and superiors who are quite different from themselves, particularly the numerous SJs who constitute an important subgroup of most churches. The beneficial effect of this broadening and deepening into introverted sensing, with its capacity for and patience with specifics, is to make inspiring projects far more effective and especially more sustainable. With such increased institutional support, ENFP leaders' energy becomes more directed and less rebellious, yet without sacrificing any of their intensity and integrity.

SHADOW PERSONALITY

5 Dominant Shadow (Challenger): Introverted Intuition

For ENFP leaders, the dominant shadow function is introverted intuition. Introverted intuition focuses on the internal world of the unconscious and thereby yields "insights into the unknowable" (Hartzler & Hartzler, 2005, p. 27). Introverted intuition orients to symbols and discerns patterns and relationships that are unconnected to external events (Berens & Nardi, 2004). Introverted intuition transcends time, moving backward to primeval origins and forward into the distant future. It affords flashes of insight that interrupt traditional patterns of thought and custom, produce new perspectives that reframe whole situations, environments and problems, or illuminates multiple perspectives simultaneously. In the twinkling of an eye, introverted intuition can drop one perspective and deploy several others.

In the case of ENFP leaders, introverted intuition shares the same function as their dominant function but expressed in the opposite direction. Beebe (2007a; 2016) articulates the atmosphere around the function in this position as an "opposing personality" carried by the archetype of the challenger. Thus, introverted intuition shows up in the psychological life of ENFP leaders with adversarial, passive aggressive or sometimes paranoid qualities. Often these aspects of introverted intuition are not acknowledged as part of themselves by ENFP leaders, but they are projected onto others who are experienced as being difficult or even persecutory. Such projection is more frequent in encounters with those types with dominant introverted intuition (INFJs and INTJs).

There are many more introverted intuitive types in Christian communities than in the general population. INTJs and INFJs are the most independent of all types and so they may seem to the extraverted intuitive types as obstinate and uncooperative. The extraverted intuitive may feel persecuted by the obscure vision that introverted intuitive types seem to "go on-and-on about" in community meetings oblivious to the eye rolling incomprehension of many in the audience. ENFP leaders may become furious that these INJs, usually subdued people, hijacked and ruined the church meeting causing members to leave before these leaders had had the opportunity to present their new project. However, the same ENFP leaders may cling to their own prognostications about the future, despite evidence to the contrary, both convictions that something *will* happen, as well as denial that something *may* happen (Berens & Nardi, 2004).

Another aspect of the oppositional dynamic between extraverted and introverted forms of intuition is that, from the perspective of the introverted intuitive types in the community, ENFP leaders may be seen as "unstable," because the latter's extraverted intuition orients to the most promising possibility in the changing external environment. Early on in their careers, ENFP leaders may be able to disregard these occasional difficult encounters, since they have the energy and outward orientation that keeps them focused on their projects.

With patience and persistence, intuition in its introverted aspect may come to feel less strange, and some of its benefits experienced and appreciated, including for example: (1) less dependence on the external environment for simulation, (2) other types especially those with a judging preference may be able to be more acknowledging of the ENFP leader because they discern an inner stability and depth of insight. Furthermore, (3) ENFP leaders may come to appreciate that intuition inwardly directed can yield profound insights, and (4) that adoption of a longer term time perspective reduces the need to rush toward immediate results.

6 Auxiliary Shadow (Critical Parent): Extraverted Feeling

For ENFP leaders, the auxiliary shadow function is extraverted feeling. Extraverted feeling attunes to how others feel, their needs and those of the group (its culture, norms, and values) and seeks to satisfy these needs, automatically adjusting their own bearing and behavior, as well as their own needs (Hartzler & Hartzler, 2005). Extraverted feeling simply "knows" what is right and appropriate in a particular social context. Extraverted feeling enables us to make decisions that will optimize the possibility of harmony.

In ENFP leaders, extraverted feeling lies in the shadow of the nurturing auxiliary function. In that position, extraverted feeling exhibits features of the critical parent and serves to block threats to survival by using shaming, blaming, put downs, and other morally questionable tactics that are intended to stop hostile force in its tracks. At first sight, extraverted feeling in the critical parent mode seems paradoxical, even contradictory. Indeed, at least until integrated, the operations of extraverted feeling under the *aegis* of the critical parent archetype is confusing and perplexing. According to Berens and Nardi (2004, p. 49), extraverted feeling often takes the form of appearing critical and disgruntled with the group. By the same token, extraverted feeling from others—that otherwise strong emotive usually shining presence—may be experienced by ENFP leaders as blocking their work and provoke them to strong criticism. This may surprise and offend not just extraverted feeling types but others in the congregation, especially when intractable argument deteriorates into an "I will fix them" attitude by one or both parties. Unless swiftly detected and diffused, this activity by ENFP leaders can undermine the feeling of community.

Often extraverted feeling types (ESFJs and ENFJs) will be the ones that trigger this reaction in ENFP leaders, which may happen quite often since extraverted feeling types may comprise from 15 to 25 percent of women active in Christian churches. The conflict may be mitigated between ENFPs and ENFJs since both are NFs and share a concern for personal growth, facility with personal communication, and an interest in a wider more inclusive vision. These shared gifts may enable them to contextualize their conflict and dialogue their way through misunderstanding. However, ESFJs are more frequent in Christian communities and as SJs they will be inclined to be tradition-oriented, and therefore often already defensive in response to the change-oriented programming that pours forth naturally from ENFP leaders.

There is, therefore, good reason for ENFP leaders to engage consciously with this critical part of their personality.

Extraverted feeling can be an ally for innovative ENFP leaders. Extraverted feeling, with its sensitivity to accepted custom and to what makes for harmony or discord, may be used (albeit unconsciously) by ENFP leaders in order to block threats to their role or their precious projects. With eventual awareness and conscious development of this function, Berens and Nardi (2004, p. 49) state that such types can at times "magically connect with the group and move it to a new place." When ENFP leaders integrate their extraverted feeling, they become able to combine their imaginative grasp of the project and the possibilities of the situation, with a concern and consideration for the culture and customs of the group. Their enhanced awareness of the human implications of any change that they are proposing will further build community support for their proposals among a variety of types for whom "change" is not an automatic virtue.

7 Tertiary Shadow (Trickster): Introverted Thinking

For ENFP leaders, the tertiary shadow function is introverted thinking. Introverted thinking is an introverted decision-making function concerned with the discernment of truth through a focus on the internal world of underlying abstract principles that precisely define a situation (Haas & Hunziker, 2006). Customs and conventional order are disregarded in the creation of the most elegant framework of principles for organizing information (Hartzler & Hartzler, 2005). Through introverted thinking, phenomena are sorted into categories which are organized in a logical way based on the consistent application of relevant principles and criteria. Berens and Nardi (2004, p. 49) summarize the activity of introverted thinking as "analyzing, categorizing, and evaluating according to principles."

For ENFP leaders, introverted thinking is carried by the trickster archetype. Under the influence of the trickster archetype, mistakes, error, and mischief accompany the operations of introverted thinking among ENFP leaders, especially before it is integrated into consciousness. This integration seldom starts before their fifties and never really completes. Introverted thinking will often get ENFP leaders into, but also out of, tricky situations. Berens and Nardi (2004) describe how ENFP leaders who are not usually interested in identifying principles or in abstract categorization, may, under stress, resort to following or defending some abstract principles deceiving themselves that this will solve the problem.

Introverted thinking is likely to be triggered in two ways for ENFP leaders: (1) when the demands of work or ministry require the services of this function, that is logical categorization based on formal rather than personal considerations and (2) when ENFP leaders directly encounter introverted thinking types (INTPs and ISTPs). However, there are few situations when introverted thinking is called for amidst the routines of Christian ministry, and by the same token, there are relatively few introverted thinking types in Christian communities. Therefore, introverted thinking remains a neglected mystery for most in Christian communities. Consequently, for most ENFPs leaders in a Christian context, learning to deal with their tricksterish introverted thinking is an internal matter, a personal struggle.

Often ENFP leaders have a naive view of introverted thinking. However, unlike the other introverted judging function (introverted feeling) that is usually well developed in this type and which is used to nurture self and others, the use of abstract principles for categorization and analysis (the quintessence of introverted thinking) is poorly understood and clumsily misapplied. For example, ENFP leaders may offer rationales that are irrelevant to the proposals being made or else supply evidence contradicting the argument that they are trying to make.

If they give time to and leave room for their introverted thinking, however, ENFP leaders may find that it helps them to escape tricky situations where they feel caught in a double bind. For example, ENFP leaders may feel trapped between conforming to prevailing norms (in order to please the many in a community with predominantly extraverted feeling preferences) and honoring their own introverted feeling inner ideals. Their introverted thinking, with its concern simply for detached consistency across comparable situations, may, however, provide a rationale that will facilitate an original solution to the situation, by which they are able both to satisfy their inner ideals and to articulate a rationale to others that goes some way toward satisfying them. Gradually, ENFP leaders may become more familiar with how introverted thinking operates, if they take leisure moments simply to play with abstract ideas and frameworks, and so learn to discern when such an activity may be useful, for example, in devising constitutional bylaws.

8 Fourth Shadow (Demon/Angel): Extraverted Sensing

For ENFP leaders, the fourth shadow function is extraverted sensing and this seldom occurs until after the mid-life passage. Extraverted sensing delights in a singularly "here and now" focus which allows us to "absorb tangible details . . . through the senses of hearing, sight, smell, taste and touch" without evaluation (Hartzler & Hartzler, 2005, p. 10). Through the operations of extraverted sensing we naturally adapt to, work with, and take pleasure in the physical world as it is. As the last function to commence integration into consciousness for ENFP leaders, extraverted sensing clashes directly with the dominant function of extraverted intuition, since both functions operate in the same (extraverted) world, but are opposing ways of perceiving and taking in information. This function is carried by the archetype of the demon/angel that has an undermining effect. When the leader in a Christian community is an ENFP, the physical side of life can be undermining, whether it is neglecting physical care, unacknowledged sexual desire, or inattention to physical hazard on a youth field trip.

There is little wisdom devoted to the extraverted sensing world in Christian literature, life and thought, just as there are few extraverted sensing types in Christian communities. And so just as with ENFP leaders' shadow function (introverted thinking), the journey to consciousness of extraverted sensing will receive little external support from the surrounding Christian cultural *ethos*. This makes problematic acting out of extraverted sensing more likely and increases the likelihood that the community's response and way of dealing with it will be destructive or at least divisive. The few extraverted sensing types in Christian communities (ESFPs and ESTPs) with their relaxed at-homeness-in-their-body and casual flexibility can help to defuse tensions and mitigate the overweening intensity that occurs from time to time in communities led by ENFP leaders. Thus, extraverted sensing, when acknowledged and allowed to contribute, can be trans-formational and provide stability to a community structure. This possibility is the basis for Beebe's hopeful surmise:

> The archetype associated with the most unconscious of regions of the mind can deliver insights that are of the highest value, as well as deprecating and undermining ones. It is truly an area of ourselves that is both Devil and Angel. (Beebe, 2007a, p. 5)

In summary, extraverted sensing usually shows up in the life of dominant extraverted intuitive types in an undermining and negative way, since extraverted intuition and extraverted sensing are contrasting ways of perceiving and processing information in the external world. However, they clash when directed in the same world, the external world, for only one kind of perceiving can operate there at the same time—just as it is not possible for the focus of a camera lens to be simultaneously adjusted for close-up portraiture and scenic vistas. The photographer feels torn. This is the experience of the dominant extraverted intuitive ENFP (or ENTP) when confronted with extraverted sensing personally in terms of a task or through sustained encounter with extraverted sensing types (ESFPs and ESTPs) in their community or other parts of their life. When the encounter is in your sphere of work, it is harder to avoid.

Chapter 18

The Enterprising Explorer

ENTP Leaders

ENTP Frequency in the Population

	Male (%)	*Female (%)*
UK	3.6	2.1
USA	6.7	2.8

ENTP PSYCHOLOGICAL TYPE PROFILE

Leading Functions

Dominant extraverted intuition with auxiliary introverted thinking

Conscious personality
1. Dominant (Hero): Extraverted Intuition
2. Auxiliary (Nurturing parent): Introverted Thinking
3. Tertiary (Eternal child): Extraverted Feeling
4. Fourth (Soul-friend): Introverted Sensing

Shadow personality

5. Dominant shadow (Challenger): Introverted Intuition
6. Auxiliary shadow (Critical parent): Extraverted Thinking
7. Tertiary shadow (Trickster): Introverted Feeling
8. Fourth shadow (Demon/Angel): Extraverted Sensing

CONSCIOUS PERSONALITY

1 Dominant (Hero): Extraverted Intuition

Extraverted intuition is the function that instantly sees patterns, connections, and inter-relationships in the external world (Hartzler & Hartzler, 2005, p. 21), and, grasping "the sensory data as a pattern of changing relationships" (Thomson, 1998, p. 197), uses this awareness to envision new possibilities. Extraverted intuition "strives to apprehend the widest range of possibilities in the objective situation" (Sharpe, 1987, p. 60) and "with an attitude of expectancy" (Jung, 1971, p. 366) senses "what is going on behind the scenes, under the surface" (Sharpe, 1987, p. 59).

As the dominant function for ENTP leaders, extraverted intuition occupies the archetypal heroic position. ENTP leaders depend on their extraverted intuition, trusting and relying on their capacity to see patterns and possibilities. Extraverted intuition is a source of stability for these leaders, and its effortlessly expansive operations are a part of feeling normal for them. Extraverted intuition is so integral to ENTP leaders' everyday functioning that they only notice it when they are prevented from using it. The effect of such deprivation is easy for all to see: ENTP leaders readily become bored and restless when they cannot envisage change.

ENTPs are not guardians of the *status quo* and serve as a natural foil to the perspectives and priorities of the sensing-judging (SJ) type group that is often the largest type cluster in Christian communities. Quenk describes them as having "a passion for new ideas and especially enjoy the pursuit of possibilities in the world." "They prefer what might be, over what is, approach the outer world with trust and optimism, and see environments as welcoming, safe, and exhilarating" (Quenk, 1993, pp. 191–192).

ENTP leaders will automatically see the "big picture" for their church and community, but miss some of the details of administration, much to the frustration of the many SJs, especially the STJs, a sentiment that may be shared at times by those in the church hierarchy, like presbytery chairpersons and bishops, who tend to be STJs. However, ENTP ministers may well feel like a "breath of fresh air" to the few NTs in the congregation, who may enjoy theological innovation, and long for an opportunity for a role that gives scope to their appetite and skill in strategy and conceptualizing current trends.

ENTP leaders need to take the time to ground their ideas or proposals in facts for the sensing types in the community and to present it in ways that respond to the values of community members for feeling types. Moreover, sensing-feeling types define the culture of many religious communities, and these types do not naturally trust or even understand NTs' ideas, especially the way NT leaders like to present them—abstractly and coining new phrases—as if they were talking to other NTs.

For ENTP leaders, using imagination to handle the world is habitual and reliable and there is often unconscious pride or even arrogance that this is the one natural way to face life's challenges: to look beyond the immediate facts of the situation and anticipate the implications. Berens and Nardi (2004, p. 40) warn that "they may overdo interpretations and read other people's minds without checking" for accuracy. They seem to exhibit a lack of realism to other types because they underestimate the time, patience, and attention to detail required for lasting change. Because of this, they may come into conflict with the ecclesiastical hierarchy. Moreover, while their peers may have sympathy for their projects, they feel that ENP leaders lack the maturity or patience to deal with the frustrations of the politics involved in renegotiating the rules and dealing with others' insecurity concerning change.

2 Auxiliary (Nurturing Parent): Introverted Thinking

The auxiliary function of ENTP leaders is introverted thinking, the "analyzer" in us (Hartzler & Hartzler, 2005), an introverted decision-making function concerned with the discernment of truth through a focus on the internal world of underlying abstract principles that serve to define a given situation or problem with precision (Haas & Hunziker, 2006, p. 83). Customs and conventional order are disregarded in the creation of the most elegant framework of principles for organizing information (Hartzler & Hartzler, 2005). Through introverted thinking, phenomena are sorted, through successive iterations if need be, into logical categories, which are in turn organized in a logical way based on the consistent application of relevant principles and criteria.

For ENTP leaders, introverted thinking is the second function to emerge into consciousness. This usually occurs in adolescence. Grant, Thompson, and Clarke (1983, p. 241) describe ENTP adolescents as "looking within, in a new way, and becoming more reflective and logical," although they frequently had "difficulty communicating that logic" to others. Furthermore, as the second function to be integrated into consciousness for ENTP leaders, introverted thinking falls under the guiding influence of the archetype of the nurturing parent. Thus, introverted thinking functions as the right hand of ENTP leaders' personality, offering a helping hand to others and to themselves. For ENTP leaders, introverted thinking is the way they most easily give to and nurture others and themselves.

The auxiliary function of introverted thinking provides balance to the personality of ENTP leaders in two respects. First, it provides access to an introverted function and the benefit of reflection. Second, it provides a judging function so that the myriad of possibilities in the outside world imagined by the intuitive function can be subjected to rational evaluation. This enables active mercurial ENTP leaders to "feel responsible for the situations they create" (Thomson, 1998, p. 206). With an inner compass they can remain stable amidst their creative juggling with the possibilities they see outside. This confidence can be very inspiring to others in the community who look to their religious life and spirituality to provide a spark to the rest of their life.

Introverted thinking enables ENTP leaders to give to their community by quickly analyzing problems. Through their introverted thinking they quickly get to the essence of the issue, discerning the relevant intersecting factors and devising a solution that provides for the maximum effect with minimal disruption and outlay of time and resources. ENTP leaders make an immense contribution in this regard, because introverted thinking is in relatively short supply in most Christian communities, since few active members are introverted thinking types. ENTP leaders provide a refreshing alternative to the prevalent SJ way of dealing with issues that require a meticulous examination of what has been done before to resolve similar problems. ENTP leaders need to develop patience, however, as others may not get to the analysis so quickly, nor be so confident to move into action afterwards. ENTP leaders may seem arrogant and condescending, especially when they do not rein in their tendency to see debate as a game to win. They readily accept the criticism to which they subject themselves, and so may be shocked to find that when they turn their logical critique to the ideas of community members, this meets with resentment. Their third or tertiary function is needed to bring real diversity.

3 Tertiary (Eternal Child): Extraverted Feeling

The tertiary function of ENTP leaders is extraverted thinking, the function that attunes to how others feel, to others' needs, and to the feelings and needs of the group, its culture, norms and values. Extraverted feeling simply "knows" what is right and appropriate in this regard. The operations of extraverted feeling enable ENTP leaders to make decisions that will optimize the possibility of harmony. Berens and Nardi (2004, p. 40) summarize the activity of extraverted feeling as "connecting and considering others and the group" in a particular social context. Extraverted feeling seeks to satisfy the needs of others, and to adjust automatically to them, altering their own behavior and bearing, and putting their own needs on one side (Hartzler & Hartzler, 2005).

As the third function to develop for ENTP leaders, extraverted feeling is mediated into consciousness through the archetype of the eternal child, the *puer aeturnus* and *puella aeterna*. Accordingly, the activity of extraverted feeling in ENTP leaders may have an innocent playful quality, but may be unreliable and subject to fatigue. The integration of extraverted feeling is a fluctuating course with many ups and downs. With the development of extraverted feeling, ENTP leaders are able to connect with a wider range of members in their community. At first, such connection takes the form of discussing preferences and opinions.

For ENTP leaders, extraverted feeling usually starts to integrate into a more conscious orientation during their twenties. Without this development, feeling types in the community feel that ENTP leaders lack empathy: they mistake cognitive understanding for actual emotional resonance. While they can quickly intuit what is going on with someone else, they may continue to struggle with communicating their own feelings, so that others actually hear them. This particularly applies to caring feelings. They may communicate for a while on a deeper emotional level and then suddenly revert to an exclusive focus on what excites them as the basis for interaction. Their quick accurate reading without emotional resonance unsettles many. At first, ENTP leaders have difficulty restraining negative emotions especially when they have felt slighted or meet resistance to their projects.

Feeling takes more time than ideas and thoughts, and it takes great patience on the part of ENTP leaders to slow down and resonate to their own and others' feeling. The benefits are significant, bringing relief and balance to the life of the community that is otherwise exhausted by the seemingly incessant excitement of ENTP leaders. However, with development of extraverted feeling, ENTP leaders find themselves giving praise more freely and being able to tune into the needs of others, wanting to take time to deal with their concerns, especially when members have been mistreated. Slowly people and their needs come to matter to ENTP leaders, almost as much as future possibilities and accurate readings and analysis of emerging trends in the local area and religious organization. Attending to the development of two or three close relationships will allow ENTP leaders to feel more settled and create the possibility of feedback from trusted *confidantes* that will decrease their isolation and prevent good programs floundering through lack of support.

4 Fourth (Soul-Friend): Introverted Sensing

The fourth function of ENTP leaders is introverted sensing, the function that registers and recalls details, relying upon "the subjective psychological impressions made by our concrete sensory experiences" (Hartzler & Hartzler, 2005, p. 15). Precisely registered present impressions trigger recall of similar past impressions that in turn determine which present impressions will remain registered in consciousness. Recall is extremely vivid and accompanied by the physical and emotional reactions associated with the original experience. Hartzler and Hartzler (2005, p. 15) label this function as the "conservator" in the human *psyche*, because of the continuity it provides between the past and present.

For ENTP leaders, introverted sensing is usually the fourth function to be integrated into the conscious orientation. As the mirror opposite of their dominant function of extraverted intuition, traditional type theory (Jung, 1971) described it as the inferior function and its unintegrated manifestations are often associated with the experience of shame (Beebe, 2007a).

For ENTP leaders, before it is integrated, introverted sensing is usually experienced as a reaction to stress. For example, usually positive and flexible ENTP leaders may become a caricature of an ISFJ or ISTJ, exhibiting an uncharacteristic pessimism, narrow focus, and "tunnel vision," once described by an ENTP as "A sense of feeling numb and frozen with no way out" (Quenk, 2000, p. 43). Other signs of an ENTP being "in the grip" of unintegrated "inferior" introverted sensing are: (1) an obsession with a few unrelated facts which are catastrophized as blocking all future developments and (2) "vacillation between over activity and withdrawal" (Quenk, 2000, p. 43). Furthermore, ENTP leaders may become so pre-occupied with their projects that they neglect their physical health. They may then veer to the other extreme of hypochondriasis imagining any physical ache or pain as a sign of a fatal disease.

What causes stress is type specific. Change, stressful to judging types, however, is stimulating to ENTP leaders. By contrast, ENTP leaders find too much routine and attention to detail stressful, along with over-close supervision and rules that stifle intuition. Unintegrated introverted sensing comes into play as a compensation for the overuse of intuition in mid-life, giving rise to un-realistic yearning for absolute stability and security on the part of ENTP leaders (Thomson, 1998).

Changes occur as introverted sensing becomes more conscious and less shameful to the dominant extraverted intuitive. For example, whereas before ENTP leaders may have neglected detailed work like record keeping, they may gradually develop more "patience for careful data gathering." They may also start to see some value in tradition including using "the work, ideas and examples of others who have come before" (Berens & Nardi, 2004, p. 49). They may start to develop a nostalgia for certain previously passed-over customs or objects from their past that may now be suffused with attractive mystery.

When ENTP leaders access the contribution of introverted sensing, they become grounded and rooted in facts and less stressed by details. The capacity for profound connection opens up even with congregants, colleagues, and superiors who are quite different from themselves, particularly the numerous SJs who constitute an important subgroup of most churches. The intensity and effort involved in the integration of introverted sensing are worthwhile. Trust will increase among sensing judging types in their inspiring and often activist ENFP leaders. The beneficial effect of broadening and deepening into sensing perceiving with its capacity for and patience with specifics is to make inspiring projects far more effective and especially more sustainable.

SHADOW PERSONALITY

5 Dominant Shadow (Challenger): Introverted Intuition

For ENTP leaders, the dominant shadow function is introverted intuition, the function that focuses on the internal world of the unconscious so as to yield "insights into the unknowable" (Hartzler & Hartzler, 2005, p. 27). Introverted intuition orients to symbols and discerns patterns and relationships that are unconnected to external events (Berens & Nardi, 2004). Introverted intuition transcends time, moving backwards to primeval origins and forward into the distant future. Introverted intuition affords flashes of insight that interrupt traditional patterns of thought and custom, producing a new perspective that re-frames whole situations, environments, and problems or else illuminating multiple perspectives simultaneously. In the twinkling of an eye, with introverted intuition, a perspective can be dropped and several others deployed.

In the case of ENTP leaders, introverted intuition shares the same function as their dominant function but is expressed in the opposite direction. Beebe articulates the atmosphere around the function in this position as an "opposing personality," carried by the challenger archetype. Thus, introverted intuition shows up in the psychological life of ENTP leaders with adversarial, passive aggressive or even sometimes paranoid qualities to its operations. Often these aspects of introverted intuition are not acknowledged as part of themselves, but projected onto others who are experienced as being difficult or even persecutory. Such projection is more frequent in encounters with those types with dominant introverted intuition.

There are many more introverted intuitive types in Christian communities than in the general population. INTJs and INFJs are the most independent of all types and so they may seem to extraverted intuitive types as obstinate and uncooperative. The extraverted intuitive type may feel persecuted by the obscure vision that introverted intuitive types seem to "go on-and-on about" in community meetings oblivious to the eye rolling incomprehension of many in the audience. ENTP leaders may become furious that these usually subdued people hijacked and ruined the church meeting causing members to leave before the ENTP leader had found the opportunity to present his/her new project. However, ENTP leaders may cling to their own prognostications about the future, despite evidence to the contrary; both convictions that something *will* happen, as well as denial that something *may* happen (Berens & Nardi, 2004).

Another aspect of the oppositional dynamic between extraverted and introverted forms of intuition is that from the perspective of the introverted intuitive types in the community, ENTP leaders may be seen as "unstable" and flaky, because the latter's extraverted intuition orients to the most promising possibility in the changing external environment. Early on in their careers, ENTP leaders may be able to shake off these occasional difficult encounters, since they have the energy and outward orientation that allows them to pursue their projects. However, with patience and persistence, intuition in its introverted aspect may come to feel less strange, and some of its benefits experienced and appreciated, including for example: (1) less dependence on the external environment for stimulation; (2) other types especially those with a judging preference may be able to be more acknowledging of the ENTP leader because they discern an inner stability and depth of insight. Furthermore, (3) ENTP leaders may come to appreciate that intuition inwardly directed can yield profound insights, and (4) that adoption of a longer-term time perspective reduces the need to rush toward immediate results.

6 Auxiliary Shadow (Critical Parent): Extraverted Thinking

For ENTP leaders, the auxiliary shadow function is extraverted thinking, the function that seeks to order external realities in a logically consistent way. Through the operations of extraverted thinking, problems are dealt with by first analyzing their causes, determining priorities, defining goals, and then sequencing activities and applying resources—both people and materials—in the service of these goals. Extraverted thinking spontaneously evaluates the present situations in terms of its proximity to these goals. For this reason, standards and rules are valued.

In ENTP leaders, as the auxiliary shadow function, extraverted thinking lies in the shadow of the nurturing parental auxiliary function. In that position, extraverted thinking exhibits the contrasting features of the critical, forbidding parent, and functions to block threats to survival by using shaming, blaming, put downs, and other morally questionable tactics that are intended to stop in its tracks any hostile force that is experienced as a threat to survival.

Particularly before the start of its integration into consciousness, which seldom occurs before mid-life, extraverted thinking often shows up under the archetypal influence of the critical parent (in the *senex*/witch position) in a crass power-oriented manner in order to resist change and new developments. The archetypes of the *senex* in male form and witch in female aspect are gendered forms of the critical negative parent. The stentorian voice of the *senex* bellows intimidation at youthful energy that is experienced as a threat, while "witch energy" defensively casts spells in a situation in order to block unheralded initiatives. When extraverted thinking is under the influence of these archetypes, ENTP leaders, invoking the violation of rational planning processes, use supposedly objective inductive logic to leverage out of the way any schemes that have not been baptized by their inspiration. Such defensiveness is confusing, particularly to those with judging preferences (the Js) in the congregation, who have seldom been enamored with ENTP leaders' lack of plan-fullness.

The potential benefit is significant for the deployment of extraverted thinking in a non-defensive way, since extraverted thinking is the function concerned with organizing the external world in a logically consistent way. There is an organizational aspect to all religious communities, and the development of extraverted thinking helps with this aspect of shared religious life. Thus, extraverted thinking empowers an administrative capacity within ENTP leaders. Moreover, learning how to work with extraverted thinking will enable ENTP leaders to build bridges to those with extraverted thinking as a dominant or auxiliary function.

7 Tertiary Shadow (Trickster): Introverted Feeling

For ENTP leaders, the tertiary shadow function is introverted feeling, a function essential for psychological completeness. Through introverted feeling, we organize our values so that we can maintain our personal identity and structure our life around these deeply held values. Introverted feeling forms the basis for developing and using *universal* values that transcend the *local* customs and conventions to which extraverted feeling is attuned.

As the tertiary shadow function, for the ENTP introverted feeling lies in the shadow of the eternally child-like tertiary function, and while it is developing in mid-life, introverted feeling falls under the influence of the archetype of the trickster. Accordingly, before it is integrated and used in a more conscious way, introverted feeling is flavored by trickster energy that makes it both unreliable and prone to deceit both of self and others. Thus, energized by the trickster archetype, the atmosphere surrounding introverted feeling is one of accident, error, mistake, and deception, especially in regard to its own limitations.

Berens and Nardi (2004, p. 41) warn that ENTP leaders are generally "not usually interested in issues of loyalty [to] or adhering to beliefs," something that introverted feeling and introverted feeling types closely monitor. However, when stressed, ENTP leaders may resort to a very personalized, even idiosyncratic system of belief, rigidly adhere to it, and in contrast to their usually elegant, precise, and salient auxiliary introverted thinking, offer very personal rationales for getting their own way, thinking that such a personal appeal will ensure success. They may also simply act in very childish ways, using such phrases as "I want" and "I don't like" (p. 41).

At other times, when all else fails, ENTP leaders may use introverted feeling in a "tricksterish" way, as a means of extricating themselves from double-binds and other awkward situations. For example, when the heat and swiftness of extraverted intuition has got ENTP leaders into a tight spot, and they are not able coolly to analyze or justify their way out, then an innocent retreat into some personal, rambling reflections on inner convictions may serve to diffuse the situation, and so enable ENTP leaders to retreat and recover.

Introverted feeling types form an important, quiet moral backbone within a congregation and may feel put off, confused, or plain distrustful of the mercurial swiftness of their ENTP leader. Introverted feeling types frequently feel confronted by what ENTP leaders have to give—their nurturing auxiliary introverted thinking—since both introverted feeling and introverted thinking are forms of introverted judgment but incompatible. Introverted feeling types appreciate their own quiet warmth being reflected back to them, but instead until introverted feeling is integrated and less in thrall to trickster influences, from their ENTP leaders they receive only cool analytic logic that is undermining to their basic way of quiet cherishing.

The gains of becoming more mindful of introverted feeling are clear—it may slow down the ENTP leaders as they learn to mull things over. This may feel at first as producing needless delay, but may enable them to bring more of the congregation along with their bold initiatives. In the presence of introverted feeling, most community members feel quietly cherished. Thus, for ENTP leaders while the passage of integration into consciousness of this understated function is not smooth, it is worthwhile and will bring greater personal peace and an ease with subjective vulnerability that will increase their personal appeal and accessibility for the variety of types that make up most congregations.

8 Fourth Shadow (Demon/Angel): Extraverted Sensing

For ENTP leaders, the fourth shadow function is extraverted sensing. Extraverted sensing delights in a singularly "here and now" focus which allows us to "absorb tangible details . . . through the senses of hearing, sight, smell, taste and touch" without evaluation (Hartzler & Hartzler, 2005, p. 10). Through the operations of extraverted sensing, we naturally adapt to, work with, and take pleasure in the physical world as it is.

Extraverted sensing clashes directly with ENTP leaders' dominant function of extraverted intuition, since both functions operate in the same (extraverted) world, but are opposing ways of perceiving and taking in information. Beebe (2007a) found that the undermining quality of the fourth shadow function gave credence to the idea of a "devil" or "demon" in every human *psyche.* It often is revealed as an oaf or beast in dreams. For ENTP leaders, the physical side of life can be undermining, whether it is neglecting physical care, unacknowledged sexual desire, or inattention to physical hazard on a youth field trip.

There is little wisdom about the extraverted sensing world in Christian life and thought, just as there are few extraverted sensing types in Christian communities. And so just as with ENTPs leaders' previous shadow function (introverted feeling), the journey to consciousness of this function will receive little external support in terms of the surrounding Christian cultural *ethos.* This makes the problematic acting out of extraverted sensing more likely and also increases the likelihood that the community's response and way of dealing with it will be destructive or at least divisive. The few extraverted sensing types in Christian communities, with their relaxed at-homeness-in-their-body and casual flexibility, can help to defuse tensions and mitigate the overweening intensity that occurs from time-to-time in a community led by an ENTP. Thus, what has been neglected (extraverted sensing), when acknowledged and allowed to contribute, can be trans-formational and provide stability to a community structure. This possibility is the basis for Beebe's optimistic surmise:

> The archetype associated with the most unconscious of regions of the mind can deliver insights that are of the highest value, as well as depreciating and undermining ones. It is truly an area of ourselves that is both Devil and Angel. (Beebe, 2007a, p. 5)

In summary, extraverted sensing usually shows up in the life of the extraverted intuitive dominant in an undermining and negative way, since extraverted intuition and extraverted sensing are contrasting ways of perceiving and processing information in the external world. However, they clash when directed in the same world, the external world, for only one kind of perceiving can operate there at the same time—just as it is not possible for the focus of camera lens to be simultaneously adjusted for close-up portraiture and scenic vistas. The photographer feels torn. This is the experience of the extraverted intuitive ENTP (or ENFP) when confronted with extraverted sensing personally in terms of a task or through sustained encounter with extraverted sensing types (ESFPs and ESTPs) in their community or other parts of their life. When the encounter is in your sphere of work, it is harder to avoid.

Chapter 19

The Enthusiastic Improviser

ESFP Leaders

ESFP Frequency in the Population

	Male (%)	*Female (%)*
UK	6.1	11.0
USA	4.0	7.2

ESFP PSYCHOLOGICAL TYPE PROFILE

Leading Functions

Dominant extraverted sensing with auxiliary introverted feeling

Conscious personality

1. Dominant (Hero): Extraverted Sensing
2. Auxiliary (Nurturing parent): Introverted Feeling
3. Tertiary (Eternal child): Extraverted Thinking
4. Fourth (Soul-friend): Introverted Intuition

Shadow personality

5. Dominant shadow (Challenger): Introverted Sensing
6. Auxiliary shadow (Critical parent): Extraverted Feeling
7. Tertiary shadow (Trickster): Introverted Thinking
8. Fourth shadow (Demon/Angel): Extraverted Intuition

CONSCIOUS PERSONALITY

1 Dominant (Hero): Extraverted Sensing

The dominant function of ESFP leaders is extraverted sensing, the information gathering or perceiving function focused on the current, objective external world. For ESFP leaders, extraverted sensing is their most reliable function, developed under the archetypal influence of the hero that equips the growing individual to cope with the challenges of life. ESFP leaders cope with life by relying on the capability of their extraverted sensing to orient them to the immediate realities of their situation. As a result, ESFP leaders are "incredibly present in the moment" and are continuously scanning for reactions and relevant information. They tune into the slightest cues of voice tone and facial expression that others offer and naturally accommodate to their own social and physical environments. They exhibit elegant simplicity in both their movements and information-seeking, asking just a few questions that key into the salient aspects of the situation for a particular individual or small group.

The swiftness of ESFP leaders to respond in a sensitive and practical manner in pressing situations will earn them respect, especially among the numerically substantial SJ type group. The spontaneity of ESFP leaders feels "like a breath of fresh air" to many other types, especially to other perceiving types such as ENFPs and ISFPs, but also to the few NTs who might otherwise be defeated in their struggle with the stodginess of the social culture prevailing in many religious groups. By the same token, their sensitivity to others' feeling will garner support from the majority who has a feeling preference. "Because of their winning way with other people, their perceptions are valued and their suggestions have a good chance of being followed" (Harbaugh, 1988, p. 54).

The humor that arises with dominant heroic extraverted sensing is often an asset among members of religious communities that are prone to take life and themselves too seriously. ESFP leaders may be able to lighten the mood of a meeting by making a humorous comment about some physical aspect of the shared environment, such as how two people look together, how someone is dressed, or what someone said. Of course this can misfire and be a cause for gossip among more staid members of the community. It may also strengthen a reputation for being distractible and unable to stay the distance with complex problems.

Part of the problem is that extraverted sensing is so familiar and adaptable for ESFP leaders that this function becomes pervasive and hence invisible, because it is assumed that this is *the* way to deal with life and *all* important problems encountered in their community. If extraverted sensing becomes inflated in this manner, then ESFP leaders may act too quickly and too confidently.

A temptation is to skip over complex problems, or else to delegate them to others without assessing the competence of these individuals or following up with them to check on progress toward a solution. This may prove disastrous for the community and for members' confidence in the reliability and judgment of their leader, but can be mitigated by connections established through the auxiliary function which for ESFPs is introverted feeling.

2 Auxiliary (Nurturing Parent): Introverted Feeling

The auxiliary function of ESFP leaders is introverted feeling, the function that allows the use of our emotions to identify what matters (Hartzler & Hartzler, 2005). By using their introverted feeling, ESFP leaders are able to hone in on and connect with their own deeply held values and those of others in their community. As the second and auxiliary function for ESFP leaders, introverted feeling is associated with, and flavored by, the archetype of the good or nurturing parent. Auxiliary introverted feeling provides a caring counterbalance to the action orientation of ESFP leaders' dominant extraverted sensing. Exhaustion and burnout become less likely with the development of this form of inner judgment. Development of introverted feeling makes it unnecessary for them to rely on feelings of fatigue and depression to escape the onslaught of external information with which they are trying to deal (Thomson, 1998). This quiet valuing, deep inside outgoing ESFP leaders, enables them to select unerringly a nuanced adaptive response to all the numerous stimuli that compose the pressing reality of the immediate situation, to which ESFP leaders are so exquisitely oriented through heroic extraverted sensing. Through such sensitivity, ESFP ministers are able to nurture others and also themselves.

Many congregants will be grateful for the deep caring of a quiet presence that they feel one-on-one with ESFP leaders. In particular, their introverted feeling will cement a firm bond with the many SFJs in the community who might be baffled and at times ruffled by their leader's unpredictability and swift twinkling humor. ESFP leaders need to maintain a good trusting relationship with the SFJs who are able to provide them with important facts and details from previous experiences in the history of the community. By the same token, senior colleagues or others, who are permitted to be *confidants* and are allowed to be in touch with ESFP leaders' introverted feeling, play an important role in building community trust by mitigating ESFP leaders' energetic fluctuations and underlining the value of their increasing predictability.

With the integration into consciousness of introverted feeling, that usually commences in adolescence and proceeds through early adulthood, ESFP leaders become able to reflect on and examine what is important to themselves and others and to connect these priorities to universal values that transcend external conventions.

Introverted feeling helps ESFP leaders to develop and maintain a firm inner integrity whereby their values are used to guide their decisions, and the welter of alternative responses are swiftly (and seemingly instinctively) sifted through their inner values. Attuned to their own inner moral compass, ESFP leaders are able to support others in maintaining their own integrity. They possess a keen sense of authenticity as well as of its eclipse and tune in readily to others' emotional states and incongruence.

Bringing introverted feeling into full consciousness is an important process. The individuation journey is worthwhile and involves many twists and turns. Thomson (1998) describes the balancing role that auxiliary introverted feeling can play in the life and work of ESFP leaders: it enables them to reflect on a situation from an introverted standpoint, and so to recognize that their responsibility to a situation outweighs some of their strong impulse toward a swift and simple solution available to them. However, while introverted feeling encourages ESFP leaders to be interested in people, they sometimes become over-involved in helping others.

3 Tertiary (Eternal Child): Extraverted Thinking

The tertiary function of ESFP leaders is extraverted thinking: the function concerned with organizing the external world in a logically consistent manner. It is mediated into consciousness through the archetype of the eternal child. Extraverted thinking in this position in the psyche is quite charming, but subject to rapid fatigue and hence its productivity is unreliable. This archetypal energy means that the use of extraverted thinking by ESFP leaders often has a disarming, even endearing innocence. Volatility characterizes the use of extraverted thinking by ESFP leaders until it becomes more fully integrated into consciousness, which seldom occurs before their thirties. For instance, they may like giving advice, but find it difficult to gauge when it is too much or too little. The integration of extraverted thinking has a fluctuating course with many ups and downs, but eventually settles down.

Once extraverted thinking is integrated into consciousness, there is enjoyment in making decisions, especially those related to goals that have been selected on the basis of explicit guiding principles. Priorities are determined on this same logical basis, and activities segmented and sequenced in pursuit of goals. When extraverted thinking is developed, ESFP leaders come to see the need for objective analysis and for relevant evidence, and so become willing to provide these to the relevant committee or ecclesiastical structure with less protest and resistance. Likewise, they accept the institutional need for the articulation of appropriate standards, rules, and regulations that are required in order to evaluate performance. They may come to feel less alienated by the religious hierarchy's concern for efficiency.

Berens and Nardi (2004) describe how, with the development of extraverted thinking, ESFP leaders may start to "enjoy organizing data, space or projects and drawing diagrams that display information, theories, or ideas in a way that others can use them" (p. 24). They accept the needs of others to have evidence and explanations for even small decisions. The development of extraverted thinking allows them to "be true to their own needs by becoming more assertive in the face of unreasonable demands by others" (Grant, Thompson, & Clarke, 1983, p. 219). This may require some adjustment from the near majority of types in most religious communities—those who boast extraverted feeling as their first or second function. These types cherish maintaining external harmony at almost any cost and wonder and worry about the new seemingly brash and even hardline approach taken by their previously easygoing leader.

By way of contrast, the ESFP leaders' newfound patience for discursive reasoning will be particularly welcomed by community members with TJ type preferences, who have extraverted thinking as their dominant or auxiliary function. In particular, the development of extraverted thinking may earn ESFP leaders new respect from many ISTJs and several ESTJs who form a significant proportion of males within the community. TJs in the church will likely appreciate ESFP leaders for their newfound concern for order and consistency regarding some projects and be impressed at the written plan that inspirational ESFP leaders have finally put together. However, because tertiary extraverted thinking is under the bipolar influence of child-like archetypal energy, these same TJ parishioners may be dismayed at the sudden wane of interest on the part of their ESFP leaders when the time comes for revisions to a particular plan, budget submissions, details of implementation, or requests for periodic review and accountability.

4 Fourth (Soul-Friend): Introverted Intuition

The fourth function of ESFP leaders is introverted intuition, an internally directed perceiving function that provides "insights into the unknowable." This inward-turned function discerns patterns and connections that are not related to external events (Hartzler & Hartzler, 2005, p. 27). It is carried by the archetype of the soul-friend. This archetype unfolds a capacity to forge connections on a profound level, providing a sense of mission, on the one hand, and a bridge to the unconscious, on the other. Full development of introverted intuition through the soul-friend archetype suffuses ESFP leaders with a grounded intensity, and capacity for depth, that provides an alluring complement to the level-headed action orientation of their dominant extraverted sensing function.

While still largely unconscious, introverted intuition is associated for ESFP leaders with being caught up in superstition, magical thinking, and needless worry about the future (Berens & Nardi, 2004, p. 25). Finding balance within the operations of introverted intuition takes time. Incorporating the opposite function to their dominant function is a challenging part of the individuation journey and involves more engagement with what is unconscious due to repression or neglect.

Stress triggers our inferior fourth function, and for ESFP leaders, the trigger usually takes one of three forms. First, because their dominant extraverted sensing has a default focus on the present, "spending a great deal of time with people who are very serious about or focused on future plans and goals trigger the inferior function" in ESTPs and ESFPs (Quenk, 2000, p. 30). Second, closing off options is also a trigger for stress. For example, ESFP leaders may often worry "What if I pick the wrong thing and have to stay with it?" (Quenk, 2000, p. 30). Third, excessive structured activity and conformity to a schedule may prove debilitating to extraverted sensing types (Quenk, 2000, p. 30). The likely frequent presence of these three stressors when leading a religious community may account in part for the under-representation of ESFP leaders in a religious context (Macdaid, McCaulley, & Kainz, 1986).

The aging process may precipitate a sense of fewer and "closed options" (Quenk, 2000). For example, ESFP leaders in a large or mid-sized religious institution realize they are unlikely to be promoted in ministry, since most senior positions in ministry favor judging types, and also in part because larger congregations require more planning. Similarly, promotion to a higher position within a religious institution requires a more structured and predictable work style. Thus, ESFP leaders in a religious context may feel closed in by life or work, or both, as they age.

Familiarity with introverted intuition yields greater powers of discrimination and, as ESFP leaders become more open to the operations of introverted intuition within themselves, images of future change transform from being full of foreboding to being energizing. Patience grows for dipping beneath the surface of experiences and appreciating what may not hitherto have been immediately apparent.

SHADOW PERSONALITY

5 Dominant Shadow (Challenger): Introverted Sensing

For ESFP leaders, the dominant shadow function is introverted sensing, an information gathering function that focuses on particular elements in order to compose the subjective internal world of current experiences, which are then compared to previous, related experiences (Haas & Hunziker, 2006).

Introverted sensing enables the registration of details that are arrayed alongside similar past experiences and empower recall, and even the re-living, of previous events. For ESFP leaders, introverted sensing seldom emerges into conscious awareness before mid-life and does so under the archetypal influence of the challenger.

In Beebe's refinement and elaboration of Jung's approach to personality typology (Beebe, 2007a), there exists a tension between sensing in its introverted and extraverted aspects, for introverted sensing is put in shadow by the habitual exercise by ESFP leaders of their dominant extraverted sensing. Because introverted sensing comprises a part of the shadow personality, before integration into consciousness, it is in fact "disowned" and projected onto other people who are experienced as "bad" characters. Thus, in the earlier stages of integration, introverted sensing is tinged with challenge for ESFP leaders and carries a passive-aggressive flavor.

Those community members with introverted sensing as their dominant function are particularly liable to fall prey to the oppositional dynamic of projection associated with introverted sensing within the ESFP leaders' psychic structure. For example, ESFP leaders may feel confined by dominant introverted sensing types' orientation to the present from the perspective of the past. ESFP leaders do well to recognize and restrain their inclination to rebel or escape in response to their experience of the structuring, or even controlling, ways of the surrounding SJs. They may be tempted to lampoon their SJ charges, "sending them up" as stuffy hypocrites. For their part, SJs may be surprised to learn that their ESFP leader responds more favorably to being encouraged to do something rather than being told what not to do.

Sensing judging types may stereotype ESFP leaders as impulsive and incorrectly conclude they must be unreliable simply because they rely on extraverted attunement to the physical environment and not on introverted sensing comparison of present to past details. SJs may also judge ESFP leaders as lazy or slack. Their free spirit may bring ESFP leaders into conflict with (and to be distrusted by) senior clerics who have introverted sensing as a dominant or auxiliary function. Accordingly, ESFP leaders may have to struggle hard against a tendency inside to feel on a perpetual crusade against the establishment, to seek escape or avoidance, or to feel driven to premature retirement. Competing expectations of leadership between SPs and SJs can and should be faced and negotiated.

Hesitation that ESFP leaders may have about over-programming in their community may be welcomed by the minority who have a perceiving preference, most numerously the ENFPs, INFPs, and ISFPs, who often feel railroaded and even stifled by the controlled and controlling culture of the majority who have judging preferences. However, ESFP leaders who succeed in religious organizations have usually found a way to accommodate the need of judging types for some structure in order to feel secure and less stressed.

6 Auxiliary Shadow (Critical Parent): Extraverted Feeling

For ESFP leaders, the auxiliary shadow function is extraverted feeling, the function that takes care to harmonize individuals with the values of the external environment. At its core, extraverted feeling maintains relationships and social networks, seeking to co-ordinate people and material resources in order "to harmoniously achieve group and individual goals" (Hartzler & Hartzler, 2005, p. 45). As the auxiliary shadow function, extraverted feeling lies in the shadow of ESFP leaders' nurturing auxiliary function of introverted feeling, the function that quietly cherishes inner universal values, on which ESFP leaders, under the influence of the archetype of the good or nurturing parent, invariably draw in order to care for others. By contrast, extraverted feeling, falls under the influence of the archetype of the critical parent, whose role is to block threats to survival by using shaming, blaming, put downs, and other morally questionable tactics that are intended to stop hostile force in its tracks (Beebe, 2007b).

The influence of the critical parent archetype is recognized when extraverted feeling is deployed protectively to block sensed threats to the conscious ego's survival. Dealing with the negative parental energy associated with extraverted feeling may be ESFP leaders' greatest challenge, first because of the generally caring role expected of the religious leader and second because extraverted feeling—along with introverted sensing—is the most frequent preference of those who join religious communities, with ISFJs and ESFJs often being the most numerous psychological types. There is, therefore, good reason for ESFP leaders to engage consciously with this critical part of their personality.

At first blush, the activity of extraverted feeling in the critical parent mode seems contradictory, for extraverted feeling is the function that attunes to how others feel, their needs and those of the group—its culture, norms, and values. Extraverted feeling seeks to satisfy these needs, automatically adjusting the individual's own bearing and behavior, as well as their own needs in order to harmonize these with those of others (Hartzler & Hartzler, 2005). Extraverted feeling simply knows what is right and appropriate in a particular social context. However, under the aegis of the critical parent archetype, extraverted feeling becomes perplexing. According to Berens and Nardi (2004, p. 49), until integrated into consciousness, the operations of extraverted feeling often take the form of appearing critical and disgruntled with the group. Indeed in the early stage of its conscious differentiation, extraverted feeling is used by ESFP leaders for these defensive purposes. ESFP leaders may simply block people with extraverted feeling whom they experience as threatening. Extraverted feeling from others, often FJs, who stress harmony with customs and convention, may be experienced by ESFP leaders as blocking their easygoing spontaneity. When others use extraverted feeling—as in expressing concern for someone else—they may view it as political manipulation. ESFP leaders do well to cultivate individual relationships with some ISFJs and ESFJs with whom they have some interests in common, including a shared preference for feeling and with whom they can consult periodically.

The struggle to bring extraverted feeling into more conscious engagement with the tasks of their life and work is worthwhile: as extraverted feeling becomes more conscious and familiar to ESFP leaders, the shadow aspect of the process decreases. Berens and Nardi (2004, p. 25) report, "At times they can magically connect with the group and move it to a new place."

7 Tertiary Shadow (Trickster): Introverted Thinking

For ESFP leaders, the tertiary shadow function is introverted thinking, the introverted decision-making function concerned with the discernment of truth through concentration on the internal world of underlying abstract principles that precisely define and name a situation (Haas & Hunziker, 2006). Through introverted thinking, phenomena are sorted into logical categories which are in turn organized in a logical way based on the consistent application of relevant principles and criteria. Berens and Nardi (2004, p. 25) summarize the activity of introverted thinking as "analyzing, categorizing, and evaluating according to principles."

Introverted thinking for ESFP leaders develops in the position managed by the trickster archetype and shares the same function as the eternally child-like tertiary function but is directed toward the opposite world, lying as it does in the shadow of their tertiary extraverted thinking. Accordingly, introverted thinking is flavored by trickster energy that makes it both unreliable and prone to deceit both of self and others, because introverted thinking in this position is unaware of its own limitations. Under the influence of the trickster archetype, mistakes, error, and mischief accompany the operations of introverted thinking for ESFP leaders, especially in the early stages of becoming more conscious.

The integration of tricksterish introverted thinking into consciousness seldom occurs before fifty years of age and is rarely completed within a human lifespan. For ESFP leaders, introverted thinking will often get them into, but also out of, tricky situations. Berens and Nardi (2004) described how ESFP leaders, though they are not usually interested in identifying principles or abstract categorization, may nevertheless under stress resort to following or defending some abstract principles, deceiving themselves that this will solve the problem.

Introverted thinking tends to be triggered in one of two ways for ESFP leaders: either when the demands of work or ministry require the services of this function (that is to say, requiring logical categorization based on formal rather than personal considerations), or when ESFP leaders directly encounter the use of introverted thinking by others, most likely dominant introverted thinking types (INTPs and ISTPs) or those with introverted thinking as an auxiliary function (ESTPs and ENTPs). Perhaps, fortunately for ESFP leaders, there are few situations when introverted thinking is called for amidst the routines of Christian ministry, and there are relatively few individuals with introverted thinking as a dominant or auxiliary function in Christian groups.

Often ESFP leaders may have a simplistic approach to this introverted judging function. Unlike the other introverted judging function (introverted feeling that is usually well-developed in this type and used to nurture self and others), the use of abstract principles for categorization and analysis (the quintessence of introverted thinking) is poorly understood and clumsily applied. For example, ESFP leaders may offer rationales that are irrelevant to the proposals being made or may supply evidence contradictory to the argument they are trying to make. They may also deceive themselves continuing to defend their own theoretical examples, while on other occasions they mishear or deliberately misinterpret another's argument.

Nevertheless, when attention is given to introverted thinking, ESFP leaders may find that it helps them escape tricky situations where they feel caught in a double bind. For example, ESFP leaders may feel trapped between honoring their own introverted feeling inner ideals and conforming to prevailing norms in order to please the many in the community with extraverted feeling preferences. In this instance, introverted thinking, with its concern simply for detached consistency across comparable situations, may provide a suitable rationale that will facilitate an original solution to the situation.

8 Fourth Shadow (Demon/Angel): Extraverted Intuition

For ESFP leaders, the fourth shadow function is extraverted intuition and this seldom develops until after the mid-life passage. Extraverted intuition is an outwardly focused perceiving function that quickly sees "patterns, connections and inter-relationships in the external world" (Hartzler & Hartzler, 2005, p. 21), synthesizes sensory data into "a pattern of changing relationships" (Thomson, 1998, p. 197), and envisions new possibilities. As the fourth shadow function for ESFP leaders, extraverted intuition is carried into consciousness by the archetype of the demon/angel.

The usual effect of the activity of the demon/angel archetype is to undermine, and occasionally to transform. Extraverted intuition is the opposite perceiving function to ESFP leaders' dominant and heroic extraverted sensing, and it *directly* clashes with the operations of extraverted sensing because it operates in the very same (extraverted) world. Accordingly, the workings of this function disrupt their habitual means of coping, especially in the first half of life when the process of integrating extraverted intuition into a conscious orientation is barely under way. At this early stage of integration, the activities of extraverted intuition, whether engaged by chance, trauma, or necessity, are often suffused with dysphoria and negative moods. Extraverted intuition is not merely unfamiliar to ESFP leaders, but something foreign in its activities, because it prevents the functioning of ESFP leaders' usual grounded easygoing extraverted sensing way of coping. Extraverted intuition undermines or even sabotages the operations of the superior extraverted sensing.

The oft-demonic fourth shadow function is "capable of great distortion, causing confusion and chaos, and disrupting trust" (Haas & Hunziker, 2006, p. 179). Boredom, tediousness, and stress for ESFP leaders can trigger "demonic" extraverted intuition. Unconscious acting out of shadow impulses may halt the development of community, undermining the trust established through the years of comfort with ESFP leaders' relaxed and low-key warm presence. Thus, it behoves ESFP leaders to be aware of their "demons," especially the one that carries this least conscious function. When ESFP leaders are "beastly," extraverted intuition is often involved. According to Beebe (2007a, p. 5), our fourth shadow function is "usually the locus of our most unyielding and unconscious flaws of character." The process of conscious integration of the fourth shadow function is a long one and seldom completed. However, engagement with this function will be less daunting if ESFP leaders have developed a solid connection with their fourth and soul-function of introverted intuition.

An incentive for ESFP leaders to get to know this neglected side of themselves is the fact that ESFP leaders may frequently encounter a trigger to their demonic function in the personal form of community members with dominant or auxiliary extraverted intuition, notably the ENFPs and INFPs. The journey toward integration has its rewards. There is the redemptive angelic aspect to extraverted intuition that appears more frequently as integration proceeds. Berens and Nardi (2004, p. 25) report that "on occasion [ESFPs] can arrive at profound interpretations that really transform situations and their daily lives."

Chapter 20

The Energetic Problem-Solver

ESTP Leaders

ESTP Frequency in the Population

	Male (%)	*Female (%)*
UK	8.2	3.7
USA	6.2	3.6

ESTP PSYCHOLOGICAL TYPE PROFILE

Leading Functions

Dominant extraverted sensing with auxiliary introverted thinking

Conscious personality
1. Dominant (Hero): Extraverted Sensing
2. Auxiliary (Nurturing parent): Introverted Thinking
3. Tertiary (Eternal child): Extraverted Feeling
4. Fourth (Soul-friend): Introverted Intuition

Shadow personality
5. Dominant shadow (Challenger): Introverted Sensing
6. Auxiliary shadow (Critical parent): Extraverted Thinking
7. Tertiary shadow (Trickster): Introverted Feeling
8. Fourth shadow (Demon/Angel): Extraverted Intuition

CONSCIOUS PERSONALITY

1 Dominant (Hero): Extraverted Sensing

The dominant function of ESTP leaders is extraverted sensing, that is (1) an information gathering or perceiving function (2) focused on the current, objective external world in order to (3) fully experience the rich details of the environment through the five senses, (4) drawing "energy and enjoyment directly from people, objects and events" (Haas & Hunziker, 2006, p. 33). For ESTP leaders, extraverted sensing is their most reliable function and develops under the archetypal influence of the hero.

ESTP leaders cope with their life by relying on the capability of their extraverted sensing to orient them to the immediate realities of their situation. As a result, ESTP leaders are present in the moment, scanning for reactions and relevant information. They are attuned to the slightest cues of voice tone and facial expression that others offer and naturally accommodate to the social and physical environments they inhabit. ESTP leaders exhibit elegant simplicity in both their movements and information-seeking, asking just a few questions that key into the salient aspects of the situation for a particular individual or small group.

The swiftness of ESTP leaders to respond in immediate practical ways, especially in pressing situations, will earn them respect, especially among the numerically substantial SJ type group. Their spontaneity feels "like a breath of fresh air" to many other types, especially to other perceiving types such as the ENFPs and ISFPs, but also to the few NTs who might otherwise feel defeated in their struggle with the stodginess of the social culture prevailing in many religious groups. ESTP leaders' coolness in tricky situations will rivet the attention and earn them the respect of other thinking types and increase their engagement in the community.

The humor that arises readily when extraverted sensing is the heroic dominant function is often an asset in religious communities whose members are prone to take life and themselves seriously. ESTP leaders may be able to lighten the mood of a meeting by making a humorous comment about some physical aspect of the shared environment, such as how two people look together, how someone is dressed, or what someone said. Of course, this can misfire and be a cause for gossip among more staid members of the community. It may also strengthen a reputation for being distractible and unable to stay the distance with complex problems. Thus, while ESTP leaders may be enviably good in the opportunity or crisis of the *present* moment, they need to draw on their less developed functions to sift through the myriad of solutions to the more complex problems that arise in religious communities.

Part of the problem is that extraverted sensing is so familiar and adaptable for ESTP leaders that this function becomes pervasive and hence invisible because it is assumed that this is *the* way to deal with life and all important problems encountered by their religious community. If extraverted sensing becomes inflated in this manner, then ESTP leaders may "act with overconfidence, feeling . . . immune to danger" (Berens & Nardi, 2004, p. 20).

The tendency is to skip over complex problems or to delegate their solution to others without assessing these individuals' competence or following up with their work. Such oversights may prove disastrous for the community and members' confidence in their leader.

2 Auxiliary (Nurturing Parent): Introverted Thinking

The auxiliary function of ESTP leaders is introverted thinking, an introverted decision-making function concerned with the discernment of truth through a focus on the internal world of underlying abstract principles that serve to define a given situation or problem with precision (Haas & Hunziker, 2006). Customs and conventional order are disregarded in the creation of the most elegant framework of principles for organizing information (Hartzler & Hartzler, 2005). With the help of introverted thinking, phenomena are sorted, through successive iterations if need be, into logical categories, which are in turn organized in a logical way based on the consistent application of relevant principles and criteria. Falling under the guiding influence of the archetype of the nurturing parent, introverted thinking serves as the right hand of the personality of ESTP leaders. Thus, introverted thinking is the way they most easily give to and nurture others and themselves.

For ESTP leaders, in adolescence there may have been an inward turning: conclusions for action were reached but the reasoning was seldom shared with others (Grant, Thompson, & Clarke, 1983). The auxiliary function of introverted thinking provides balance to the personality of ESTP leaders in two respects. First, it provides access to an introverted function and offers the benefit of reflection. Second, introverted thinking provides a function of judgment so that numerous details of the present situation can be swiftly sifted according to the most salient criteria related to action. The swift elegance of their response may earn ESTP leaders respect from the sensing judging types who may have considered them previously as indulgent, distracted, or ill-disciplined.

Introverted thinking enables ESTP leaders to give to their community by quickly analyzing problems and taking prompt action. Through their introverted thinking, they strike to the heart of the situation, discerning the relevant intersecting factors and devising a solution that provides for the maximum effect with minimal disruption and outlay of time and resources. ESTP leaders make an immense contribution in this regard, because introverted thinking is in short supply in most Christian communities.

ESTP leaders provide a refreshing alternative to the prevalent sensing-judging way of dealing with issues that stipulates a meticulous examination of what has been done previously to resolve similar problems. ESTP leaders need to develop patience, however, as others may not get to the analysis so quickly nor be so confident to move into action afterwards. ESTP leaders may seem arrogant and condescending, especially when they fail to rein in their tendency to see debate as a game to win. They enjoy debate and can play the devil's advocate, but may prolong the argument past the point of usefulness, since enthralled in the delight of the play of ideas they miss how others are reacting and feeling.

ESTP leaders have no trouble accepting the criticism to which they subject themselves, and so may be shocked to find that when they turn their logical critique to the ideas of others, this meets with resentment. They also provide such an elaborate analysis that others have trouble seeing the point. Their tertiary function is needed to bring real diversity.

3 Tertiary (Eternal Child): Extraverted Feeling

The tertiary function of ESTP leaders is extraverted feeling; the function that attunes to how others feel, to their needs, and to the feelings and needs of the group. Extraverted feeling simply "knows" what is right and appropriate in a particular social context and seeks to satisfy the needs of others, enabling automatic adjustment to them, altering their own behavior and bearing, and putting their own needs on one side (Hartzler & Hartzler, 2005). Berens and Nardi (2004, p. 20) summarize the activity of extraverted feeling as "connecting and considering others and the group." Once developed, the operations of extraverted feeling enable ESTP leaders to make decisions that will optimize the possibility of harmony between people.

As the third function to develop for ESTP leaders, extraverted feeling is mediated into consciousness through the archetype of the eternal child. Accordingly, the activity of extraverted feeling in ESTP leaders may have an innocent playful quality, but may be unreliable and subject to fatigue. The integration of extraverted feeling is a fluctuating course with many ups and downs.

For ESTP leaders, extraverted feeling usually starts to integrate into a more conscious orientation in their twenties. Before this development occurs feeling types often perceive ESTP leaders as devoid of empathy. Once extraverted feeling becomes more a part of their consciousness, ESTP leaders find themselves enjoying making connections with others. However, for ESTP leaders, extraverted feeling may retain a child-like fluctuating reliability and their strengthened emotional resonance with others is inconstant and may feel duplicitous to some. Some ESTP leaders may feign caring more about others than is really the case, using their charm to gain advantage. Only gradually does extraverted feeling become freed from the volatility associated with archetypes of the eternal child. Indeed trusting the emotional realm is a winding road for ESTP leaders: they may continue to have difficulty expressing their care, and, if they do, they are confused when they later discover that others did not hear it (Berens & Nardi, 2004). Feeling types puzzle over their ESTP leaders' ability to connect easily and read others at one level, but seem maladroit at deeper levels of emotional resonance.

The incentive for ESTP leaders to be more conscious of their volatile extraverted feeling is obvious, since the many unconscious aspects of this function in the eternal child position could undermine the trust that the feeling majority in most religious communities need to place in their leader in order for their sense of community to flourish. Both the large group with extraverted feeling preferences (ESFJ, ENFJ, ISFJ, and INFJ) and the significant group with introverted feeling preferences (ENFP, ESFP, INFP, ISFP) need to be able to trust their leader on this emotional level. While they observe with admiration an ESTP leader's ability to respond swiftly to snuff out a tangible crisis facing the community, these feeling types need reassurance that ESTP leaders can also build enduring relationships based on values that they can instinctively trust. Fortunately, those ESTP leaders taking leadership roles in a religious community as a second career may have already started along the path of integrating and stabilizing their extraverted feeling.

4 Fourth (Soul-Friend): Introverted Intuition

The fourth function of ESTP leaders is introverted intuition, an internally directed perceiving function that provides "insights into the unknowable" and that discerns patterns and connections unrelated to external events (Hartzler & Hartzler, 2005, p. 27). For ESTP leaders, the integration of introverted intuition into conscious awareness seldom begins before the mid-thirties and does so under the archetypal influence of the soul-friend. More conscious contact with this archetype enables a capacity to forge connections on a profound level, providing both a bridge to the unconscious and a sense of mission.

Full development of introverted intuition through the soul-friend archetype suffuses ESTP leaders with an inspiring intensity and with a capacity for deep connection, thus providing an alluring complement to the level-headed action orientation of their dominant extraverted sensing. Introverted intuition puts the specific moment in a universal perspective. When both functions are consciously developed, extraverted sensing and introverted intuition together form a strong psychic spine for the journey of individuation. Incorporating the opposite function to the dominant function is a challenging part of the individuation journey and involves engagement with what is unconscious due to repression or neglect. There are particular challenges and stresses when leading a religious community that may account in part for the under-representation of ESTP leaders in religious settings (Macdaid, McCulley, & Kainz, 1986). However, from the dual perspective of psycho-spiritual development and cultural diversity, there are real benefits when ESTPs do offer leadership and it is received. For in so doing, ESTP leaders may be challenged to come to terms with their less developed functions earlier in their life cycle than other ESTPs who are in more purely action-oriented vocations.

The aging process itself may precipitate a sense of "closed options" for ESTP leaders. For example, in a large or mid-sized religious institution, they may realize that they are unlikely to be promoted in ministry since most senior positions in ministry favor judging types. Thus, ESTP leaders in a religious context may feel closed-in by life or work, or both, as they age. However, ESTP leaders working in a religious context are likely to face these challenges to engage their less conscious processes earlier than ESTPs outside the religious community, and also compared to the significant number of clergy with introverted sensing preferences, who fit perhaps too comfortably with the similarly large numbers of SJs in the religious community. From a lifespan developmental perspective, this prod to individuate might prove an advantage.

In the early stages of integrating introverted intuition, ESTP leaders may feel out of their depth when others immediately grasp the significance of an event or remark. When others do not provide the sequence of steps that took them to a conclusion they may feel irritated. ESTP leaders may confront others with the question "What does this have to do with reality?" Conversely, at other times, they may show absolute unwavering faith in others, which may lead them all too easily to accept groundless theories.

Familiarity with introverted intuition yields greater powers of discrimination and, as ESTPs become more open to the operations of introverted intuition within themselves, images of future change transform from being full of foreboding to being energizing. Patience grows for dipping below the surface of experiences and appreciating what may not be readily apparent. Their swift responsiveness starts to be informed by "inner intuitions of what's really about to happen" (Berens & Nardi, 2004, p. 21).

SHADOW PERSONALITY

5 Dominant Shadow (Challenger): Introverted Sensing

For ESTP leaders, the dominant shadow function is introverted sensing, an information-gathering function that focuses on particular elements to compose the subjective internal world of present experience, which is then compared to previous related experiences (Haas & Hunziker, 2006). Introverted sensing enables the registration of details that are arrayed alongside similar past experiences and empower recall and even the re-living of previous experiences. For ESTP leaders, introverted sensing seldom emerges into conscious awareness before mid-life and does so under the archetypal influence of the challenger.

There exists a tension between sensing in its introverted and extraverted aspects, for introverted sensing is put into shadow by the habitual exercise on the part of ESTP leaders of their dominant extraverted sensing. Before such time as introverted sensing is integrated and "owned" in consciousness, it is "disowned," and projected onto other people who are experienced as "bad" characters, and are judged as prone to display oppositional or another kind of problematic behavior. In the earlier stages of integration, introverted sensing is expressed within ESTP leaders as tinged with challenge.

Those community members with introverted sensing as their dominant function are particularly liable to fall prey to the oppositional dynamic of projection associated with the introverted sensing within ESTP leaders' psychic structure. Accordingly, the impact of this oppositional projection within ESTP leaders is significant in most religious communities because of the considerable number of church members who have introverted sensing as their auxiliary or dominant function (ISFJs, ISTJs, ESFJs, ESTJs). For example, ESTP leaders may feel confined by the SJ types' orientation to the present from the perspective of the past. Sensing-judging types for their part may stereotype ESTP leaders as impulsive and incorrectly conclude they must be unreliable simply because they rely on extraverted attunement to the physical environment and not on an introverted sensing comparison of present to past details. They may judge ESTP leaders as lazy or slack.

The free spirit of ESTP leaders may bring them into conflict with (and to being distrusted by) senior clerics who are even more likely than congregants to have introverted sensing as a dominant or auxiliary function. Accordingly, ESTP leaders may have to struggle hard against a tendency to feel, on the inside, being on a perpetual crusade against the establishment while, on the outside, seeking escape, or avoidance, or premature retirement.

Extraverted sensing is a function that is in short supply in most religious groups. The integration of introverted sensing into a conscious orientation will be a long personal journey for most ESTP leaders, but one rewarded by more satisfying working and personal relationships with the J majority in the congregation. Integration of introverted sensing that otherwise may show up in oppositional ways, both inside and outside religious communities, is a significant accomplishment for ESTP leaders. It deepens their effectiveness as leaders by establishing their actions in a tradition without eclipsing their flair and energy for action, something they may have initially feared. If ESTP leaders rise to the personal growth challenge through their commitment to wholeness and balance in themselves; their *joie de vivre* will make an important contribution to the vitality of the religious tradition of which they are a part, as well as to the communities beyond in society at large.

6 Auxiliary Shadow (Critical Parent): Extraverted Thinking

For ESTP leaders, the auxiliary shadow function is extraverted thinking, an organizing function that seeks to order external realities in a logically consistent way. Through the operations of extraverted thinking, problems are dealt with by analyzing their causes, determining priorities, defining goals, sequencing activities, and then applying resources, both people and materials, in the service of these goals. Extraverted thinking spontaneously evaluates the present situations in terms of its proximity to these goals. For this reason, standards and rules are valued.

Being in the auxiliary shadow position for conscious development among ESTP leaders, extraverted thinking lies in the shadow of the nurturing parent auxiliary function. In that position, extraverted thinking exhibits the contrasting features of the critical, forbidding parent, and functions to block threats to survival by using shaming, blaming, put-downs, and other morally questionable tactics that are intended to stop any hostile force in its tracks. It is carried by the archetype of the critical parent.

How might the alarming archetypal energies of the critical parent play out in interaction with the rational external structuring activity of extraverted thinking in the usually cool headed spontaneous action-oriented ESTP leaders? Whereas younger ESTP leaders probably tended to rebel against structure and saw schedules as a constraint on their freedom of action, in mid-life extraverted thinking may show itself in a negative parent mode in being "critical and disgruntled with disorder," inefficiency, and the absence of logic (Berens & Nardi, 2004, p. 21).

When others use extraverted thinking, ESTP leaders may feel their survival threatened. This may happen with some frequency, especially when interacting with males in their community, for ISTJs (who have auxiliary extraverted thinking) are often the most frequent types among males in religious groups, especially the more conservative ones, with ESTJs also (who have extraverted thinking as their dominant function) usually ranking in the five largest type groups among religiously affiliated men. Extraverted thinking finds expression in segmenting, systematizing, and organizing for efficiency, and ESTP leaders must learn to control their impulse to denigrate those who organize others well, a self-defeating act for religious leaders who want to establish strong, stable, and dynamic religious communities.

In regard to their own deployment of extraverted thinking, some ESTP leaders say they have belittled others for being illogical and have used logic to silence others in an argument rather than engage in a sympathetic meeting of minds on an issue. While extraverted thinking in a somewhat strident mode might be effective for some institutional roles required of religious leadership, the same strident extraverted thinking will feel harsh and controlling in pastoral roles.

In conclusion, there is significant potential benefit from the deployment of extraverted thinking in a non-defensive and non-power-oriented manner, since extraverted thinking is the function concerned with organizing the external world in a logically consistent fashion. Thus, extraverted thinking empowers a valuable administrative capacity within ESTP leaders. Moreover, learning how to work with extraverted thinking will enable ESTP leaders to build bridges to those with extraverted thinking as a dominant or auxiliary function, who form a significant part of religious communities.

7 Tertiary Shadow (Trickster): Introverted Feeling

For ESTP leaders, the tertiary shadow function is introverted feeling; a function essential for complete psychological functioning; it enables us to use our emotions "to identify what is important to us" (Hartzler & Hartzler, 2005, p. 52). Through introverted feeling, we organize our values so that we can maintain our personal identity and structure our life around these deeply held values (Hartzler & Hartzler, 2005). Introverted feeling forms the basis for developing and using *universal* values that transcend the *local* customs and conventions to which extraverted feeling is attuned.

As the tertiary shadow function, for ESTP leaders, introverted feeling lies in the shadow of the eternally child-like tertiary function, and while it is developing in mid-life introverted feeling falls under the influence of the archetype of the trickster. Accordingly, before it is integrated and used in a more conscious way, introverted feeling is flavored by trickster energy that makes it unreliable and prone to deceit of both self and others.

Berens and Nardi (2004) note that ESTPs are not usually interested in issues of loyalty, value, and belief, something that those with introverted feeling as their dominant or auxiliary function (INFPs and ISFPs, and ENFPs and ESFPs, respectively) may find unsettling, since for these types, monitoring congruence with personal beliefs is important and ongoing. However, ESTP leaders when stressed may resort to a highly subjective, even an idiosyncratic system of belief, rigidly adhere to it, offering very personalized rationales for getting their own way, thinking that such a personal appeal will ensure success. They may also simply act in very childish ways, using such phrases as "I want" and "I don't like" (Berens & Nardi, 2004, p. 21). Furthermore, introverted feeling types appreciate their own quiet warmth being reflected back, but are more likely to receive instead cool analytic logic of introverted thinking from ESTP leaders.

While introverted feeling remains under the influence of trickster energy, more congregants than those who are introverted feeling types may feel alarmed when ESTP leaders unconsciously draw on their trickster introverted feeling seemingly to rationalize any means toward a valued end. In turn, when church members use introverted feeling, ESTP leaders may feel manipulated by these expressions of their members' values. ESTPs also struggle with "moral" decision-making, in contrast to their usual fast-paced decision-making based on those logical principles deemed relevant to a situation.

The gains of becoming more mindful of introverted feeling are clear—it may slow down the ESTP leaders as they learn to mull things over. At first, this may frustrate them, but it may also enable them eventually to bring more of the congregation along with them on bold initiatives, and thereby build community. In the presence of introverted feeling, community members feel quietly cherished. Although the passage of integration into consciousness is not smooth, it is worthwhile both to self and to others, especially in a religious context where moral values are central to a culture founded on shared faith.

For ESTP leaders themselves conscious development of introverted feeling will help bring greater personal peace and an ease with subjective vulnerability that will increase their own happiness, appeal, and accessibility to the variety of types making up congregations.

8 Fourth Shadow (Demon/Angel): Extraverted Intuition

For ESTP leaders, the fourth shadow function is extraverted intuition. Extraverted intuition is an outwardly focused perceiving function that quickly sees patterns, connections, and inter-relationships in the external world (Hartzler & Hartzler, 2005), and which instantly synthesizes sensory data into "a pattern of changing relationships" (Thomson, 1998, p. 197) and then envisions new possibilities. As the fourth shadow function for ESTP leaders, extraverted intuition is carried into consciousness by the archetype of the demon/angel.

The usual effect of the demon/angel archetype is to undermine, and occasionally to transform, a situation or relationship. Extraverted intuition is the opposite perceiving function to that of ESTP leaders' dominant and heroic extraverted sensing, and it *directly* clashes with the operations of extraverted sensing because it operates in the very same (extraverted) world that their dominant function also inhabits. Extraverted intuition, therefore, may be disruptive and even destructive for ESTP leaders, especially in the first half of life when the integration of its operations into a conscious orientation is barely under way. At this early stage of integration extraverted intuition, whether engaged by chance, trauma, or necessity, is often suffused with dysphoria and negative moods. Extraverted intuition prevents the exercise of ESTP leaders' usual grounded easygoing extraverted sensing way of coping. Extraverted intuition undermines or even sabotages the operations of the superior extraverted sensing. When extraverted intuition is encountered or called forth, it is impossible for the same individual to continue to engage in extraverted sensing and remain purely rooted in what is being currently encountered, since activation of extraverted intuition necessitates instant transport to consideration of future possibilities, demanding a shift away from the pressing present.

Extraverted intuition has the effect of interfering with the customary coping and functioning of ESTP leaders. The oft-demonic fourth shadow function is "capable of great distortion, causing confusion and chaos, and disrupting trust" (Haas & Hunziker, 2006, p. 179). Boredom, tediousness, and stress for ESTP leaders can trigger "demonic" extraverted intuition. Unconscious acting out of such shadow impulses may devastate the development of community and undermine the trust gradually established over years. Thus, it behoves ESTP leaders to be aware of their "demons" especially the one that carries their least conscious function. When ESTP leaders are "beastly," extraverted intuition is often involved. According to Beebe (2007a), the fourth shadow function is "usually the locus of our most unyielding and unconscious flaws of character" (p. 5).

Developing patience with the felt intensity of extraverted intuition, both in themselves and others, will pay dividends in the long run, helping all perceiving types to work together to articulate alternative, more flexible approaches to the rule- and closure-oriented culture favored by the J majority in religious groups, thereby, broadening the appeal of the religious group by making its culture more attractive to a wider type spectrum in society at large. However, for the ESTP leader, conscious integration of their fourth shadow function is a long process and is seldom completed even by life's end. There will always be the liability of a shadow aspect to extraverted intuition for ESTP leaders of which they are wise to remain aware.

When others use extraverted intuition, ESTP leaders may just feel swamped by too many ideas. An incentive for ESTP leaders to get to know this neglected side of themselves is the fact that ESTP leaders may frequently encounter a trigger to their demonic function in the personal form of community members who have extraverted intuition as their dominant or auxiliary function, notably the ENFPs and INFPs. The journey toward integration has its rewards. There is the redemptive angelic aspect to extraverted intuition that appears more frequently as integration proceeds. Berens and Nardi (2004, p. 21) report that "on occasion [ESTPs] can arrive at profound interpretations that really transform situations and their daily lives."

Conclusion

This book has set out to explore the implications of psychological type theory for leaders in religious communities, with relevance across diverse faiths and spiritual traditions. It is a book that discusses in detail a nuanced and dynamic theory of psychological development. It is a book rooted in two traditions of human psychological science, in (1) the individual differences tradition that values the importance of self-awareness and the awareness of the different selves of others; (2) the analytical psychology of Carl Jung where awareness of psychological type and archetypal patterns is regarded as contributing to the unfolding of the individual, the process of individuation. In writing the book, the authors have approached this complex task in two stages. In part one, we set out the building blocks, taking seriously two distinctive components of psychological type theory that are often overlooked in the kind of introductory books on the topic often accessible to religious leaders.

The first distinctive component concerns moving beyond the conceptualization of the four psychological functions (sensing, intuition, feeling, and thinking) to the conceptualization of the eight psychological function-orientations (introverted sensing, extraverted sensing, introverted intuition, extraverted intuition, introverted feeling, extraverted feeling, introverted thinking, and extraverted thinking). The location and integration of these eight psychological function-orientations highlights the richness of Jungian analyst John Beebe's differentiation between the conscious personality and the shadow personality. According to this model, there is much more about the self to discover and much more about the self of which to be aware and to draw into conscious recognition.

The second distinctive component concerns drawing attention to the developmental positioning of the eight function-orientations within each of the 16 complete psychological types. Within our chosen model, this component itself contains two features. First, each function-orientation has been assigned to its location within the following structure: dominant function, auxiliary function, tertiary function, fourth function, dominant shadow function, auxiliary shadow function, tertiary shadow function, and fourth shadow function. Second, following John Beebe's model, each of the developmentally positioned functions has been aligned with an archetype that carries the associated function into consciousness: the dominant function with the hero archetype, the auxiliary function with the nurturing parent archetype, the tertiary function with the eternal child archetype, the fourth function with the soul-friend archetype, the dominant shadow function with the challenger archetype, the auxiliary shadow function with the critical parent archetype, the tertiary shadow function with the trickster archetype, and the fourth shadow function with the demon/angel archetype. It is these archetypes that help to nuance and texture the location of the eight function-orientations within the emerging developmental structure of each of the 16 complete psychological types. For example, in this way the dominant function is nuanced and textured by the power of heroic strength, while the fourth shadow function is nuanced and textured by the danger of the demonic pitfalls.

As two academics (rooted in the psychology of religion and in empirical theology), we have set out to write with clarity and academic rigor. We have tried to establish the theory in a clear and documented manner. However, as two practitioners (one engaged in psychotherapeutic practice, the other in ministerial formation), we recognize that the transformative power of psychological type theory for shaping religious leaders and for promoting stability and growth in religious communities is not actually realized by the intellectual grasp of abstract theory. As practitioners, our experience tells us that religious leaders best grasp the power of psychological type theory when they experience it at work. Our practice is to facilitate professional development workshops for religious leaders, perhaps over one full day, but preferably over three full days in a residential context. In such workshops, we have learned how to structure experience within type-alike groups. Sometimes these type-alike groups will work at the level of distinguishing among the four functions, and sometimes at the level of distinguishing among the eight function-orientations.

What type-alike groups achieve is to allow the voices of distinctive types to clarify and to sharpen their distinctive perspective. For example, Francis, Strathie, and Ross (in press) established workshops to invite dominant introverted intuitive types and dominant introverted sensing types to explore the same section of a sacred text. Disclosure took place when the two groups met to share their deliberations. The INFJs and INTJs who comprised the group of dominant introverted intuitive types and the ISFJs and ISTJs who comprised the group of dominant introverted sensing types not only generated distinctively different content and reported distinctively different experiences of working in their type-alike group but also found the reports of the other group quite difficult to appreciate and to comprehend. Looking at the developmental sequencing of the function-orientations within the two groups is revealing. While for INFJs and INTJs introverted intuition is their dominant function carried by the strong hero archetype, for ISJFs and ISTJs it is their fourth shadow function, carried by the usually undermining—but occasionally transforming—demon/angel archetype. While for ISFJs and ISTJs introverted sensing is their dominant function carried by the strong hero archetype, for INFJs and INTJs it is their fourth shadow function carried by the undermining demon/angel archetype. Here is the strongest clash when the directly opposing functions are operating in the same (introverted) orientation.

What we would like our book to achieve is the opening up of a deeper and richer application of psychological type theory within both the initial and the continuing formation of religious leaders. However, for such a vision to be realized, the first step must be for seminaries to develop a rigorous program of postgraduate clinical training, at both masters and doctoral level, to equip a new generation of faculty professionally equipped in the disciplines both of theology and psychology. This new generation of seminary faculty professionally trained in both theology and psychology is needed to facilitate the formation of religious leaders with the intellectual understanding, the professional skills, and the personal self-awareness necessary to release the capacity of psychological type theory for nurturing religious leaders on their own personal spiritual journey and for fostering stronger and growing religious communities.

References

Anchors, S. (1989), 'Type Development and Different Types', *Bulletin of Psychological Type*, 21: 10–12.

Arraj, T. and Arraj, J. (1988), *Tracking the Elusive Human: Volume 1, a Practical Guide to C. G. Jung's Psychological Types, W. H. Sheldon's Body and Temperament Types and their Integration*, Chiloquin, OR: Inner Growth Books.

Beebe, J. (1988), 'A New Model of Psychological Types', C. G. Jung Institute of Chicago, Evanston, IL, April 9–10. (Recorded workshop).

Beebe, J. (1991), Personal Communication to Christopher Ross.

Beebe, J. (2004), 'Understanding Consciousness through the Theory of Psychological Types', in J. Cambray and L. Carter (eds), *Analytical Psychology: Contemporary Perspectives in Jungian Analysis*, 83–115, New York, NY: Brunner Routledge Press.

Beebe, J. (2006a), 'Psychological Types', in R. Papadopoulos (ed), *The Handbook of Jungian Psychology*, 130–52, New York: Brunner Routledge Press.

Beebe, J. (2006b), 'Evolving the Eight-function Model', *Australian Psychological Type Review*, 8 (1): 39–43.

Beebe, J. (2007a), 'Type and Archetype, Part 1: The Spine and Its Shadow', *Australian Psychological Type Review*, 9 (2): 1–6.

Beebe, J. (2007b), 'Type and Archetype, Part 2: The Arms and their Shadow', *Typeface*, 18 (3): 22–7.

Beebe, J. (2016), *Energies and Patterns in Psychological Type: The Reservoir of Consciousness*, London: Routledge.

Berens, L. V. and Nardi, D. (2004), *Understanding Yourself and Others: An Introduction to the Personality Type Code*, Huntington Beach, CA: Telos Publications.

Berwick, R. C. and Chomsky, N. (2016), *Why Only Us: Language and Evolution*, Cambridge, MA: MIT Press.

Bramer, P. and Ross, C. F. J. (2012), 'Type Patterns Among Evangelical Protestants in Ontario', *Mental Health, Religion & Culture*, 15: 997–1007.

Brownsword, A. W. (1987), *It Takes All Types!*, Port Richmond, CA: Baytree Publishing Company.

Brownsword, A. W. (1988), *Psychological Type: An Introduction*, Port Richmond, CA: Baytree Publishing Company.

Bruner, J. (1979), *Knowing for the Left Hand*, Cambridge, MA: Harvard University Press.

Detloff, W. (1972), 'Psychological Types: Fifty Years After', *Psychological Perspectives*, 3 (1): 62–73.

Fowler, J. W. (1976), *Stages of Faith: The Psychology of Human Development and the Quest for Meaning*, New York, NY: Harper & Row.

Francis, L. J., Craig, C. L., Whinney, M., Tilley, D. and Slater, P. (2007), 'Psychological Profiling of Anglican Clergy in England: Employing Jungian Typology to Interpret Diversity, Strengths, and Potential Weakness in Ministry', *International Journal of Practical Theology*, 1: 266–84.

Francis, L. J., Robbins, M. and Craig, C. L. (2011), 'The Psychological Type Profile of Anglican Churchgoers in England: Compatible or Incompatible with their Clergy?' *International Journal of Practical Theology*, 15: 243–59.

Francis, L. J., Strathie, D. and Ross, C. F. (in press), 'Reading the Beatitudes (Matthew 5: 1–10) through the Lenses of Introverted Intuition and Introverted Sensing: Perceiving Text Differently', *HTS Theological Studies*.

Freud, S. (1989), *Civilization and Its Discontents*, New York, NY: W. W. Norton.

Fuller, R. C. (2001), *Spiritual, but Not Religious: Understanding Unchurched America*, Oxford: Oxford University Press.

Grant, W. H., Thompson, M. and Clarke, T. (1983), *From Image to Likeness: A Jungian Path in the Gospel Journey*, New York: Paulist Press.

Haas, L. and Hunziker, M. (2006), *Building Blocks of Personality Type: A Guide to Using the Eight Process Model of Personality*, Huntingdon Beach, CA: Telos Publications.

Haas, L., McAlpine, R. and Hartzler, M. (2001), *Journey of Understanding: MBTI© Interpretation Using the Eight Jungian Functions*, Palo Alto, CA: Consulting Psychologists Press.

Hammer, A. and Mitchell, W. D. (1996), 'The Distribution of MBTI Types in the US by Gender and Ethnic Group', *Journal of Psychological Type*, 37: 2–14.

Hartzler, G. and Hartzler, M. (2005), *Functions of Type*, Huntingdon Beach, CA: Telos Publications.

Hartzler, M. T., McAlpine, R. and Haas, L. (2005), *Introduction to Type and the Eight Functions*, Mountainview, CA: Consulting Psychologists Press.

Jung, C. G. (1970), *Psychology and Religion, West and East: Collected Works of C. G. Jung*, vol. 11, Princeton, NJ: Princeton University Press.

Jung, C. G. (1971), *Psychological Types: Collected Works of C. G. June*, vol. 6, Princeton, NJ: Princeton University Press.

Jung, C. G. (1973), *Experimental Researches: Collected Works of C. G. Jung*, vol. 2, Princeton, NJ: Princeton University Press.

Jung, C. G. (1977a), *The Symbolic Life: Collected Works of C. G. Jung*, vol. 18, Princeton, NJ: Princeton University Press.

Jung, C. G. (1977b), *Two Essays on Analytical Psychology: Collected Works of C. G. Jung*, vol. 7, Princeton, NJ: Princeton University Press.

Juergensmeyer, M. (2003), *Terror in the Mind of God: The Global Rise of Religious Violence*, Berkeley, CA: University of California Press.

Keirsey, D. and Bates, M. (1978), *Please Understand Me: Character and Temperament Types*, Del Mar, CA: Prometheus Nemesis Books.

Kendall, E. (1998), *Myers-Briggs Type Indicator European English Edition Manual Supplement*, Oxford: Oxford Psychologists Press.

Lacan, J. (2001), *Ecrits: A Selection*, trans. Alan Sheridan, London: Routledge.

Loomis, M. E. (1991), *Dancing the Wheel of Psychological Types*, Wilmette, IL: Chiron Publications.

Macdaid, G. P., McCaulley, M. H. and Kainz, R. I. (1986), *MBTI Atlas of Type Tables: Vol. 1 & 2*, Gainesville, FL: Center for Applications of Psychological Type.

McAlpine, R., Shumate, C., Evers, A. and Hughey, D. (2009), *Function Archetype Decoder*, Louisville, KY: Type Resources. Available online: https://www.type-resources.com/login-links.html.

McGuire, W. and Hull, R. F. C. (eds) (1977), *C. G. Jung Speaking: Interviews and Encounters*, Princeton, NJ: Princeton University Press.

Myers, I. B. (1980), *Gifts Differing*, Palo Alto, CA: Consulting Psychologist Press.

Myers, I. B. (1987), *Introduction to Type*, 3rd edn, Palo Alto, CA: Consulting Psychologist Press.

Pascal, B. (1670), *Of the Means of Belief*, http://www.leaderu.com/cyber/books/pensees/pensees.html.

Quenk, N. L. (1993), *Besides Ourselves: Our Hidden Personality in Everyday Life*, Palo Alto, CA: Consulting Psychologists Press.

Quenk, N. L. (2000), *In the Grip: Understanding Type, Stress and the Inferior Function*, Palo Alto, CA: Consulting Psychologists Press.

Ragan, K. (1998), *Fearless Girls, Wise Women and Beloved Sisters: Heroines in Folktales from Around the World*, New York: W. W. Norton.

Robards, M. J. (1986), *Insight: A Perspective on Personality*, Laguna Beach, CA: Martine Robards.

Ross, C. F. J. (1992), 'Orientation to Religion and the Feeling Function in Jung's Personality Typology', *Studies in Religion*, 21: 305–20.

Ross, C. F. J. (1993), 'Type Patterns among Active Members of the Anglican Church: Comparisons with Catholics, Evangelicals, and Clergy', *Journal of Psychological Type*, 26: 28–36.

Ross, C. F. J. (1995), 'Type Patterns among Catholics: Four Anglophone Congregations Compared with Protestants, Francophone Catholics, and Priests', *Journal of Psychological Type*, 33: 33–42.

Ross, C. F. J. (2011a), 'Jungian Typology and Religion: A Perspective from North America', *Research in the Social Scientific Study of Religion*, 22: 166–91.

Ross, C. F. J. (2011b), 'Type-wise: Using Jung's Theory of Psychological Types in Teaching Religious Studies Undergraduate and Graduate Students', in K. Bulkeley and C. Weldon (eds), *Teaching Jung*, 127–48, Oxford: Oxford University Press.

Ross, C. F. J. (2015), 'The Way of Personality Type', in D. Bryant (ed), *Ways of the Spirit: Persons, Communities and Spiritualities*, 117–32, Waterloo, ON: Pandora Press.

Ross, C. (2019), 'Type and Reconciliation across Life Span and Lifetimes', *Personality Type in Depth.* Available online: http://typeindepth.com.

Ross, C. F. J. and Francis, L. J. (1998), 'The Perceiving Function and Christian Spirituality: Distinguishing between Sensing and Intuition', *Pastoral Sciences*, 16: 93–103.

Saunders, F. W. (1991), *Katherine and Isabel: Mother's Light, Daughter's Journey*, Palo Alto, CA: Consulting Psychologists Press.

Segovia, M. (2005), Personal Communication to C. Ross.

Sharpe, D. (1987), *Personality Types: Jung's Model of Typology*, Toronto: Inner City Books.

Sheehy, G. (1995), *New Passages: Mapping your Life across Time*, New York: Random House.

Spoto, A. (1989), *Jung's Typology in Perspective*, Boston, MA: Sigo Press.

Thompson, H. (1996), *Jung's Function-attitudes Explained*, Watkinsville, GA: Wormhole Publishing.

Thomson, L. (1998), *Personality Type: An Owner's Manual*, Boston, MA: Shambhala Publications Inc.

von Franz, M. L. (1970), *Puer Aeturnus*, Thompson, CT: Spring Publications.

von Franz, M. L. and Hillman, J. (1971), *Lectures on Jung's Typology*, Thompson, CT: Spring Publications.

Wheelright, J. B. (1971), *The Analytic Process: Aims, Analysis, Training: The Proceedings*, New York: Putnam for the C. G. Jung Foundation for Analytical Psychology.

Zhuang, Tzu. (2002), *Zhuang Tzu*, Beijing: China Social Science Publisher. (Original work written about 300 B.C.).

Index

About the Authors

Christopher F. J. Ross, PhD, is a clinical psychologist and a psychologist of religion. His clinical work has included appointments at the Centre for Mental Health and Addiction (CAMH) in Toronto, and the Southdown Institute, Holland Landing, Ontario, that was founded to address the needs of clergy and members of religious congregations with issues related to mental health and addictions. After establishing a psychotherapy practice in Toronto that included minsters of the United Church of Canada and the Anglican Church of Canada, and members of Catholic and Anglican religious communities, Dr. Christopher Ross taught and researched in the psychology of religion in the Department of Religion and Culture at Wilfrid Laurier University, Waterloo, where he is Emeritus Associate Professor. He is currently adjunct faculty at Martin Luther University College, and provides psychotherapy and psychotherapy supervision in his psychology practice in Waterloo. His previous publications include "Personality, Individuation, Mindfulness" in *Transforming Wisdom*, with Felicity Kelcourse, 2015; "The Way of Personality Type" in *Ways of the Spirit: Persons, Communities and Spiritualities*, 2015; "Buddhism, Healing and Pastoral Care" with Robert Doering in *Psychotherapy: Cure of the Soul*, 2014; and "Type-wise: Using Jung's Theory of Psychological Types in Teaching Religious Studies Undergraduate and Graduate Students" in *Teaching Jung*, 2011.

The Revd Canon Professor **Leslie J. Francis**, PhD, ScD, DD, DLitt (an Anglican priest) has served as Professor of Pastoral Theology at Lampeter, Wales, and as Professor of Practical Theology at Bangor, Wales, before moving to the University of Warwick, England, as Professor of Religions and Education. He is also Honorary Distinguished Canon at Manchester

Cathedral, England, Canon Theologian at Liverpool Cathedral, England, and Honorary Distinguished Canon at the Diocese of Eastern Newfoundland and Labrador. His recent books include *Anglican cathedrals in modern life* (2015), *Diversity and intersectionality: Studies in religion, education and values* (2016), *Lessons in spiritual development* (2017), and *Values, human rights and religious education* (2018).

www.ingramcontent.com/pod-product-compliance
Ingram Content Group UK Ltd.
Pitfield, Milton Keynes, MK11 3LW, UK
UKHW012037150926
475560UK00001B/47

9 781793 605825